P9-DEC-822

GATHERINGS

A collection of highly entertaining menus by the Junior League of Milwaukee.

Editor & Food Stylist
F. Lynn Nelson

Art Direction & Design
Rachel J. Stephens

Photography
Scott Lanza

This book represents the efforts and dedication of the members of the Junior League of Milwaukee, Inc.

Copyright © 1987 by Junior League of Milwaukee, Inc.

Photographs Copyright © 1987 Lanza Advertising Photography, Inc.

All rights reserved. Printed in the United States of America. No part of this book may be used or reproduced in any manner whatsoever without written permission except in the case of brief quotations embodied in critical articles and reviews. For information address JLM, Inc., 626 North Broadway, Milwaukee, WI 53202.

FIRST EDITION

ISBN 0-9618294-0-0

The purposes of this corporation are exclusively educational and charitable and are as follows:

- to promote voluntarism;
- to develop the potential of its members for voluntary participation in community affairs; and
- to demonstate the effectiveness of trained volunteers.

Proceeds from the sale of GATHERINGS will be returned to the community through support of the Junior League of Milwaukee's projects.

Photographs

TABLE OF CONTENTS

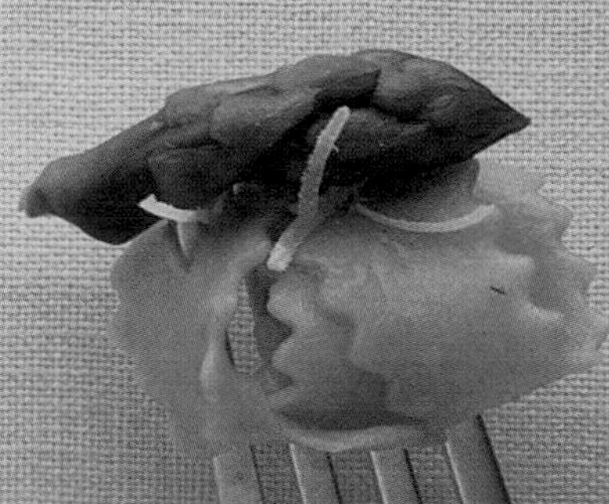

GATHERINGS.

In the language of the Potawatomi Indians native to our region, "Milwaukee" means "gathering place by the waters."

Thus, GATHERINGS—the best recipes gathered from our Great Lakes community and arranged into ten chapters of complete menus. Chapters create a mood to fit every dining occasion. Menus present a mélange of contemporary yet classic Midwest cooking which forms the foundation of heartland cuisine. Boldfaced recipes are featured with accompanying serving suggestions.

All of this is designed to conserve every cook's most precious commodity—time.

The editors selected recipes which highlight Wisconsin products. "America's Dairyland" ingredients include products such as cream, butter, cheese and frozen custard. Wisconsin also stars in the roles of producer of wild rice, cranberries and mushrooms; grower of fresh fruits and vegetables; supplier of bountiful fresh water fish; provider of prime veal, ham, lamb, pork and sausages; and brewer of Old World beverages like beer, malt and ale.

GATHERINGS represents nearly two years of work by dedicated groups of Junior League of Milwaukee volunteers, community advisors and culinary professionals. They gathered and triple-tested the book's 400 recipes, transforming them into this 200-page menu showcase illustrated with 31 poster-quality color pages.

Experience the joy of your own special GATHERINGS with this classic cookbook presented by the Junior League of Milwaukee.

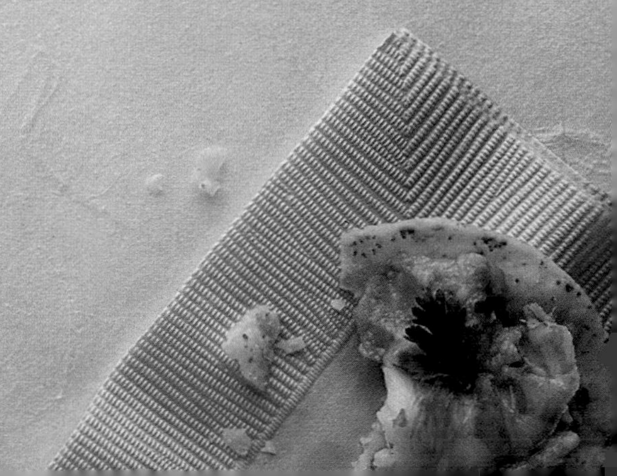

Quiet Gatherings

easy elegance for family or friends

MENU

Poulet Provençale

Baked Onions

Lentil Garden Salad

State Fair Cream Puffs

California Red Zinfandel

•

On a balmy summer evening, vaguely reminiscent of Mediterranean nights, use red geraniums, Milwaukee's official flower, as the centerpiece on top of a green & white striped or checked cloth.

Poulet Provençale

•

4 boneless, skinless chicken breast halves, pounded thin
2 tablespoons flour
1 tablespoon fines herbs
salt & pepper
2 tablespoons butter
2 tablespoons olive oil
1 clove garlic, minced
1 small onion, chopped
3 plum tomatoes, peeled, seeded & chopped
½ cup red wine
½ cup pitted, chopped Niçoise or Kalamata olives

Combine flour, herbs, salt & pepper. Lightly dredge chicken in flour to coat both sides. Heat butter & oil in large skillet. Sauté chicken 3 minutes each side. Remove to a plate. Sauté garlic & onion 3 minutes. Add tomatoes & wine. Return chicken to pan. Spoon sauce over chicken. Lower heat. Simmer until sauce is slightly thickened. Garnish with olives.

4 servings

Baked Onions

•

5 tablespoons butter, divided
½ pound fresh mushrooms, sliced
1 tablespoon flour
1 teaspoon balsamic vinegar
¾ cup light cream
1½ pounds sweet onions, sliced ¼-inch thick, separated into rings
¼ teaspoon pepper
½ pound Swiss or Gruyère cheese, grated
6-8 French bread slices, ½-inch thick
soft butter

Preheat oven to 350°F. Butter a 13x9-inch baking dish.

Melt 3 tablespoons butter in saucepan. Add mushrooms. Sprinkle with flour. Cook over medium heat, stirring occasionally 8-10 minutes. Add vinegar. Slowly stir in cream. Cook & stir until mixture thickens. Add pepper. Set aside.

Sauté onion rings with 2 tablespoons butter in a large skillet 10-15 minutes. Arrange onions in baking dish. Sprinkle cheese over onions. Top with mushroom sauce. Butter bread slices on both sides. Arrange on top. Bake 30 minutes.

6-8 servings

Lentil Garden Salad

•

8-ounces dried lentils
2 teaspoons salt, divided
½ cup red wine vinegar
¼ teaspoon fresh ground pepper
1 clove garlic, minced
½ cup olive oil
4 cups assorted vegetables:
chopped cauliflower
cucumber
broccoli
celery
scallions
1 cup julienned ham, optional
½ cup crumbled feta or blue cheese, optional

Wash lentils. Cook in boiling water to cover with 1 teaspoon salt until tender, not overcooked, 10 minutes. Drain.

Combine vinegar, pepper, garlic & 1 teaspoon salt. Stir in oil. Marinate lentils & vegetables in dressing overnight in refrigerator. Add ham & cheese, if desired, at serving time. Be creative in your choice of vegetables to make it as appetizing & eye appealing as possible. Use Egyptian lentils for colorful orange-yellow pizzaz.

8-10 servings

MENU

Grilled
Strip Sirloin
Steaks

Italian Mushroom Salad

Pasta with Gorgonzola Sauce

Raspberry Tart

Chianti Riserva

•

Wind surfing, sailing, water skiing, swimming, sunning & water volleyball have filled your day. Come home, light the coals & toss the salad. Serve!!!

SALAD

Italian Mushroom Salad

•

½ pound mushrooms, sliced
2 cups sliced zucchini
1 cup halved cherry tomatoes
1 cup pitted ripe olives
⅓ cup olive oil
⅓ cup red wine vinegar
2 tablespoons capers
1 clove garlic, minced
¼ teaspoon rosemary, crumbled
¼ teaspoon oregano, crumbled

Combine mushrooms, zucchini & tomatoes. Arrange in large glass dish or pan. Combine remaining ingredients. Pour over vegetables. Cover & refrigerate.

6 servings

PASTA

Pasta with Gorgonzola Sauce

•

3 tablespoons butter
1½ pints heavy cream
¼ cup fresh grated Parmesan
½ pound gorgonzola cheese
white pepper
12 ounces rotelle or spiral shaped pasta, cooked & drained
fresh grated Parmesan
fresh ground black pepper

Melt butter. Add cream. Simmer about 5 minutes until thickened slightly. Add Parmesan, gorgonzola & white pepper. Cook, stirring until cheeses are melted. Toss with pasta. Serve with additional grated Parmesan & fresh ground black pepper.

4 servings

DESSERT

Raspberry Tart

•

½ cup butter, softened
2½ tablespoons sugar
½ cup finely chopped walnuts
1 egg, beaten
1⅓ cups flour
¾ cup chocolate chips
2 egg yolks
2½ tablespoons sugar
2 tablespoons cornstarch
1 teaspoon vanilla
⅔ cup milk
3 tablespoons butter, softened
3 cups sweetened raspberries, reserve juice
3 tablespoons cornstarch

Preheat oven to 350°F. Butter an 11-inch tart pan.

Cream butter & sugar. Add walnuts, egg & flour. Press onto bottom & sides of pan. Refrigerate 30 minutes.

Bake 15-20 minutes. Immediately sprinkle with chocolate chips. When softened, spread chocolate over crust.

In a bowl, beat egg yolks, sugar, cornstarch & vanilla until pale & thick. Heat milk in heavy saucepan. Combine milk with yolk-mixture. Return mixture to saucepan. Whisk over medium heat until very thick. Pour mixture into bowl. Beat 5 minutes. Add butter, one tablespoon at a time. Cool filling.

In a small saucepan, combine cornstarch with reserved raspberry juice. Cook until thick. Add raspberries stirring until coated.

Spread custard mixture on chocolate crust. Top with raspberry sauce. Refrigerate at least 2 hours.

Top with whipped cream if desired.

8-10 servings

MENU

Beth's Sherried Wild Rice Soup

Cranberry Pork Chops

Scalloped Potatoes

Zucchini with Toasted Walnuts

Crème de Menthe Parfaits

California Gerwürztraminier

•

Return after an evening of cross-country skiing to the smells of pork chops & scalloped potatoes filling the house. Light a fire in the fireplace & relax!!!

SOUP

Beth's Sherried Wild Rice Soup

•

2 tablespoons butter
1 tablespoon minced onion
¼ cup flour
4 cups chicken stock
½ teaspoon salt
1 cup light cream
¼ cup dry sherry
½ cup wild rice, cook according to package directions
minced parsley or chives

Melt butter in saucepan. Add onion. Cook to light golden. Blend in flour, broth & salt, stirring constantly until thickened. Simmer 5 minutes. Blend in cream & sherry. Simmer until heated through.

To serve, place ⅓ cup wild rice in bottom of soup bowl. Ladle soup over rice. Garnish with parsley or chives.

6 servings

Pictured page 58.

ENTREE

Cranberry Pork Chops

•

6 pork chops
salt & pepper
1 cup whole berry cranberry sauce
½ cup crushed pineapple
¼ cup fresh orange juice
1 teaspoon grated orange peel

Trim fat from chops. Place fat in skillet. Sauté fat until crispy. Reserve. Season chops with salt & pepper. Brown on both sides. Remove to a buttered baking dish. Combine remaining ingredients. Pour over chops. Cover & bake at 325°F. 45-60 minutes. Sprinkle with cracklings.

4-6 servings

VEGETABLE

Zucchini with Toasted Walnuts

•

6 medium zucchini, sliced ½-inch thick
2 tablespoons butter
1 teaspoon salt
½ teaspoon pepper
1 cup chopped, toasted walnuts

Sauté zucchini in butter until tender but still firm. Season with salt & pepper. Toss walnuts with zucchini. Serve.

4 servings

MENU

Veal in Madeira & Cream Sauce

Feather Biscuits

Sautéed Matchsticks of Zucchini, Carrots & Turnips

Chilled Tangerine Soufflé

California Sonoma Chardonnay

•

Stay out of the kitchen heat in summer with this quickly prepared menu. Enjoy the summer's evening with friends & a chilled glass of wine.

Veal in Madeira & Cream Sauce

•

1 pound veal round steak
¼ cup flour
2 tablespoons butter
1 tablespoon vegetable oil
salt & pepper
⅓ cup Madeira
½ cup heavy cream
¼ teaspoon salt

Cut veal into serving pieces. Dredge in flour. In a skillet large enough to hold the veal in one layer, heat butter & oil. Brown veal over medium-high heat 3-4 minutes on each side until golden. Remove from pan. Season with salt & pepper.

Add Madeira to pan. Reduce heat to medium, stirring up brown bits on bottom of pan. When wine begins to boil, stir in cream & salt. Boil until thickened. Season to taste. Return veal to pan. Simmer, covered, 20 minutes.

2-3 servings

Feather Biscuits

•

1 package yeast
¼ cup water
2½ cups flour
1 teaspoon baking powder
1 teaspoon salt
¼ cup sugar
½ cup shortening
1 cup buttermilk

Preheat oven to 400°F.

In small bowl, dissolve yeast in warm water. Set aside.

Mix dry ingredients. Cut in shortening. Stir in buttermilk & yeast mixture. Blend thoroughly. Dough may be covered in a lightly oiled bowl in refrigerator at this point.

Turn out dough onto a floured surface. Knead lightly. Roll out ½-inch thick. Cut with a biscuit cutter. Place on buttered baking sheet. Let biscuits rise 40 minutes. Bake 10 minutes until lightly browned.

18-24 biscuits

Chilled Tangerine Soufflé

•

2 cups heavy cream
1 teaspoon vanilla
3 egg yolks
¾ cup superfine sugar
½ cup tangerine juice
¼ cup grated tangerine peel, divided
¼ cup cold water
1 package gelatin
¼ cup hot water
4 egg whites

Whip cream. Add vanilla. Chill.

Beat yolks. Add sugar, tangerine juice & 3 tablespoons grated peel.

Add cold water to gelatin. When soft, add hot water & dissolve completely over very low heat. Add tangerine mixture to gelatin.

Beat egg whites until stiff. Fold into mixture. Fold in cream. Pile into soufflé dish or bowl. Top with reserved tangerine peel. Chill at least 6 hours. Can be frozen. Any citrus fruit may be substituted for tangerine.

8 servings

MENU

Spinach Melon Salad

Sourdough Rolls

Oriental Roast Pork Tenderloin

Parmesan Onions

Hot Fudge Sundaes

Spanish Pink Cordornieu

•

How about a bridge party in front of the fire? Serve buffet-style on black plates!

Spinach Melon Salad

¼ cup vegetable oil
1 tablespoon vinegar
¼ teaspoon salt
¼ teaspoon celery seed
¼ teaspoon Dijon-style mustard
4 cups torn spinach
2 cups cantaloupe balls
1 cup quartered, thinly sliced zucchini
2 tablespoons chopped scallions

Combine oil, vinegar, salt, celery seed & mustard in a cruet. Cover & shake. Refrigerate.

Combine spinach, cantaloupe, zucchini & onion in a bowl. Toss with dressing prior to serving.

6 servings

Oriental Roast Pork Tenderloin

Marinade:
1 cup chicken stock
¼ cup soy sauce
¼ cup honey
2 tablespoons sherry
1 tablespoon lemon juice
1 clove garlic, crushed
1 teaspoon cinnamon
¼ teaspoon fresh grated ginger

3 pork tenderloins
2 tablespoon cornstarch

Combine marinade ingredients. Marinate pork 2 hours, turning frequently. Drain meat, reserve marinade. Coat meat with cornstarch. Place in a shallow roasting pan. Bake at 325°F. 45 minutes, basting frequently with reserved marinade.

8 servings

Parmesan Onions

1 large onion per person
1 tablespoon butter
3 tablespoons freshly grated Parmesan cheese

Peel & quarter onion. Place on a square of aluminum foil. Place butter & cheese on top. Fold up foil, securing edges & ends well. Place packages on grill or in 350°F. oven 1 hour.

1 serving

MENU

Shasti's Navarin

Sautéed Mushrooms & Tomatoes

Roquefort-Stuffed Potatoes

Cheesecake with Fresh Fruit

Spanish Red Rioja

•

A wonderful winter's meal after a night of ice skating. Serve hot toddies while you are warming up, & the dinner is being prepared.

Shasti's Navarin

•

4 slices bacon
1 medium onion, chopped
1 pound lean lamb cubes or leftover lamb
1 tablespoon flour
1 tablespoon sugar
salt & pepper
2 cups beef stock
3-4 tablespoons tomato paste

Crisp-cook bacon in skillet. Remove bacon & crumble. Set aside.

Brown onions in bacon fat. Reserve. Brown lamb. Return crumbled bacon & onions to pan. Blend in flour, sugar, salt & pepper. Cook mixture over medium-low heat 7 minutes. Blend stock & tomato paste. Slowly stir into pan. Cover & simmer on low heat 1 hour. Add liquid if needed. Stir.

4 servings

Sautéed Mushrooms & Tomatoes

•

1½ pounds mushrooms, quartered
2 tablespoons chopped onions
2 cloves garlic, minced
4 tablespoons butter
2 tablespoon olive oil
4 tomatoes, peeled, wedged
1½ teaspoons salt
¼ teaspoon pepper
1 teaspoon sugar
¼-½ teaspoon marjoram

Sauté mushrooms with onion & garlic in butter & oil 10 minutes. Add tomatoes. Stir in salt, pepper, sugar & marjoram. Cook, uncovered, until liquid is evaporated.

4-6 servings

Roquefort-Stuffed Potatoes

•

6 large baking potatoes
¼ cup butter
3 tablespoons warm milk
1 cup sour cream
4-5 ounces crumbled Roquefort cheese
2 tablespoons minced chives
1 teaspoon salt
freshly ground pepper

Preheat oven to 450°F.

Wash & dry potatoes. Rub skins with vegetable oil. Bake until tender, about 45 minutes. Cut in half & scoop out pulp, being careful not to puncture skins. Mash potatoes. Beat in butter, warm milk & sour cream until mixture is light & fluffy. Stir in cheese. Add chives, salt & pepper. Put into shells, mounding slightly. Return to oven 8-10 minutes to heat through.

12 servings

Four Cheese Puffs

•

1 pound loaf unsliced white bread
½ cup butter
¼ cup grated mozzarella cheese
¼ cup grated sharp cheddar cheese
¼ cup grated Swiss cheese
1 package (3 ounces) cream cheese, softened
½ teaspoon dry mustard
⅛ teaspoon cayenne
pinch salt
2 egg whites

Trim & discard crusts from top, bottom & sides of loaf. Cut bread into 1-inch cubes. Set aside.

In saucepan, combine butter & cheeses. Stir over moderate heat until melted. Add mustard, cayenne & salt. Remove from heat.

Beat egg whites until stiff. Fold into cheese mixture. Using a fondue fork or skewer, spear bread cubes one at a time & dip into mixture until well coated.

Arrange cubes on a baking sheet. Freeze immediately until firm, preferably overnight. Remove puffs from baking sheet. Store in plastic bags in freezer until ready to use.

At serving time, place frozen cubes on baking sheet. Bake at 400°F. 10 minutes, until nicely browned.

50 puffs

Split Pea & Pepper Soup

•

1 pound dried split peas
6 cups chicken stock
2 meaty ham bones
3 celery stalks with leaves, chopped
1 bay leaf
1 teaspoon thyme
2 tablespoons butter
3 sweet peppers (green, yellow, red), chopped
1 large onion, chopped
½ cup dry white wine
½ teaspoon grated nutmeg
salt & pepper
sour cream
popcorn

Boil peas, stock, ham bones, celery, bay & thyme 45 minutes. Purée 1 cup celery & peas in blender. Return to pan. Stir to blend.

In skillet, over medium heat, melt butter. Sauté peppers & onions 5 minutes. Add wine & nutmeg. Simmer 3 minutes. Season to taste. Pour into soup mixture. Serve garnished with a dollop of sour cream & popcorn.

6 servings

Cranberry Shortcakes

•

1 cup sugar
3 tablespoons butter
1½ cups flour
1½ teaspoons baking powder
½ teaspoon salt
¾ cup milk
2 cups halved cranberries

Glaze:
½ cup butter
½ cup light cream
½ cup brown sugar
½ cup white sugar

Cream butter & sugar. Add dry ingredients. Stir in milk. Add cranberries. Stir just to mix. Pour into 9-inch square pan. Bake 375°F. 40-45 minutes. When nearly cool, cut into squares. For glaze, boil butter, cream, brown sugar & white sugar over low heat 15 minutes. Serve hot over warm shortcakes.

8-12 servings

Pictured page 8.

MENU

Four Cheese Puffs

Tender Dandelion Greens Salad

Split Pea & Pepper Soup

Braided Italian Bread

Cranberry Shortcakes

Italian Red Valtellina Inferno

•

It is always said, "Splitting firewood warms you twice . . ." Now here's a way to warm you three times!!!!

MENU

Mom Terschan's Beef Goulash

Buttered Brussel Sprouts

Lois' Pilaf

Bibb Lettuce with Lemon Vinaigrette

Savory Topped Rolls

Cherries Jubilee over Vanilla Custard Ice Cream

French Rhône Tavel

•

This meal is one to be made the day before. Finish watching that all-important football game. Then put together the last minute items, & serve.

Mom Terschan's Beef Goulash

•

- 5 tablespoons vegetable oil, divided
- 6 medium onions, sliced & separated into rings
- 3 pounds beef chuck, cut into 1½-2-inch cubes
- 2 teaspoons paprika
- 1 teaspoon salt
- 1 tablespoon vinegar
- 1 tablespoon tomato paste
- ½ teaspoon caraway seed, finely ground
- 1 clove garlic, minced
- 1½ cups beef stock
- 2 teaspoons flour

Heat 2 tablespoons oil. Sauté onion rings until transparent. Remove onions, reserve. Add remaining oil. Brown meat over medium-high heat. Add paprika & salt. Stir. Return onions. Add vinegar & tomato paste. Add caraway seed, garlic & 1 cup stock. Simmer until meat is tender, about 2 hours. Mix flour & remaining stock. Add to pan. Blend well. Simmer a few minutes. Serve. Best if made the day before!

5-6 servings

Lois' Pilaf

•

- 1½ cups fine noodles
- ½ cup butter
- 1 cup rice
- 1 small onion, chopped
- 2 cups chicken stock
- 1½ cups water
- ½ teaspoon salt or other herbs pepper

Brown noodles in butter. Add remaining ingredients. Bring to boil. Immediately turn down heat. Simmer covered, 25 minutes. Pilaf can be held for a long time if serving is delayed.

6-8 servings

Savory Topped Rolls

•

- ½ cup mayonnaise
- ½ cup Parmesan cheese
- ¼ cup finely chopped red onion
- 5 dinner rolls

In a small bowl, mix mayonnaise, cheese & onion. Break rolls in half. Spread broken surfaces of roll with cheese mixture. Toast under broiler until brown. Serve immediately.

5 servings

MENU

Seafood Gratiné

Vermicelli

Florentine Tomatoes

Julie's Wheat Bread

Orange Custard with Ginger Cookies

California Mendocino Chenin Blanc

•

Remember that luncheon you have been wanting to give? Here's the perfect menu. Set your table with white lace & yellow daffodils galore.

Seafood Gratiné

•

1 pound cooked shrimp, split lengthwise
1 cup cooked, flaked crab meat
½-¾ cup chopped green pepper
¼ cup finely chopped onions
1 cup thinly sliced celery
1 cup mayonnaise
1 teaspoon white wine-Worcestershire sauce
½ teaspoon salt
¼ teaspoon pepper
1 cup fresh bread crumbs
1 tablespoon butter

In a medium bowl, combine shrimp, crab, green pepper, onion, celery, mayonnaise & seasonings. Spread mixture in 13x9-inch casserole. Top with bread crumbs & butter. Bake in 350°F. oven 30 minutes, until lightly browned.

8-10 servings

Florentine Tomatoes

•

4 medium tomatoes, hollowed
2 cups packed, cooked chopped spinach
1 cup sour cream
2 tablespoons minced onion
½ teaspoon seasoned salt
chopped parsley

Combine spinach, sour cream, onion & seasoned salt. Fill tomatoes & bake, uncovered, in muffin tin 30 minutes at 325°F. Decorate tops with chopped parsley if desired.

4 servings

Julie's Wheat Bread

•

3 cups warm water
3 packages yeast
3 cups whole wheat flour
½ cup honey
2 teaspoons salt
¼ cup vegetable oil
3-4 cups flour
milk

Combine water, yeast & whole wheat flour. Cover. Let rest 15 minutes. Add honey, salt & oil. Mix well. Add 3-4 cups flour. Knead on floured surface 5-10 minutes, adding flour if needed.

Place in oiled bowl, turning dough to coat. Cover, let rise one hour until doubled.

Preheat oven to 450°F. Butter 2, 9x5-inch loaf pans.

Punch down. Divide into two loaves. Place in loaf pans. Cover, let rise one hour. Place in oven. Immediately reduce heat to 375°F. Bake 35-45 minutes. Remove from pans. Brush with milk & cover with towels a few minutes until crust is soft.

2 loaves

MENU

Egg Drop Soup

Chinese Spareribs

Fried Rice

Broccoli with Lemon Mustard Cream Sauce

Mocha Ice Cream Dessert

Chinese Beer

•

Fill a Chinese lantern with a string of small white Christmas lights. Hang from the ceiling or outdoors in the trees & plug in. Use bright colored tablecloths & dishes. Of course use chop sticks only.

Chinese Spareribs

•

- 4 pounds pork spareribs
- 2 cups water
- ½ cup liquid from braising
- ½ cup honey
- ¼ cup soy sauce
- ½ cup ketchup

Braise spareribs & 2 cups water at 350°F. 1 hour & 20 minutes.

Place spareribs in a large pan. Combine braising liquid, honey, soy & ketchup. Warm this mixture, pour over ribs. Allow meat to marinate in refrigerator at least overnight. Broil, or roast meat at 450°F. ½ hour, until crispy & brown.

4 servings

Broccoli with Lemon Mustard Cream Sauce

•

- 1½-2 pounds broccoli
- ½ cup mayonnaise
- 2 tablespoons lemon juice
- 1 tablespoon Dijon-style mustard
- ⅓ cup heavy cream, whipped

Steam broccoli until just tender.

Whisk together mayonnaise, lemon juice, & mustard. Fold in whipped cream. Pour sauce over hot broccoli & serve.

4-6 servings

Mocha Ice Cream Dessert

•

- 24 cream-filled chocolate cookies
- ⅓ cup butter, melted
- ½ gallon coffee ice cream, softened
- 3-ounces unsweetened chocolate
- 2 tablespoons butter
- 1 cup sugar
- pinch salt
- 1 can (11 ounces) evaporated milk
- ½ teaspoon vanilla
- 1½ cups heavy cream, whipped
- 1½ ounces coffee-flavored liqueur
- powdered sugar to taste
- ¾ cup chopped pecans

Crush cookies in blender or food processor. Combine crumbs with butter. Press into a buttered 13x9-inch pan. Chill. Spoon softened ice cream on chilled crust & freeze.

Melt chocolate & butter. Add sugar, salt & milk. Bring mixture to boil. Stir until thickened. Remove from heat. Add vanilla. Chill. Spread on top of ice cream & freeze.

Add powdered sugar & liqueur to whipped cream. Spread over chocolate layer. Sprinkle with chopped nuts. Freeze.

25 servings

MENU

A Veal Caper

Buttered Spinach Noodles with Poppy Seeds

Cabbage & Grapes

Cranberry Crisp

California Pinot Noir

•

The combination of colors in this menu is a delight to the eye. Serve on yellow or white plates with pale green linens. Rave reviews!

❦

ENTREE

A Veal Caper

•

2 pounds veal stew meat
2 stalks celery, cut into 2-inch lengths
1 small whole onion
1½ cups chicken stock
6 peppercorns
2 tablespoons butter
2 tablespoons flour
2 tablespoons lemon juice
2 teaspoons capers
salt & white pepper

Preheat oven to 350°F.

Place meat, celery, onion, stock & peppercorns in 2-quart covered casserole. Bake 1-1½ hours until meat is fork tender. Discard celery, onion & peppercorns. Reserve pan juices.

In small saucepan, melt butter. Add flour. Mix well. Add juice from meat. Cook until thick & smooth. Add lemon juice, capers & meat. Season with salt & white pepper. Serve over rice or noodles.

4 servings

VEGETABLE

Cabbage & Grapes

•

1 small head red cabbage
½ cup seasoned, toasted bread crumbs
2 tablespoons butter, divided
1 cup seedless grapes, halved
1 tablespoon flour
1 cup milk
¼ teaspoon salt
¼ teaspoon pepper
¼ teaspoon curry powder
pinch cayenne pepper
½ pound Gruyère cheese, grated
1 tablespoon white wine

Preheat oven to 300°F. Butter a 13x9-inch baking dish.

Chop cabbage into bite-size pieces or wedges. Boil in salted water 5-6 minutes. Drain.

Sauté bread crumbs with 1 tablespoon of butter. Set aside. Melt 1 tablespoon butter in medium saucepan. Add flour & cook 2 minutes. Add milk, salt, pepper, curry powder & cayenne pepper. Stir until thickened. Add cheese to mixture, stirring until melted. Add white wine. Combine cabbage, grapes & white sauce. Place in baking dish. Top with crumbs. Bake 15-20 minutes. Try red cabbage with green grapes, green cabbage with red grapes.

8-10 servings

Pictured page 174.

DESSERT

Cranberry Crisp

•

1 pound fresh cranberries
¾ cup sugar, divided
¼ cup chopped nuts
1 egg, beaten
½ cup flour
¼ cup butter, melted
whipped cream

Preheat oven to 325°F. Butter an 8-inch pie pan.

Cover bottom of pan with cranberries. Sprinkle cranberries with ¼ cup sugar & nuts. Add remaining sugar to beaten egg. Add flour & melted butter. Pour over cranberries. Bake 45 minutes. Serve warm with fresh whipped cream.

6-8 servings

MENU

Orange Roughie Dijonnaise

Ancini di Pepe Pasta

Beets Romaine

Velvet Pound Cake

Sliced Nectarines

French White Burgundy Mâcon-Villages

•

The menu tastes as outstanding as it looks. Served to family or guests, anyone would feel particularly special.

ENTREE

Orange Roughie Dijonnaise

•

Sauce:
- 2 tablespoons butter
- 1 small onion, chopped
- 2 tablespoons flour
- ⅓ cup dry white wine
- ¼ cup water
- salt & pepper
- 1 tablespoon Dijon-style mustard
- ⅓ cup milk or light cream
- ⅓ cup grated mozzarella cheese
- 1 peeled, seeded & chopped tomato

- 2 pounds orange roughie fillets
- 2 tablespoons butter, melted
- 2 tablespoons fresh lemon juice
- salt & pepper

For the sauce, melt butter in saucepan over medium heat. Sauté onion 3-5 minutes. Add flour. Cook 2 minutes. Add wine, water, salt, pepper & mustard. Stir & cook until thickened. Add milk & cheese. When cheese melts add tomato. Remove from heat. Cover & keep warm.

Preheat broiler. Arrange fillets on broiler pan, turning under thin ends. Brush with melted butter. Sprinkle with lemon, salt & pepper. Broil 4-inches from heat 8-10 minutes until fish flakes with a fork. Cover fillets with sauce. Return to broiler until sauce is lightly browned, 2-3 minutes.

4 servings

SALAD

Beets Romaine

•

French Dressing:
- ½ cup vegetable oil
- ⅛ cup red wine vinegar
- 1 tablespoon water
- 1 tablespoon tomato paste
- 1 clove garlic, minced
- pinch salt, pepper & sugar

- 2 cups cooked, julienned beets
- 1 tablespoon prepared horseradish
- 1 tablespoon grated onion
- 1 head romaine lettuce, torn into bite-size pieces

Combine ingredients for dressing. Toss beets with horseradish, onion & ½ the dressing. Refrigerate several hours. Toss romaine with remaining dressing. Arrange on flat serving platter. Arrange beets in center.

4 servings

DESSERT

Velvet Pound Cake

•

- 1½ cups butter, softened
- 1 teaspoon almond extract
- 1 pound powdered sugar
- 6 extra large eggs
- 3 cups cake flour

Preheat oven to 350°F. Butter & flour a 10-inch tube pan.

Beat butter & extract until very light & fluffy. Add sugar, a little at a time. Add eggs alternately with flour, beating well after each addition. Bake 1 hour 10 minutes. Cool 10 minutes. Remove from pan. Cool on wire rack. Will stay fresh tightly covered 5 days or frozen 1-2 months. Serve with berries or sliced fruits.

12-15 servings

MENU

Flank Steak with Red Wine & Shallot Sauce

Corn-on-the-Cob with Blue Cheese Butter

Garlic Primavera

Brown Bag Apple Pie

French Red Bordeaux Saint Émilion

•

Treat yourselves on a Sunday afternoon of cleaning the garage or basement to a repast instead of supper. Grill the Steak if you like.

ENTREE

Flank Steak with Red Wine & Shallot Sauce

•

- 1½-2 pounds flank steak
- soy sauce
- freshly ground pepper
- 1 teaspoon dried thyme
- 1¼ cups chopped shallots
- 1½ cups red Bordeaux or Burgundy wine
- ½ cup butter
- 2 tablespoons finely chopped parsley

Heat Broiler or prepare grill.

Brush both sides of steak with soy sauce, twice. Sprinkle with pepper & thyme. Broil or grill 3-4 minutes each side.

In saucepan, bring shallots & wine to boil. Cook 10 minutes. Off heat, add butter & several grinds pepper. Stir until butter melts. Add parsley.

To serve, slice steak very thinly on diagonal. Ladle sauce over steak on serving platter.

4 servings

PASTA

Garlic Primavera

•

- ½ pound vermicelli, cooked & drained
- 1½ cups mayonnaise
- 2 teaspoons mashed garlic pepper
- 1 tablespoon vinegar
- 4 asparagus spears, cut in 1-inch lengths
- 2 cups sliced zucchini
- ½ cup peas
- 1 cup broccoli flowerets
- ¼ pound mushrooms, sliced
- 2 tomatoes, sliced
- ¼ cup chopped parsley
- 3 tablespoons chopped fresh basil

Rinse pasta with cold running water. Drain.

Blend mayonnaise, garlic, vinegar & pepper. Set aside.

Blanch asparagus, zucchini, peas & broccoli 1-2 minutes. Rinse in ice cold water. Drain well. Toss blanched vegetables, spaghetti, mushrooms, tomatoes, dressing, parsley & basil in large bowl. Chill until served.

8-10 servings

DESSERT

Brown Bag Apple Pie

•

- 1 unbaked 9-inch pie crust, pierced with fork
- 4 cups sliced MacIntosh or Granny Smith apples
- 2 tablespoons lemon juice
- 1 cup sugar, divided
- ½ cup plus 2 tablespoons flour
- ½ teaspoon nutmeg
- ½ cup butter
- whipped cream garnish

Preheat oven to 425°F.

Toss apples with lemon juice in bowl. Arrange on pastry. In small bowl, combine ½ cup sugar, 2 tablespoons flour & nutmeg. Mix well. Sprinkle over apples.

Combine remaining sugar & flour. Cut butter into mixture to make coarse crumbs. Sprinkle over apples.

Slide pie into large brown paper bag. Fold end over twice & secure with paper clips. Put on baking sheet. Bake 1 hour. Garnish with whipped cream.

6-8 servings

Casual Gatherings

informal, picnics & grilled foods

MENU

Carrot Soup

Shaved Smoked Turkey Breast on Herb Rolls

Hot Mustard Sauce

Horseradish Sauce

Green Beans with Green Pepper Dressing

Drambuie Cake

A portable Soup & Sandwich supper can be hearty & extremely appetizing. Serve the soup at your next tailgate party in mugs topped off with sour cream or croutons. The Drambuie Cake can be made into muffins for individual servings. Everything tastes better if made in advance!

Carrot Soup

2 slices bacon, chopped
½ cup chopped onion
1 clove garlic, minced
3 cups chicken stock
2 cups chopped carrots
1 cup peeled, seeded & chopped tomatoes
1 cup diced potatoes
1 teaspoon salt
white pepper
Seasonings to taste: ginger, cinnamon & lemon juice; or, dill & paprika; or, coriander & ginger
sour cream

Cook bacon, onion & garlic in large saucepan until bacon is crisp. Drain fat. Add stock, carrots, tomatoes, potatoes, salt & pepper. Heat to boiling. Reduce heat. Add your choice of seasonings. Cover & simmer 20 minutes until carrots are tender. Blend smooth in blender or processor. Best to make 1 day in advance. Reheat to boiling. Serve hot garnished with sour cream.

4 servings

Hot Mustard Sauce

4-ounces dry mustard
½ cup tarragon vinegar
1 egg, slightly beaten
½ cup sugar

Put mustard & vinegar in top of double boiler. Let stand overnight. Heat over boiling water. Add beaten egg & sugar. Cook until thick & smooth. Stir often. Remove from heat. Beat with mixer until steam is gone. Mustard steam will smart your eyes.

1 pint

Horseradish Sauce

2 egg yolks
2 tablespoons prepared horseradish
1 tablespoon water
1 tablespoon butter
½ teaspoon sugar
pinch salt
1 cup heavy cream, whipped

In top of double boiler, combine yolks, horseradish, water, butter, sugar & salt. Blend well. Cook over low heat until thick, stirring constantly. Cool completely. Fold cream into cooled mixture. Chill overnight. Prepare 1 day before serving.

1½ cups

Drambuie Cake

2½ cups unbleached flour
pinch salt
1 teaspoon baking powder
1 teaspoon baking soda
1 cup butter, softened
1 cup sugar, divided
3 eggs, separated
1 tablespoon grated orange peel
1¼ cups sour cream
2 tablespoons Drambuie liqueur

Sauce:
½ cup sugar
½ cup orange juice
¼ cup Drambuie liqueur

Preheat oven to 325°F.

Sift flour, salt, baking powder & soda.

Cream butter & ⅔ cup sugar until light & fluffy. Add yolks, one at a time, beating one minute after each addition. Add orange rind. Add Drambuie. Alternately add dry ingredients & sour cream.

In small bowl, beat egg whites until soft peaks form. Gradually add remaining ⅓ cup sugar, beating until stiff & glossy. Gently fold into batter. Pour into a 10-inch tube or bundt pan. Bake 1 hour 20 minutes.

For the sauce, combine sugar & orange juice in small saucepan. Cook mixture until sugar dissolves & mixture boils 1-2 minutes. Remove from heat. Add Drambuie. Pour over hot cake. Poke holes in cake to absorb sauce. When cool to the touch, turn out cake onto plate. Chill.

20 servings

MENU

Marinated Chuck Roast

Potatoes & Beer

Milwaukee's Country French Bread

Tomato, Zucchini & Onion Salad

Cherry Pie à la Mode

French Red Bordeaux Côte de Bourg

•

Invite the Grandparents over for a Sunday afternoon of storytelling with the grandchildren, "What it was like when you were young?"

Marinated Chuck Roast

•

4 pounds chuck roast
1 clove garlic

Marinade:
½ cup soy sauce
½ cup water
1 tablespoon sugar
3 tablespoons wine vinegar

Rub meat with garlic clove on both sides. Let stand ½ hour. Pierce meat thoroughly with fork. Combine marinade ingredients. Marinate four hours. Broil or grill 12-15 minutes on each side, 4-inches from heat. Warm leftover marinade to use as au jus.

6 servings

Potatoes & Beer

•

4 medium potatoes, thinly sliced
1 large onion, thinly sliced
4-5 tablespoons butter
salt & pepper
2 cups beer
1 cup heavy cream

Preheat oven to 525°F.

Overlap potatoes & onions in 11x9-inch pan. Dot with butter. Salt & pepper to taste. Pour beer over potatoes. Bake 10 minutes. Reduce heat to 375°F. Continue baking 40 minutes. Add cream. Bake an additional 10 minutes.

4 servings

Milwaukee's Country French Bread

•

2¼ cups water
¾ cup beer
1½ packages active dry yeast
1 tablespoon salt
7 cups flour
1 egg white, lightly beaten

Preheat oven to 375°F.

In a large bowl, combine water, beer, yeast, salt & 3 cups flour to make a pancake-type batter. Allow to rest at least one hour in a covered bowl. Turn out onto a floured surface. Add enough additional flour to make a smooth ball. Knead 10-15 minutes. Form into a large round loaf, or two small loaves. Place on buttered baking sheet to let rise, covered, one hour. Brush with egg white or sprinkle with water to make crusty. Bake one hour.

1 large loaf or 2 small loaves

MENU

Yellow Cherry Tomatoes Stuffed with Herbed Goat Cheese

Grilled Swordfish Steaks

Rice & Green Chilies

Strawberry Muffins

California Chardonnay

•

This is a beautiful menu when presented on white plates with white napkins on a white tablecloth surrounded with crystal vases filled with white Lilies of the Valley. Use crystal oil-burning candles to give a soft sheen to the whole meal.

Grilled Swordfish Steaks

•

6 swordfish steaks, 1-inch thick
½ cup olive oil
1 cup dry white wine
1 small onion, chopped
juice of 1 lemon
2 teaspoons salt
2 teaspoons oregano
1 clove garlic, minced
mayonnaise

Place steaks in shallow baking dish. Mix oil, wine, onion, lemon juice, salt, oregano & garlic. Pour over steaks & let stand one hour at room temperature. Drain. Baste steaks with mayonnaise. Grill 4-inches from coals, 6-8 minutes each side, basting several times with mayonnaise.

6 servings

Rice & Green Chilies

•

1 cup uncooked rice
½ pound Monterey Jack Cheese, coarsely grated
1 can (4 ounces) chopped green chilies
2 cups sour cream
2 tablespoons butter

Cook rice according to package directions. Add cheese to hot rice. Add green chilies & sour cream. Mix well. Put in buttered casserole dish. Dot with butter. Bake 350°F. 30 minutes until bubbly.

4 servings

Strawberry Muffins

•

2 cups strawberries
1¼ cups sugar, divided
1½ cups flour
½ teaspoon baking soda
1 teaspoon cinnamon
½ teaspoon nutmeg
2 eggs, beaten
¾ cup vegetable oil
1 teaspoon vanilla
¾ cup chopped walnuts

Preheat oven to 350°F. Butter a muffin pan.

Clean, hull & chop strawberries. Combine with ¼ cup sugar. Let stand one hour. Combine flour, soda, cinnamon & nutmeg. Mix eggs & oil. Add 1 cup sugar. Stir until well blended. Add vanilla & strawberry mixture. Blend together. Add nuts. Fold into dry ingredients. Mix only until moistened. Fill 12 muffins tins ¾-full. Bake 25 minutes.

12 muffins

MENU

Italian Sausages

Blue Cheese Potato Salad

Cucumbers & Yellow Tomatoes

Poppy Seed Cookies

Italian Red Vino Nobile di Montepulciano

•

Going to the Brewers baseball game? Make Sausages the night before & reheat before departing. Take along plenty of napkins.

Italian Sausages

•

12 Italian sausages
3 medium onions, sliced
2 cans (12 ounces each) tomato paste
3 cups water
2 tablespoons sweet basil
2 tablespoons oregano
1 teaspoon parsley
2-3 bay leaves
salt & pepper
3 large sweet green peppers, sliced

In a 3-quart saucepan, brown sausage. Remove to plate. Sauté onions. Add tomato paste, water, basil, oregano, parsley, bay leaves, salt & pepper. Heat thoroughly. Add sausage & simmer one hour. Cover & refrigerate overnight. Before serving, add green peppers. Simmer one hour. Serve in Italian sausage buns.

6 servings

Blue Cheese Potato Salad

•

8 to 10 new potatoes, unpeeled
½ cup blue cheese, crumbled
1 cup chopped celery
2 tablespoons chopped chives
2 tablespoons sliced scallions
¾ cup sour cream
¾ cup mayonnaise
3 tablespoons vinegar
½ teaspoon salt
¼ teaspoon pepper

Wash potatoes. Cook in boiling water until tender. Slice with skins. Combine with blue cheese, celery, chives, & scallions. In a separate bowl, combine sour cream, mayonnaise, vinegar, salt & pepper. Stir until blended. Fold into potatoes. Chill thoroughly.

6-8 servings

Poppy Seed Cookies

•

1 cup butter
½ cup sugar
2 egg yolks
1 teaspoon vanilla
2 cups flour
¼ teaspoon salt
3 tablespoons poppy seed
sugar

juice glass

Preheat oven to 375°F. Butter a baking sheet.

Cream butter, sugar & egg yolks. Add remaining ingredients. Mix well. Chill 1 hour. Roll 1 teaspoon dough into a ball. Place on baking sheet. Fill sheet with dough balls. Dip bottom of juice glass into sugar & press dough balls flat. Bake 10 minutes. Cool 2 minutes. Remove from pan to cooling rack.

4 dozen

MENU

Marinated Vegetables on Skewers

Jack Birchhill's Beef Barbeque

Sliced Goat Cheddar & Colby

Grilled Corn-on-the-Cob

Cucumber-Pimiento Salad

Mrs. Repetti's Cupcakes

Homemade Ice Cream

Spanish Red Rioja

•

Picnic supper before the 4th of July neighborhood fireworks display. Serve cupcakes & ice cream after the walk back to the house.

SANDWICH

Jack Birchhill's Beef Barbeque

•

6 pounds beef chuck roast
1 cup chopped celery
1 large onion, chopped
1 large green pepper, chopped
1 bottle (10 ounces) ketchup
3 tablespoons barbeque sauce
3 tablespoons vinegar
1½ cups water
1 teaspoon hot pepper sauce
2 tablespoons chili powder
2 teaspoons salt
1 teaspoon pepper

Cut meat into large pieces. Place in roaster or dutch oven. Combine remaining ingredients. Pour over meat. Cover. Bake 6 hours at 300°F. Stir several times during cooking. Shred meat with 2 forks. Discard fat. Continue cooking 15 minutes, uncovered. Serve in assorted hard rolls.

2½-3 dozen

SALAD

Cucumber-Pimiento Salad

•

3 cucumbers
5 tablespoons lemon juice
2 tablespoons honey
¾ teaspoon salt
¼ teaspoon white pepper
1 small onion, chopped
½ cup sour cream
¼ cup mayonnaise
1 jar (4 ounces) chopped pimientos
leaf lettuce

Score cucumbers. Cut in half lengthwise. Remove seeds. Slice thin. Pat dry. Combine lemon juice, honey, salt, pepper & onion. Toss with cucumbers. Cover & refrigerate 1-2 hours, stirring occasionally. Combine sour cream, mayonnaise & pimientos. Cover & chill 1-2 hours. Drain cucumbers, reserving 3 tablespoons marinade. Whisk marinade into sour cream mixture. Add to cucumbers. Serve in bowl lined with leafy lettuce.

4-6 servings

DESSERT

Mrs. Repetti's Cupcakes

•

1 package (8 ounces) cream cheese, softened
1 egg
⅓ cup sugar
⅛ teaspoon salt
1 cup semi-sweet mini chocolate chips
1½ cups flour
1 cup sugar
¼ cup cocoa
1 teaspoon baking soda
⅛ teaspoon salt
1 cup water
⅓ cup vegetable oil
1 teaspoon vinegar
1 teaspoon vanilla
powdered sugar

Preheat oven to 350°F. Butter 18 muffin cups.

In a small bowl, beat cream cheese, egg, sugar & salt. Stir in chocolate chips. Set aside.

In a large bowl combine flour, sugar, cocoa, soda & salt. Add water, oil, vinegar & vanilla. Fill muffin cups ½-full with cocoa batter. Top each with 1 heaping teaspoon cream cheese mixture. Sprinkle with powdered sugar. Bake 30-35 minutes. Can also be made in 13x9-inch pan. Drop cream cheese mixture evenly over top of cake. Bake 40-45 minutes.

18 servings

MENU

Cold
Cucumber Soup

Martini Sole on the Grill

Cashew Rice with Scallions

Braised
Kale

Sauce for a Summer Sundae

French White Sancerre

•

A meal for a night on the deck when the lake is quiet, the moon is just coming up over the horizon as the sun sets in a multitude of harmonious colors . . .

Martini Sole on the Grill

•

2 tablespoons butter
1 teaspoon chopped shallots
4 fillets of sole
pinch seasoned salt
⅓ cup dry vermouth
1 teaspoon cornstarch
1 tablespoon gin
2 teaspoons chopped parsley
sliced green olives

Warm butter & shallots in flat pan inside covered grill. Sprinkle sole on both sides with seasoned salt. Arrange in pan with shallots & butter. Mix vermouth, cornstarch & gin. Pour over fish. Grill 5-6 minutes. Sprinkle with parsley. Baste fish with the pan juices. Cook another 5 minutes. Serve with a few sliced green olives.

4 servings

Pictured page 60.

Cashew Rice with Scallions

•

2 cups long grain rice
3½ cups cold water
1 teaspoon salt
¼ cup chopped scallions
½ cup cashew halves
2 tablespoons honey

Place rice, water & salt in medium saucepan. Bring to a boil. Boil 4 minutes. Cover & cook on low heat 15-20 minutes, until liquid is absorbed. Remove from heat. Let rest 10 minutes. Fluff rice & add green onions, cashews & honey.

8-10 servings

Sauce for a Summer Sundae

•

½ cup raspberry jelly
1½ tablespoons cornstarch
1 cup orange juice
2 tablespoons orange-flavored liqueur
1 cup sliced, unpeeled nectarines
½ cup raspberries
½ cup blueberries

Melt jelly in small pan over low heat. Mix cornstarch, orange juice & salt. Stir into melted jelly. Cook, stirring constantly. Boil mixture gently until sauce is clear. Add orange liqueur & fruit. Chill. Serve over vanilla or lemon custard ice cream.

3 cups

MENU

Green Chili Bites

Flank Steak with Asparagus & Broccoli

Sour Cream Potato Salad

Romaine & Spinach Salad

Brandy Alexanders

Italian Red Chianti

•

A wonderful weekend at the cabin with friends. Take a short walk while the appetizers are baking.

Green Chili Bites

•

8-ounces whole green chilies
10-ounces sharp cheddar cheese, grated
3 eggs, beaten
1 tablespoon prepared mustard
dash Worcestershire sauce
dash hot pepper sauce
paprika

Preheat oven to 350°F. Butter a 9x9-inch pan.

Remove seeds from green chilies, rinse & drain well. Mix cheese, eggs, mustard, Worcestershire & hot pepper sauce. Mixture will be thick. Line pan with green chilies. Spread cheese mixture over the top. Sprinkle with paprika. Bake 25 minutes. Cut into small squares & serve hot.

8 servings

Flank Steak with Asparagus & Broccoli

•

¾-pound flank steak
1 can (12 ounces) beer
½ cup soy sauce
½ teaspoon ground coriander
¾ pound fresh asparagus, sliced diagonally
1 bunch broccoli, cut into flowerets
1 red pepper, thinly sliced

Dressing:
⅓ cup soy sauce
¼ cup white vinegar
3 tablespoons sesame oil
1½ tablespoons grated fresh ginger root
1 teaspoon sugar
freshly ground pepper

Marinate flank steak in beer, soy sauce & coriander 4 hours or overnight. Remove from marinade, grill or broil to desired doneness. Slice thinly. Blanch asparagus, broccoli & peppers in salted water for 30 seconds. Drain & cool. Set aside. Combine ingredients for dressing. When ready to serve, combine steak, vegetables & dressing. Serve at room temperature. 8-ounces water chestnuts & 2-ounces pimiento may be substituted for asparagus when not in season.

4 servings

Sour Cream Potato Salad

•

⅓ cup vinaigrette dressing
7 medium pototoes, cooked, peeled & sliced
¾ cup celery
⅓ cup sliced scallions, including tops
4 hard-cooked eggs
1 cup mayonnaise
½ cup sour cream
1 tablespoon prepared horseradish
salt & pepper
1 cucumber, peeled & diced, optional

Pour dressing over warm potatoes. Chill at least two hours. Chop egg whites. Add to potatoes with celery & onion. Sieve egg yolks & mix with mayonnaise, sour cream & horseradish. Gently fold mixture into salad. Add salt & pepper to taste. Chill 2 hours longer. Garnish with cucumbers.

8 servings

MENU

Ultimate Grilled Cheese Sandwich

Creole Onion Soup

Chocolate Chocolate-Chip Cookies

Coffee Ice Cream

Spanish Red Rioja

•

Take a break from snow shoveling or cleaning the basement & enjoy this hearty meal. Use all the chunks & pieces of cheese in the refrigerator for the Sandwich.

SANDWICH

Ultimate Grilled Cheese Sandwich

•

- 1 small loaf French bread, halved lengthwise
- 2 tablespoons prepared mustard
- ½ pound cheese, grated, preferably more than 1 type
- ¼ cup butter, softened
- ½ teaspoon Worcestershire sauce
- 1 egg
- 4 slices crisp-cooked bacon, crumbled
- 2 scallions, chopped

Spread cut sides of bread with mustard. Mix cheeses, butter, Worcestershire, egg, bacon & scallions in mixer or food processor. Spread mixture on bread. Place on baking sheet. Broil until puffed & lightly browned, 5 minutes. Serve immediately. Can be cut into one inch strips & served as appetizers too!!!

4 servings

SOUP

Creole Onion Soup

•

- 8 cups heavy cream
- 1 cup chicken stock
- 9 tablespoons unsalted butter, divided
- 4 medium onions, shaved
- 2 tablespoon flour
- 1-2 tablespoons Curry Mix, recipe follows
- freshly ground white pepper

Curry Mix:

- 1½ teaspoons cumin seed
- 1 teaspoon coriander seed
- 1 teaspoon whole black pepper
- 1 teaspoon turmeric
- 1 teaspoon dried chili pepper
- ½ teaspoon ground ginger
- ½ teaspoon hot pepper
- ¼-½ teaspoon cinnamon

Scald cream & chicken stock in a heavy saucepan over low heat. Remove from heat. Set aside. Melt 6 tablespoons butter in heavy saucepan over medium heat. Add onions. Sauté until onions are soft, 6-7 minutes. Remove onions with a slotted spoon to a small bowl. Reserve. Add remaining 3 tablespoons butter to saucepan. Stir in flour. Cook, stirring often, 3-4 minutes. Add curry mix. Cook, stirring constantly, 2 minutes. Add hot cream mixture in a steady stream, whisking constantly. Cook until smooth & begins to thicken. Heat to boiling. Reduce heat to low. Simmer 15-20 minutes. Add reserved onions to soup. Season with salt & white pepper. Thin soup with additional stock if desired.

For curry mix, grind ingredients in a mortar or electric grinder until powdered. Put ingredients through sieve.

8 servings

DESSERT

Chocolate Chocolate-Chip Cookies

•

- 1 cup butter, softened
- 1½ cups sugar
- 2 eggs
- 1 teaspoon vanilla
- 1 tablespoon coffee-flavored liqueur
- 2 cups flour
- ⅔ cup cocoa
- ¼ teaspoon baking soda
- ½ teaspoon salt
- 2 cups chocolate chips

Preheat oven to 350°F.

Cream butter, sugar, eggs, vanilla & liqueur. Combine flour, cocoa, baking soda & salt. Blend into creamed mixture. Add chips. Drop by teaspoonfuls 2-inches apart on baking sheets. Bake 8 minutes. Leave on sheets to cool 2 minutes before removing.

4 dozen

MENU

Our Best Barbecued Ribs

Harvest Corn Relish

Sugar Snap Peas

Corn Muffins

Sour Cream Apple Squares

Lager Ale

•

The day was filled with raking & leaf fights. It will feel good to kick off your shoes, relax when you get inside & smell the aroma from the oven.

Our Best Barbecued Ribs

•

1½ cups ketchup
1 cup sour mash whiskey
¾ cup chili sauce
½ cup vinegar
⅓ cup Worcestershire sauce
⅓ cup firmly packed brown sugar
3 tablespoons fresh lemon juice
1 tablespoon paprika
2 teaspoons salt
1 clove garlic, crushed
¼ teaspoon hot pepper sauce
5 pounds pork back ribs
salt & pepper
thin slices onion
thin slices lemon

Preheat oven to 450°F.

Combine ketchup, whiskey, chili sauce, vinegar, Worcestershire, brown sugar, lemon juice, paprika, salt, garlic & hot pepper sauce in large sauce pan. Heat to boiling. Reduce heat. Simmer 30-45 minutes until sauce is slightly thickened.

Cut meat into 3-4 rib portions. Season with salt & pepper. Put on rack in shallow baking pan. Bake 30 minutes. Remove from rack. Drain off fat. Return ribs to baking pan, meaty-side down. Brush with sauce. Reduce heat to 300°F. Bake 30 minutes. Turn ribs & brush with sauce. Top each rib with an onion slice. Bake 1 hour, brushing with remaining sauce until ribs are tender & brown. Add lemon slices to ribs during last ½ hour of baking.

6 servings

Harvest Corn Relish

•

4 cups whole kernel corn
1 cup chopped celery
⅓ cup chopped onion
⅓ cup sugar
⅓ cup vinegar
¼ cup chopped dill pickles
2 tablespoons cornstarch
1 teaspoon salt
1 teaspoon caraway seed
¼ teaspoon dry mustard
pepper
3 tablespoons chopped pimiento

Combine ingredients, except pimiento in saucepan. Stir to dissolve cornstarch. Cook, stirring constantly, until thickened. Remove from heat. Stir in pimiento. Pour into jars. Cover tightly. Refrigerate. Keeps several weeks. Great with grilled meats.

3 pints

Sour Cream Apple Squares

•

2 cups flour
2 cups brown sugar
½ cup butter, softened
1 cup chopped nuts
1½ teaspoons cinnamon
1 teaspoon baking soda
½ teaspoon salt
1 cup sour cream
1 teaspoon vanilla
1 egg
2 cups finely chopped, peeled apples

Preheat oven 350°F.

In large bowl, combine flour, brown sugar & butter. Mix on low speed until crumbly. Stir in nuts. Press 2¾ cups crumb mixture into a 13x9-inch pan.

Add cinnamon, soda, salt, sour cream, vanilla & egg to remaining mixture. Blend well. Stir in apples. Spoon evenly onto crust. Bake 30-35 minutes, until toothpick comes out clean. Cut into squares. Serve warm with whipped cream or ice cream.

12 servings

MENU

Bacon Artichoke Dip

Grilled Salmon with Cucumber Dill Sauce

Bibb Lettuce with Fresh Lemon Cream Dressing

Croissants

Frozen Raspberry Soufflé

French White Burgundy Chablis

•

A wonderfully light meal to serve after going to the matinée of the marvelous play that every one is talking about. The Artichoke Dip & Soufflé are made the day before, making your afternoon an unhurried one!!!

APPETIZER

Bacon Artichoke Dip

•

1½ cups cooked artichoke hearts, chopped
4 slices crisp-cooked bacon, crumbled
2 tablespoons chopped onion
2 tablespoons fresh lemon juice
½ cup mayonnaise
cayenne
1 teaspoon white wine-Worcestershire sauce
additional crisp-cooked bacon, crumbled

Combine ingredients. Cover & chill several hours or overnight. Use additional bacon pieces on top of dip as garnish.

1 cup

ENTREE

Grilled Salmon with Cucumber Dill Sauce

•

Cucumber Dill Sauce:
½ cucumber, peeled, seeded, diced into ¼-inch pieces
1 cup sour cream
1 tablespoon chopped fresh dill
1 tablespoon lemon juice
salt & pepper

2 pounds salmon fillets, with skin
½ lemon
dash pepper

Place diced cucumbers in sieve. Drain 30 minutes. Pat dry on paper towels. Combine cucumber, sour cream, dill & lemon juice, salt & pepper. Cover & chill several hours. Stir just before serving.

Prepare charcoal fire. Place salmon, skin side down, directly on grill. Season with juice of half lemon & pepper. Cover grill. Cook 15 minutes until salmon flakes with a fork. Remove from grill with spatula. Remove skin. Serve with dill sauce.

4 servings

SALAD

Bibb Lettuce with Fresh Lemon Cream Dressing

•

1 tablespoon finely minced onion
1 pint whipping cream
1 teaspoon sugar
salt & pepper
juice of 2 lemons
Bibb lettuce

Combine onion, cream, sugar, salt & pepper. Just before serving add lemon juice. Toss with bibb or any soft-leaf lettuce.

2½ cups

MENU

Bleu Caesar

Baked Potatoes

Grilled Bourbon Beef

Quick French Bread

Chocolate Devil's Food Cake

California Zinfandel

•

The neighbors just moved in last week. Their boxes are piled high. Invite them over for a chance to relax & become acquainted. This meal is a delightful, easy way to break the ice.

Bleu Caesar

•

1 clove garlic, finely chopped
½ cup vegetable oil
1 head romaine lettuce
2 heads iceberg lettuce
1 head bibb lettuce
1 tablespoon white wine-Worcestershire sauce
¼ teaspoon salt
¼ teaspoon pepper
¼ lemon juice
1 egg
¼ cup fresh grated Parmesan cheese
¼ cup crumbled bleu cheese
2 cups garlic croutons

Add garlic to oil. Set aside several hours.

In a large bowl, tear lettuce into bite-size pieces. Chill, covered.

Blend seasonings, lemon & egg with garlic oil. Toss with greens. Sprinkle with cheeses & croutons. Toss. Serve immediately.

8 servings

Grilled Bourbon Beef

•

1 4-pound English cut or arm bone chuck roast, 2-inches thick

Marinade:
1 cup bourbon
½ cup brown sugar
4 tablespoons soy sauce
juice of one lemon

Combine marinade ingredients. Marinate meat several hours or overnight in refrigerator. Grill 15-20 minutes each side over hot coals. Baste with marinade. Cut into slices.

6 servings

Quick French Bread

•

1 package rapid-rise yeast
1 cup very warm water
3 cups bread flour
1 teaspoon salt
1 egg, beaten

In a small bowl, dissolve yeast in warm water.

Mix 2½ cups of bread flour with salt in large bowl. Make well in center. Add yeast-water mixture. Mix well. When dough forms a ball, continue kneading about 5 minutes. Add more flour if too sticky.

Preheat oven to 375°F.

Place dough in buttered bowl. Cover and let rise in warm place until double in bulk, 30-45 minutes. Punch down. Form into two long loaves. Place on lightly buttered baking sheet. Score with sharp knife in 3 places. Let rise until doubled, about 30 minutes. Brush with beaten egg. Bake 35 minutes.

2 loaves

MENU

Zoo Concert Quiche

Molded Grapefruit Salad

Soft Bread Sticks

Ravani Greek Almond Cake

Spanish White Rioja

•

On a warm summer's evening, take this to the zoo in a gorgeous basket. Wrap quiche in foil & newspapers to keep warm. Pull out a red-checked table cloth, silver candelabra & fresh flowers. Serve on disposable plates!

ENTREE

Zoo Concert Quiche

•

2 unbaked 9-inch pie crusts
juice of one lemon
1/8 cup grated lemon peel
3/4 pound cooked shrimp
2 cups sliced mushrooms, sautéed
1/2 pound Swiss cheese, grated
1/2 cup chopped celery
1/2 cup chopped scallions
1/2 cup chopped tops of scallions
1 cup mayonnaise
2 tablespoons flour
1 cup dry white wine
4 large eggs beaten

Squeeze juice of lemon over both crusts. Allow to absorb. Sprinkle each with lemon peel.

Combine shrimp with mushrooms. Add remaining ingredients in order listed. Divide evenly between 2 pie shells.

Bake pies at 350°F. 45 minutes, until middle is set & knife inserted comes out clean.

May be frozen before baking. Thaw at room temperature 45 minutes. Bake at 375°F. 60 minutes.

12-16 servings

SALAD

Molded Grapefruit Salad

•

3 packages unflavored gelatin
1 cup cold water
1 cup sugar
1 cup boiling water
3 large grapefruit
1 can (8 ounces) crushed pineapple, drained
1 cup chopped pecans
1 tablespoon lemon juice

Soak gelatin in cold water. Add sugar & boiling water. Stir until gelatin & sugar dissolve. Halve grapefruit & scoop out pulp, removing seeds. Add grapefruit pulp, juice, pecans & pineapple to gelatin mixture. Mix well. Add lemon juice. Pour into a 6-cup mold. Refrigerate until set, about 4-6 hours.

8 servings

DESSERT

Ravani Greek Almond Cake

•

1 cup sugar
1 cup butter, softened
5 eggs
1 teaspoon almond extract
2 cups self-rising flour
1 cup sugar
1 1/2 cups water
fresh fruits, sliced berries, nectarines, etc.

Preheat oven to 350°F. Butter a 13x9-inch pan.

Cream butter & sugar. Add eggs, extract & flour. Pour mixture into pan. Bake 20-25 minutes.

Boil sugar & water 5 minutes. Cool. Pour over hot baked cake. Serve with fruit on the side.

8-10 servings

MENU

Heart of Wisconsin Dip

Bratwurst à la Vern

Creamy Vegetable Slaw

Cheesy Bean Bake

Fudgey Brownie Sundaes

Milwaukee's Finest, Ice Cold Beer

•

Typically Wisconsin, this winter meal only needs a crackling fire, 10 inches of snow, a good football game & plenty of Milwaukee's golden brew.

Heart of Wisconsin Dip

•

½ pound cheddar cheese, grated
¼ cup sour cream
1 clove garlic, chopped
½ tablespoon Worcestershire sauce
½ cup beer, room temperature
dash cayenne pepper
round loaf dark rye bread or French bread

Combine ingredients except bread. May be served at room temperature, or hot in fondue pot with French bread. Or, hollow out an unsliced round rye bread. Fill with dip. Wrap with foil & bake at 400°F. 15 minutes. Serve with cubed rye bread.

2 cups

Bratwurst à la Vern

•

6 onions, sliced

Sauce:
1 cup chili sauce
1 tablespoon Worcestershire sauce
1 cup ketchup
2 tablespoons vinegar
½ teaspoon salt
2 tablespoons brown sugar
½ teaspoon paprika

6 grilled bratwurst
1 can (12 ounces) beer

Put onions & sauce ingredients in dutch oven. Add sausage & beer. Simmer, covered, 15-20 minutes, until onions are tender. Serve hot in bratwurst buns.

6 servings

Cheesy Bean Bake

•

1 cup chopped onions
½ cup chopped green pepper
2 tablespoons vegetable oil
3 cups cooked pinto, red or kidney beans
1 cup cooked rice
1 cup cottage cheese
3 cups grated cheddar cheese

Preheat oven to 350°F.

Sauté onion & pepper in oil until tender. Fold into beans with rice, cottage cheese & cheddar cheese. Spoon into 2-quart casserole. Bake 30 minutes or until bubbly.

6 servings

MENU

Asparagus Salad

Salmon Bisque

Wisconsin Cheese Plate

Beer Bread

Swedish Cream

Wisconsin Red Ruby Gamay

•

With the sport of salmon fishing booming in Wisconsin, there is often a prize catch in the freezer. Serve Bisque in mugs, with or without rice, for a casual dining event. Bake Beer Bread in an interesting mold.

Salmon Bisque

•

4 slices bacon, cut into 1-inch pieces
½ medium green pepper, chopped
1 large onion, chopped
2 red potatoes, peeled & chopped
3 cups chopped plum tomatoes, including juice
1 cup dry vermouth
1 tablespoon Worcestershire sauce
3 bay leaves
2 cloves garlic, minced
2 pounds salmon, cut into ½-inch pieces
salt & pepper
cayenne
1 cup rice, cook according to package instructions
dill sprigs
sour cream or crème fraîche

In a 5-quart pan over medium heat, cook bacon until crisp. Add green pepper, onion & potatoes. Cook 5 minutes. Add tomatoes & their juice. Stir in vermouth, Worcestershire, bay leaves & garlic. Cover & simmer until potatoes are tender, 30 minutes. May be prepared in advance to this point. Add fish. Cover & cook until fish flakes easily, 5-6 minutes. Season with salt, pepper & cayenne. To serve, place cooked rice in bottom of soup bowl. Ladle hot bisque over rice. Garnish with dill & a dollop of sour cream or crème fraîche.

6-8 servings

Beer Bread

•

3 cups self-rising flour
3 tablespoons sugar
1 can (12 ounces) light or dark beer
¼ cup butter, melted

Preheat oven to 350°F. Butter a 9x5-inch loaf pan.

Combine flour, sugar & beer. Pour into prepared loaf pan. Pour melted butter over top. Bake 50 minutes. Cool completely in pan. Serve with onion conserve.

1 loaf

Swedish Crème

•

2¼ cups heavy cream
1 cup sugar
1 teaspoon unflavored gelatin
2 cups sour cream
1 teaspoon vanilla, or other extract, (lemon, almond, etc.)
2 cups sweetened, chopped fresh fruit

Combine cream, sugar & gelatin in medium-size saucepan. Heat gently, stirring, over low heat 5 minutes until gelatin has dissolved. Remove from heat. Cool until slightly thickened. Fold in sour cream & vanilla. Pour into parfait glasses or dessert dishes. Chill, covered, several hours or overnight. Before serving, top with fruit.

8 servings

MENU

Sausage & Potato Soup

Mixed Greens with Leona's Sour Cream Dressing

Whole Wheat Sour Dough Bread

Super Lemon Pie

Italian Red Brunello di Montalcino

•

It's a cool autumn day. The smell of fall is in the air & a sweater feels good. What a day to go leaf peeping!

SOUP

Sausage & Potato Soup

•

1 pound Italian sausage, sliced 1⁄3-inch thick
1 tablespoon vegetable oil
1⁄2 cup chopped onion
2 pounds tomatoes, peeled, chopped
4 potatoes, peeled, chopped
1⁄4 cup finely chopped parsley
1 cup celery, sliced diagonally
2 tablespoons finely chopped celery leaves
1 1⁄2 cup beef stock
1 bay leaf
1⁄2 teaspoon thyme
1 tablespoon lemon juice
salt & pepper

Brown Italian sausage slices in oil. Add chopped onions. Cook 5 minutes. Add remaining ingredients. Bring to a boil, reduce heat. Simmer, uncovered, until potatoes are tender, 40 minutes.

4-6 servings

SALAD

Mixed Greens with Leona's Sour Cream Dressing

•

1 clove garlic
1 teaspoon salt
3 scallions including greens, chopped
1⁄2 cup parsley, chopped
1 cup sour cream
1 cup mayonnaise
1 teaspoon Worcestershire sauce
1⁄4 teaspoon hot pepper sauce
1 tablespoon lemon juice
2 quarts mixed greens, field lettuces, mâche, arugula, etc.

Mince or mash garlic & place in a small sauce dish. Cover with salt & let rest 15-20 minutes. Mix scallions, parsley, sour cream, mayonnaise, Worcestershire sauce, hot pepper sauce, vinegar & lemon juice; add garlic. Mix well & refrigerate. Will keep for two weeks.

At serving time toss dressing with lettuces. Pass pepper mill.

3 cups

DESSERT

Super Lemon Pie

•

3 eggs separated
grated peel & juice of 1 lemon
4 tablespoons boiling water
1 cup powdered sugar, sifted
1 baked 9-inch pie shell

Beat egg whites until stiff.

Beat yolks until lemon colored. Add peel & juice of lemon. Gradually add boiling water. Add sugar. Cook mixture in a double boiler 3-4 minutes, until thickened. Cool. Fold in beaten egg whites. Pour mixture into pie shell. Bake 2-4 minutes at 400°F. until pie turns light golden brown on top.

6 servings

Simple Gatherings

uncomplicated & convenient

MENU

Dairyland Crab Spread

Sautéed Chicken Tarragon

Orzo with Parmesan & Pimientos

Julienned Beets

Brandied Peaches

Peach Ice Cream

French White Burgundy Meursault

•

A simple three-course meal to put you completely at ease. Use placemats & everyday dinnerware to keep it comfortable for everyone.

APPETIZER

Dairyland Crab Spread

•

2 packages (3 ounces each) cream cheese, softened
¾ cup mayonnaise
½ pound cheddar cheese, grated
1 can (4 ounces) chopped ripe olives
½ pound cooked, flaked crab meat
¼ cup finely chopped onion
2 hard-cooked eggs, chopped
1 teaspoon dry mustard
½ teaspoon paprika
½ teaspoon pepper

Combine cream cheese & mayonnaise. Stir in remaining ingredients. Chill. Serve with a variety of crackers or vegetable crudités. May be broiled on wheat crackers or toast cutouts to serve hot.

2½ cups

ENTREE

Sautéed Chicken Tarragon

•

4 chicken breast halves, skinned & boned
2 tablespoons butter
salt & pepper
1 teaspoon cornstarch
¼ teaspoon salt
1½ teaspoons chopped fresh tarragon or ½ teaspoon dried
1 teaspoon capers, crushed

Pound chicken breasts between sheets of plastic to ¼-inch thick. Melt butter in pan over medium heat until it sizzles. Sauté chicken 1-2 minutes per side. Remove to heated platter. Season with salt & pepper. Combine remaining ingredients. Add to pan. Bring to boil. Stir & cook until thickened. Spoon over chicken.

4 servings

DESSERT

Brandied Peaches

•

Per serving:
1 peach half
1 tablespoon butter
2 teaspoons dark brown sugar
1 tablespoon brandy

Place peaches, pitted side up, in pie plate or shallow container to fit. Add butter, sugar & brandy to center of each peach. Broil 3-5 minutes until bubbly. Serve hot with ice cream if desired. Use rum, cognac, hazelnut or another liqueur in place of brandy.

MENU

Smoked Oysters
or Scallops
& Melon Kebobs

Grilled Marinated Pork Chops

Au Gratin
Potatoes

Sweet-Sour Vegetables Pommery

Chocolate Mousse Pie

French
Red Rhône
Côte Rotie

•

Midsummer's night entertaining with emphasis on style & ease & out of the kitchen. The cold & hot, sweet & sour contrasts will pique everyone's palate.

Grilled Marinated Pork Chops

•

Marinade:
1 cup fresh orange juice
2 cloves garlic, minced
2 tablespoons light soy sauce

4 pork chops, 1-inch thick

Combine marinade ingredients. Put chops in pan to fit. Pour marinade over chops. Turn to coat. Marinate at least 4 hours, preferably overnight, turning occasionally. Grill over hot coals or broil. Warm remaining marinade. Serve with chops.

4 servings

Sweet-Sour Vegetables Pommery

•

2 cups broccoli flowerets
2 cups caulifloweretts
1 small red pepper, cut into 1-inch pieces
¾ cup sliced scallions

Dressing:
½ cup vegetable oil
½ cup white wine vinegar
½ cup sugar
2 tablespoons Pommery or whole-grain mustard
salt & pepper

¼ cup toasted pine nuts

Combine vegetables in bowl. Mix dressing ingredients. Toss with vegetables. Marinate over night. Before serving, sprinkle with pine nuts.

4-5 servings

Chocolate Mousse Pie

•

½ cup butter
1 cup flour
1 tablespoon sugar
⅛ teaspoon salt

Filling:
1 package (6 ounces) semi-sweet chocolate chips
1 egg
2 egg yolks
1 teaspoon rum
2 egg whites, beaten stiff
1 cup heavy cream, whipped
whipped cream for garnish
1 square baking chocolate, shaved

Preheat oven to 450°F.

Cut butter into flour, sugar & salt. Mix well. Press into 9-inch pie pan. Bake 10 minutes. Cool on wire rack.

Melt chocolate chips. Beat in egg & yolks, one at a time. Blend well. Add rum. Fold in egg whites. Fold in 1 cup of the whipped cream. Spoon into pie shell. Chill several hours or overnight. Garnish with whipped cream & shaved chocolate.

6-8 servings

MENU

Quick Baked Haddock

Cabbage Slaw for Keeps

Savory Baked Beans

Half Rye Bread

Poires au Gratin

German White Rheingau Spätlese

•

Milwaukee is famous for its Friday Night Fish Fry. No need to go out when the menu is this easy & delicious.

ENTREE

Quick Baked Haddock

•

- 1/3 cup bread crumbs
- salt & pepper
- 1 tablespoon minced herbs
- 2 pounds haddock fillets, pat dry with toweling
- 1 egg, beaten
- 1/2 cup butter, melted
- paprika
- lemon wedges

Preheat oven to 375°F. Butter a 13x9-inch pan.

Combine bread crumbs, salt, pepper & herbs. Dip fillets in egg, then crumbs. Place fillets in pan. Drizzle with melted butter. Bake 30 minutes. Sprinkle paprika on top. Serve with lemon.

4 servings

SALAD

Cabbage Slaw for Keeps

•

- 1 medium head cabbage, finely shredded
- 1 onion, chopped
- 1 green pepper, chopped
- 1/4 cup sliced pimiento-stuffed olives
- 1/2 cup sugar

Dressing:

- 1 cup white vinegar
- 1/2 cup vegetable oil
- 1/2 cup sugar
- 1 teaspoon salt
- 1 teaspoon celery seed
- 1 teaspoon prepared mustard
- 1/4 teaspoon pepper

Place vegetables in large bowl. Combine dressing ingredients in saucepan. Boil 3 minutes. Add hot dressing to cabbage. Mix well. Cover. Chill at least 24 hours. Keeps until gone!

10 servings

DESSERT

Poires au Gratin

•

- 4 ripe, but firm, pears, peeled, cored & sliced 3/8-inch thick
- cinnamon-sugar
- 1/3 cup apricot jam
- 1/4 cup dry white vermouth
- 4-5 dried macaroon or amaretti cookies
- 2 tablespoons butter, cut into pieces
- ice cream or whipped cream

Preheat oven to 325°F. Butter a shallow 1-quart baking dish.

Arrange pear slices in prepared dish. Sprinkle with cinnamon-sugar. Blend jam & vermouth. Pour over pears. Crumble macaroons on top. Dot with butter pieces. Bake 25-30 minutes until pears are tender. Serve hot or cold with vanilla ice cream or whipped cream.

4-6 servings

MENU

Country Bean Soup

Cucumber Orange Spinach Salad with Caraway Seed Dressing

Refrigerator Bran Muffins

California Burgundy

•

Just home from work & dinner is in the refrigerator! Prepare Soup, Muffin batter & Dressing in advance. 30 minutes after arriving home, a warm & satisfying meal.

Country Bean Soup

•

½ pound northern beans
½ pound red kidney beans
½ pound pinto beans
water
2 tablespoons butter
1 onion, chopped
1½ pounds smoked pork hocks
1 bay leaf
¾ pound Polska Kielbasa, sliced ½-inch thick
1 tablespoon thyme
salt & pepper

Rinse beans. In stockpot, heat beans & 8 cups water to boiling. Boil 2 minutes. Remove from heat. Cover. Let stand 1 hour. Drain beans in colander & rinse in cold water.

Return pan to heat. Sauté onion in butter 5 minutes. Add hocks, bay leaf & 7 cups water. Heat to boiling. Return beans to pan. Simmer 45 minutes. Add sausage. Cook 15-20 minutes. Remove bay leaf & hocks. Cool slightly. Trim hocks. Add meat to soup. Add thyme, salt & pepper. Best if made 1 day in advance.

8-10 servings

Cucumber Orange Spinach Salad with Caraway Seed Dressing

•

2 bunches spinach, torn into bite-size pieces
2 cups mandarin oranges
1 large cucumber, peeled, seeded & julienned

Dressing:
¾ cup mayonnaise
1 tablespoon honey
1 teaspoon lemon juice
1 teaspoon caraway seed

⅓ cup toasted almonds

Add spinach, oranges, cucumbers to salad bowl. Cover & chill. Combine dressing ingredients. Cover & chill. Toss salad with dressing & almonds just before serving.

6-8 servings

Refrigerator Bran Muffins

•

3 eggs
3 cups buttermilk
2¼ cups white or brown sugar
¾ cup vegetable oil
3 cups all bran cereal
1 cup raisins
2 teaspoons baking soda
¼ cup boiling water
4 cups graham flour
3 teaspoons baking powder
2 teaspoons salt

Combine eggs, buttermilk, sugar, oil, bran, raisins, baking soda & water. Let stand. Mix flour, baking powder & salt. Combine with bran batter. Store in refrigerator. Use as needed. Pour into muffin tins. Bake 20 minutes at 450°F.

3 dozen

MENU

Chicken Marsala

Green Bean Bundles

Shredded Red Cabbage & Red Onion Salad

Oven-Browned Potatoes

Lemon Pepper Loaf

Rich Chocolate Cake

Italian Red Bardolino or Gattinara

•

Large family birthdays or gatherings can be hosted with joy utilizing the oven-cooked menu.

Chicken Marsala

•

36 pieces chicken
salt & pepper
paprika
¾ cup butter, divided
1 pound mushrooms, sliced
¼ cup flour
1½ cups chicken stock
6 tablespoons dry Marsala wine
3 sprigs fresh rosemary or ½ teaspoon dried

Season chicken with salt, pepper & paprika. In a large skillet, brown chicken in ½ cup butter. Remove to baking pans. Add remaining butter. Sauté mushrooms 5 minutes. Add flour. Stir until smooth. Add stock, Marsala & rosemary. Cook until thick. Pour over chicken. Bake, covered, at 350°F. 1 hour.

18 servings

Green Bean Bundles

•

2 pounds whole green beans, trimmed
8 scallions including long green stems
1 red pepper, cut into ¼-inch thick strips
⅓ cup butter
1 clove garlic, finely chopped
½ teaspoon crushed thyme
¼ teaspoon white pepper

Cook beans in salted water 3 minutes. Plunge into ice water. Drain. Blanch scallions 15 seconds. Remove & pat dry. Cut onion off stem.

Gather a serving-size bundle of green beans. Tie scallion stem around beans. Knot. Place bundles in buttered 8-inch square pan. Slip several red pepper strips under knot.

Melt butter in small pan. Sauté garlic 3 minutes. Add thyme & pepper. Pour over beans. Cover & refrigerate. Bring to room temperature. Bake at 375°F. 7-10 minutes until heated through.

8 servings

Lemon Pepper Loaf

•

1 pound loaf unsliced white bread
½ cup butter, softened
1 tablespoon chopped chives
½ teaspoon grated lemon peel
½ tablespoon lemon juice
¼ teaspoon freshly ground black pepper
1 tablespoon Dijon-style or other prepared mustard
2 teaspoons poppy seed
8 slices crisp-cooked bacon, crumbled
½ pound Swiss cheese, sliced

Cut bread into 9 slices, cutting into, but not through, bottom crust. In small bowl, cream butter until light & fluffy. Add chives, lemon peel, lemon juice & pepper. Mix thoroughly. Add mustard, poppy seed & bacon. Set aside 3 tablespoons butter mixture. Spread remainder on all cut surfaces of bread. Place 1 slice cheese in each cut. Spread reserved butter mixture on top & sides of loaf. Bake at 350°F. 15-20 minutes.

9 servings

MENU

Fresh Asparagus with Herbed Caper Dip

Vermouthy Veal

Pilaf

Fruit & Lettuce Salad with Orange Yogurt Dressing

Chocolate-Dipped Madeleines

California Napa Chardonnay

•

Elegant May dinner when flowers are from the garden, asparagus is fresh from the market & you want sprightliness on the table.

Fresh Asparagus with Herbed Caper Dip

•

Herbed Caper Dip:
1 package (8 ounces) cream cheese, softened
½ cup sour cream
3 scallions, minced
2 tablespoons capers
2 tablespoons minced parsley
1 tablespoon Dijon-style mustard
1 teaspoon Herbs de Provence
salt & pepper

2 pounds fresh asparagus, trimmed

For dip, beat cream cheese & sour cream until light & fluffy. Stir in remaining ingredients. Chill. Best made 1 day in advance. Keeps up to 5 days. Serve asparagus spears in pretty basket with dip.

1½ cups

Vermouthy Veal

•

2 pounds very thin veal slices
3-4 tablespoons flour
⅓ cup butter
1 clove garlic, minced
1 small onion, chopped
1 small green pepper, chopped
1 small red pepper, chopped
½ pound mushrooms, chopped
1 tablespoon lemon juice
½ cup dry vermouth

Lightly flour veal. Melt butter in sauté pan. Brown veal pieces. Add garlic, onions, peppers & mushrooms. Sprinkle with lemon juice. Add vermouth. Can be made in advance to this point. Cover & cook on low heat 25 minutes until veal is tender. Substitute turkey slices or chicken breasts for veal.

6 servings

Fruit & Lettuce Salad with Orange Yogurt Dressing

•

4 cups torn Boston lettuce
1 can (11 ounces) mandarin oranges, drained
1-2 bananas, sliced
½ cup dried black currants
½ cup chopped Macadamia nuts, almonds or cashews
½ cup mayonnaise
½ cup mandarin orange yogurt

Place lettuce in bowl. Top with fruits, currants & nuts.

Combine mayonnaise & yogurt. Chill several hours. Serve dressing with salad.

4 servings

MENU

Mushroom Canapés

Grilled Lamb Chops

Basil Spaghetti Carbonara

French Apple Pie

Italian Red
Brunello di Montalcino

•

The Canapés are in the freezer, light the grill & sit back to enjoy the evening. Pop the Dessert in the oven while you assemble the Pasta. You'll entertain often when it's this easy.

Mushroom Canapés

•

¼ cup butter
1 cup finely chopped onion
1 pound mushrooms, finely chopped
⅓ cup flour
⅓ cup milk
½ teaspoon salt
⅛ teaspoon pepper
1 pound loaf extra-thin sliced bread (white, dill, rye, etc.)
grated Parmesan cheese
sliced pimento-stuffed olives, optional

Melt butter in skillet. Sauté onions & mushrooms 10 minutes until liquid is nearly evaporated. Add flour. Cook 1 minute. Add milk, salt & pepper. Cook until mixture is very thick. Set aside to cool. Trim crusts from bread. Cut bread into triangles or variety of shapes with canapé cutters. Spread mixture on bread. Arrange on baking sheets. Sprinkle with Parmesan. Freeze until firm. Place in plastic bags until needed. To serve, preheat broiler. Arrange canapés on baking sheets. Broil 5 minutes until browned. Garnish with olive slice.

30 servings

Basil Spaghetti Carbonara

•

3 slices bacon, chopped
½ pound prosciutto ham, julienned
1 small onion, sliced
½ cup sliced mushrooms
3 tablespoons dry Marsala
3 tablespoons butter
8-ounces thin spaghetti, cooked & drained
1 egg, beaten
salt & pepper
3 tablespoons sliced fresh basil leaves
¼ cup freshly grated Parmesan cheese

In a large skillet, brown bacon. When almost crisp, add prosciutto. Cook 3 minutes. Remove to plate. Sauté onion 3 minutes. Return bacon & ham to pan. Add Marsala. Simmer 2 minutes. Add butter. Remove from heat. Add hot spaghetti to pan. Toss. Add egg, salt & pepper. Toss again. Pour onto warm serving platter. Sprinkle with basil & Parmesan.

2-4 servings

French Apple Pie

•

6 cups peeled, sliced apples
½ teaspoon nutmeg
½ teaspoon cinnamon
1¼ cups sugar, divided
2-3 tablespoons butter
1 egg, beaten
¾ cup flour
1 teaspoon baking powder
¼ teaspoon salt
whipped cream or ice cream

Preheat oven to 375°F. Arrange apple slices in buttered 10-inch pie pan.

Combine nutmeg, cinnamon & ½ cup of the sugar. Sprinkle over apples. Dot with butter. Combine egg, flour, baking powder, salt & remaining sugar. Sprinkle over top of pie. Bake 50 minutes. Serve warm or cold with whipped cream or a scoop of ice cream.

6 servings

MENU

Snapper Amande

Garlic-Dill
Extra-Fine
Egg Noodles

Broiled Blue Cheese Tomatoes

Marcie's Grasshoppers

French White Muscadet

•

Intimate dinner for two after a hard day's work. Dinner takes very little time to prepare. Spruce up your table & refresh yourselves with an inviting menu to linger over.

ENTREE

Snapper Amande

•

- ¼ cup coarsely chopped almonds
- 3 tablespoons butter, softened
- 1 tablespoon grated lemon peel
- ½ teaspoon paprika
- ¼ teaspoon salt
- ⅛ teaspoon pepper
- 1 pound snapper fillets

Preheat oven to 350°F. Butter a 1-quart baking dish.

Combine almonds, butter, lemon peel, paprika, salt & pepper. Place fillets, skin side down, in baking dish. Top fillets with butter-nut mixture. Bake 15-20 minutes until fish flakes easily.

2 servings

VEGETABLE

Broiled Blue Cheese Tomatoes

•

- 4 medium tomatoes, halved
- salt & pepper
- 1 clove garlic, minced
- 1 medium onion, minced
- 3 tablespoons fresh bread crumbs
- 4-ounces blue cheese, crumbled

Preheat oven to 350°F.

Season tomatoes with salt & pepper. Arrange in muffin tin. Combine garlic & onions. Divide evenly over tomatoes. Combine bread crumbs & cheese. Sprinkle over tomatoes. Bake 20-25 minutes or broil 5 minutes until cheese is light brown & tomatoes are heated through.

8 servings

DESSERT

Marcie's Grasshoppers

•

- ½ gallon French vanilla ice cream, softened
- ½ cup crème de menthe
- ⅓ cup white crème de cacao
- chocolate twigs garnish

Blend ice cream & liqueurs. Refreeze. To serve, remove from freezer 5-10 minutes before scooping into parfait glasses or ice cream dishes. Garnish with chocolate twigs.

8-10 servings

MENU

Celery Pinwheels

Old Fashioned Cream of Tomato Soup

Salmon Stuffed Potatoes

Dinner Salad

Frozen Chocolate Tofu Ice Cream

California Gamay Beaujolais

•

After a day of holiday shopping, munch on the Pinwheels with a mug of Soup while the Potatoes are heating. Toss the salad with your favorite dressing. Your evening will be free to wrap the gifts!

Celery Pinwheels

•

- 5 stalks celery
- 1 package (8 ounces) cream cheese, softened
- 4-5 tablespoons ground toasted almonds

Clean, trim, & dry celery. Beat cream cheese until light & fluffy. Add almonds. Pack cheese into celery ribs. Fill liberally. Press stalks together pinwheel fashion, one inside the other until a tight circle is formed. Tie at each end. Wipe away excess cheese. Chill until firm. To serve, slice stalks crosswise, ⅜-inch thick. Use as garnish or an hors d'oeuvre.

12-16 pieces

Old Fashioned Cream of Tomato Soup

•

- 6 tablespoons butter
- 6 tablespoons flour
- ¾ teaspoon salt
- 3 cups milk
- 3 cups peeled, quartered tomatoes
- 2 bay leaves
- 1 small onion, chopped
- pinch baking soda
- salt & pepper
- ½ cup heavy cream, whipped

Melt butter in saucepan over low heat. Blend in flour & salt. Cook 2-3 minutes. Add milk. Stir until mixture thickens & bubbles. Set aside.

In another saucepan, cook tomatoes, bay leaves & onions 10 minutes over low heat. Add soda just before removing from heat. Discard bay leaves.

Combine cream sauce & tomato mixture. Season with salt & pepper. Top each serving with 1 tablespoon whipped cream.

4-6 servings

Salmon Stuffed Potatoes

•

- 4 large baked potatoes
- ¼ cup milk
- 2 tablespoons butter
- 1 egg, beaten
- 3 tablespoons grated Parmesan cheese
- 2 scallions, finely chopped including greens
- salt & pepper
- 8-ounces cooked, flaked salmon

Cheese Sauce:

- 2 tablespoons butter
- 2 tablespoons flour
- 1 cup milk
- salt & pepper
- 1 teaspoon dry mustard
- 8-ounces Bel Paese cheese, cubed

Cut baked potatoes in half. Scoop out pulp. Mash potatoes with milk, butter, egg & Parmesan. Stir in scallions, salt & pepper. Fold in salmon. Mound into potato shells. Bake at 375°F. 20 minutes.

For the sauce, in a small saucepan over medium heat melt butter. Add flour, salt, pepper & mustard. Cook 1-2 minutes. Add milk. Stir until smooth & thickened. Add cheese. Stir until melted. Serve sauce over potatoes.

4 servings

MENU

Tomato-Mustard Chicken

Parmesan-Eggplant Strata

Broccoli

Strawberry Meringues

California Mendocino Chardonnay

•

A snappy menu for entertaining casually with panache. Top the table with a bright red cloth & a bowl brimming with yellow daisies. Use yellow bandana 'kerchiefs as napkins. Pzazz!

❦

Tomato-Mustard Chicken

•

1 tablespoon butter
1 tablespoon vegetable oil
4 skinless, boneless chicken breast halves, sliced thin
1 onion, chopped
½ teaspoon thyme
½ teaspoon tarragon
¼ cup dry white wine
1 cup chicken stock
2 cups seeded, chopped tomatoes
1½ tablespoons tomato paste
1 clove garlic, minced
1 tablespoon Dijon-style mustard
3 tablespoons minced parsley

Heat butter & oil in skillet over medium heat. Sauté chicken slices 3-4 minutes. Remove from pan. Add onion & herbs. Cook 5 minutes. Add wine, broth, tomatoes, tomato paste & garlic. Simmer, stirring occasionally, 10 minutes. Increase heat to high. Cook 3 minutes. Stir in mustard & chicken. Cook 2 minutes. Sprinkle with parsley. Serve with pasta or noodles if desired.

4 servings

Parmesan-Eggplant Strata

•

1 large eggplant, peeled & diced
½ loaf white bread, crusts trimmed & diced
8 slices crisp-cooked bacon, crumbled
6 eggs, beaten
1 cup milk
1 teaspoon Italian herbs
salt & pepper
½ cup grated Parmesan cheese
3 tablespoons butter

Preheat oven to 325°F. Butter a 2-quart baking dish.

Parboil eggplant in salted water 5 minutes. Drain well. Combine eggplant, bread & bacon. Pour into baking dish. Combine eggs, milk, herbs, salt & pepper. Pour over eggplant. Top with cheese. Dot with butter. Bake 45 minutes until golden brown.

8 servings

Strawberry Meringues

•

3 egg whites, room temperature
¼ teaspoon cream of tartar
½ cup superfine sugar
¾ teaspoon vanilla
1 cup heavy cream
2 teaspoons sugar
2 tablespoons orange-flavored liqueur
1 quart strawberries, sliced

Preheat oven to 350°F. Line baking sheets with paper.

Beat egg whites & cream of tartar until soft peaks form. Beat in sugar, 2 tablespoons at a time. Add vanilla. Spoon meringue onto baking sheets in mounds of desired size. Make "nest" shape with spoon in middle of mound. Bake 1 hour until set. Cool 10 minutes. Carefully remove from sheets. Store in air-tight container.

Whip cream with the sugar until soft peaks form. Stir in liqueur. Spoon cream into meringues. Top with berries.

4-6 servings

MENU

Mock Crab

Sausage & Lentil Soup

Bermuda Delights

Fresh Fruit & Cheese

California Fumé Blanc

•

After the first softball game, invite the team for an informal dinner to discuss strategies. Bermuda Delights may be served as an open-face sandwich or appetizer.

Mock Crab

•

1 can (8 ounces) sauerkraut, rinsed & drained
1 cup grated sharp cheddar cheese
2 tablespoons chopped green pepper
2 tablespoons chopped pimiento
2 tablespoons chopped onion
2 tablespoons bread crumbs
1 tablespoon sugar
dash hot pepper sauce
¼-½ cup mayonnaise
1 cup cooked tiny shrimp
lemon slices
parsley

Finely cut sauerkraut with scissors. Combine with remaining ingredients. Chill at least 2 hours. Serve garnished with lemon slices & parsley. Serve with wheat crackers.

2 cups

Sausage & Lentil Soup

•

1 pound lentils
9 cups water
½ teaspoon thyme
1 teaspoon salt
1 teaspoon pepper
1 bay leaf
1 pound pork sausage
1 pound hot Italian sausages
1 cup sliced carrots
1 cup sliced celery
1 clove garlic
1 cup chopped onion
1 can (28 ounces) plum tomatoes, chopped
2 teaspoons Italian herbs
1 cup dry white wine
½ cup broken spaghetti pieces

Rinse lentils. Combine with water, thyme, salt, pepper & bay leaf. Bring to boil. Simmer, covered, 20 minutes.

In a large skillet, brown sausages. Cut Italian sausages into ½-inch pieces. Add to soup. Sauté carrots, celery, garlic & onions in skillet 6 minutes. Add to soup with tomatoes & herbs. Simmer 1 hour. 15 minutes before serving, add wine & spaghetti.

8 servings

Bermuda Delights

•

Dijon-style mustard
thin-sliced whole grain wheat bread
thin slices Bermuda onion
thin slices ripe tomato
thin slices goat's milk cheddar or sharp cheddar cheese

Spread Dijon-style mustard on bread slices. Top with onion & tomato. Place 2 strips goat cheddar criss-crossed on tomato. Broil until cheese melts. Use cocktail rye for hors d'oeuvres.

Luncheon Gatherings

fresh daytime entertaining

MENU

Fresh Virgin Marys

Eggs Sonora

Mexican Rice

Julienned Cactus & Lettuce Salad

Hard Rolls

Melon Wedges

This versaule brunch, lunch, or light dinner menu will become a favorite.

BEVERAGE

Fresh Virgin Marys

- 7½ pounds tomatoes, coarsely chopped
- 1 cup chopped celery
- 2 cups chopped onion
- 1 clove garlic, minced
- ⅛ cup sugar
- 1 tablespoon salt
- ½ teaspoon pepper
- 1 teaspoon horseradish
- 3 tablespoons fresh lemon juice
- 1 teaspoon Worcestershire sauce

Combine tomatoes, celery, onion & garlic in 6-quart pan. Bring to boil over medium-high heat. Reduce heat. Simmer 20 minutes. In blender, whirl mixture until smooth in batches. Pour into sieve. Discard pulp & seeds. Stir in sugar, salt, pepper, horseradish, lemon juice & Worcestershire. Store in freezer containers. Best to make in advance if using fresh.

3 quarts

ENTREE

Eggs Sonora

- 1 can (10 ounces) enchilada sauce
- 2¼ cups chopped tomatoes
- ¼ cup chopped green chilies
- ¼ cup chopped celery
- ¼ cup chopped green pepper
- ½ cup chopped onion
- salt & pepper
- pinch sugar
- 2 ripe avocados, mashed
- 2 teaspoons fresh lemon juice
- 2 cups refried beans, heated
- 8 corn tortillas, warmed
- 1 cup grated cheddar cheese
- 1 cup grated Monterey Jack cheese
- 1 pound bacon, crisp-cooked & crumbled
- 12 eggs, scrambled
- sour cream

In a saucepan, combine enchilada sauce, tomatoes, chilies, celery, green pepper, onion, salt, pepper & sugar. Simmer 20-30 minutes. Combine avocado & lemon juice. Set aside.

On warmed tortillas, place a layer of beans, cheeses, bacon, eggs, sauce & avocado. Top with a dollop of sour cream.

8 servings

RICE

Mexican Rice

- 1 large onion, chopped
- 4 tablespoons olive oil
- 2 cloves garlic, minced
- 2 cups long grain rice
- 1½ cups peeled, chopped tomatoes
- 4 cups beef consommé
- 1½ teaspoons cumin
- salt

In large saucepan over medium heat, sauté onion in oil until tender, not browned, 3-5 minutes. Add garlic & rice. Cook 3-5 minutes, stirring often. Add tomatoes, consommé, cumin & salt. Bring to boil over high heat. Reduce heat. Simmer, covered, until liquid is absorbed 20 minutes. Fluff with fork before serving.

10-12 servings

MENU

Chicken Confetti Salad

Shaved Cucumber & Onion Salad

Walnut Bread

Marbleridge Farm Tea

Pineapple Sorbet with Sugar Cookies

Lemon Flavored Sparkling Water

•

What a delightful patio luncheon for 12. Use brightly colored paper plates, napkins & plenty of flowers.

Chicken Confetti Salad

•

1 head lettuce, torn into bite-size pieces
1 head cauliflower, separated into flowerets
1 Bermuda onion, sliced
1 sweet red pepper, chopped
1 cup broccoli, chopped
¾ pound bacon, crisp-cooked & crumbled
2 cups diced, cooked chicken

Dressing:
3 tablespoons sugar
1½ cups mayonnaise
¾ cup grated Parmesan or romano cheese
1 tablespoon crushed green peppercorns
2 tablespoons milk

Combine lettuce, cauliflower, onion, red pepper, broccoli, bacon & chicken. Chill 1 hour. Mix dressing ingredients, Refrigerate until serving time. Toss salad with dressing just before serving.

12 servings

Walnut Bread

•

2 packages dry yeast
¼ cup warm water
4-5 cups bread flour
½ tablespoon salt
4 teaspoons sugar
½ cup walnuts, finely chopped
1 cup milk
2 tablespoons vegetable oil
2 eggs

Mix yeast with warm water. Set aside 10 minutes until dissolved. In mixing bowl, combine flour, salt, sugar & nuts. Add milk, oil, eggs & yeast mixture.

Beat on low speed with mixer or bread hook. When blended, adjust speed to medium. Mix 15 minutes. If dough hook is not available, mix half of flour with other ingredients until well blended. Stir in remaining flour by hand. Knead 10 minutes. Cover & let stand 15 minutes.

Preheat oven to 375°F. Butter a baking sheet. Turn out dough, cut into 6 pieces. With floured hands, knead into loaf shapes. Place on baking sheet. Cover. Let loaves rise until doubled in bulk. Bake 25-30 minutes, until golden brown.

Dough can be shaped into 2 loaves & baked in two 9x5-inch pans.

6 small or 2 large loaves

Marbleridge Farm Tea

•

6-ounces frozen lemonade concentrate, thawed
1 cup packed, fresh garden mint leaves
4 tea bags
6 cups cold water

Combine ingredients in a 2-quart pitcher. Stir with a wooden spoon to bruise mint leaves. Steep 24 hours in refrigerator. Remove tea bags & mint leaves. Stir & serve over ice.

2 quarts

MENU

Assorted Cheeses

Spring Soup

Salad of Mixed Greens

Toasted Celery Seed Bread

Tipsy Peach Cake with Brown Butter Frosting

Washington State Johannisberg Reisling

•

A great light dinner after work or play. Soup & Cake should be made the day before. For last minute guests, put a cloth on the kitchen table & add candles.

S O U P

Spring Soup

•

- 2 tablespoons butter
- 2 leeks, cleaned & chopped, including tender greens
- 1 small onion, chopped
- 6 cups hot water
- 2 potatoes, peeled & thinly sliced
- 2 carrots, peeled & thinly sliced
- 2 teaspoons salt
- ¼ cup uncooked rice
- 8 stalks asparagus, cut into ½-inch pieces
- ½ pound spinach, chopped
- 1 cup light cream

Melt butter in large pan. Add leeks & onion. Simmer over low heat until tender, 5 minutes. Add hot water, potatoes, carrots & salt. Bring to a boil. Reduce heat. Simmer 15 minutes. Add rice & asparagus. Simmer 25 minutes. Add spinach & simmer 10 minutes. Stir in cream. Bring to a boil. Note: Flavor improves if soup is chilled overnight. Heat through before serving time.

6-8 servings

B R E A D

Toasted Celery Seed Bread

•

- ¾ cup butter, softened
- ¼ teaspoon salt
- cayenne pepper
- ⅜ teaspoon paprika
- ¾ teaspoon celery seed
- 1½ pound loaf white bread, unsliced, crusts removed

Preheat oven to 450°F.

Blend butter & seasonings. Cut loaf in half lengthwise, almost through to bottom. Cut at 2-inch intervals crosswise, almost to bottom. Spread butter mixture over all cut surfaces except bottom. Can be assembled in advance. Bake on baking sheet 5 minutes.

8 servings

D E S S E R T

Tipsy Peach Cake with Brown Butter Frosting

•

- ½ cup shortening
- 2 cups sugar
- 2 eggs
- 2½ cups flour
- 1½ teaspoons baking soda
- ¼ teaspoon baking powder
- 1½ teaspoon salt
- ¾ teaspoon cinnamon
- ½ teaspoon ginger
- ½ teaspoon allspice
- 3 large peaches, pitted
- ½ cup bourbon
- ½ cup water
- ¼ teaspoon almond extract
- ½ cup pecans
- 1 cup raisins

Brown Butter Frosting:

- ⅓ cup butter
- 3 cups powdered sugar, sifted
- ½ teaspoon vanilla
- 3 tablespoons heavy cream

Preheat oven to 350°F. Butter & flour a 13x9-inch pan.

Cream shortening & sugar. Add eggs. Sift dry ingredients. Add to creamed mixture.

Put peaches, unpeeled into blender. Add bourbon, water & extract. Purée & measure. Add more peaches, if needed, to make 2½ cups. Mix peaches with batter. Add raisins & nuts. Blend well. Pour into pan. Bake 60-65 minutes until cake tests done. For frosting, brown butter over medium heat until a delicate brown, not scorched. Blend butter with sugar. Stir in vanilla & cream. Mix until smooth. Frost cake.

12-15 servings

MENU

Mugs of Chunky Potato Soup

Ratatouille en Croûte

Bibb Lettuce with Pecans & Oranges

Carrot Cake

California Gewürztraminer

•

Light the fireplace, sip a glass of wine while the Ratatouille bakes. Spread a cloth in front of the fire to have a picnic on a winter's afternoon.

Ratatouille en Croûte

•

1 small eggplant, cut into 1-inch cubes
1 medium onion, sliced
1 clove garlic, chopped
2 tablespoons olive oil
3 tomatoes, peeled & cut into wedges
1 medium zucchini, sliced
½ green pepper, cut into strips
¼ cup snipped parsley
1 teaspoon salt
¼ teaspoon pepper
½ teaspoon basil
1 package (3 ounces) cream cheese
½ pound puff pastry
1 egg, beaten with 1 teaspoon water

Preheat oven to 425°F.

Cook onion & garlic in oil in large skillet until tender. Add eggplant, tomatoes, zucchini, green pepper, parsley, salt, pepper & basil. Simmer 10 minutes. Cool.

Roll pastry into a 16x9-inch rectangle on a floured surface. Spoon ratatouille lengthwise down center of pastry. Dot with cream cheese. Blend egg & water. Brush edges of pastry. Fold pastry over to enclose filling. Secure edges with tines of a fork. Place on a baking sheet. Slash top in four places with point of a sharp knife, cutting through pastry. Brush with egg-water mixture. Bake 20-30 minutes until puffed & golden. Slice to serve.

6 servings

Bibb Lettuce with Pecans & Oranges

•

4 heads Bibb lettuce
¾ cup pecan halves, toasted
2 oranges, peeled & sliced
⅓ cup vinegar
½ cup sugar
1 cup vegetable oil
1 teaspoon salt
½ small onion, chopped
1 teaspoon dry mustard
2 tablespoons water

Place lettuce, pecans & oranges into a salad bowl.

Combine vinegar, sugar, oil, salt, onion, mustard & water in a blender. Dressing can be made ahead & refrigerated. Toss with salad just before serving.

8 servings

Carrot Cake

•

2 cups flour
1 teaspoon baking soda
2 teaspoons cinnamon
1 teaspoon salt
2 cups sugar
1½ cups vegetable oil
3 eggs
2 cups finely grated carrots
1 cup crushed pineapple, well drained
1 cup shredded coconut
1 cup chopped walnuts
1 teaspoon vanilla

Frosting:
1 package (8 ounces) cream cheese, softened
½ cup butter, softened
2 teaspoons vanilla
4 cups sifted powdered sugar

Preheat oven to 350°F. Butter & flour a 13x9-inch pan.

Sift flour, soda, cinnamon & salt. Set aside. Beat sugar, oil & eggs until well blended. Gradually add flour mixture. Fold in carrots, pineapple, coconut, walnuts & vanilla. Pour into pan. Bake 1 hour. Cool.

For frosting, beat cream cheese, butter & vanilla. Gradually add powdered sugar, beating until smooth. Frost cake.

12-15 servings

MENU

Country Pâté
with
French Bread

Lemon-Sherry Chicken Supreme

Dilled Broccoli Salad

Milwaukee Million Dollar Pie

California Chardonnay

•

Use fresh broccoli from your garden or the farmer's stand. Gather a large bunch of broccoli & secure with a fat rubber band. Tie with ribbon. Trim stems evenly to stand as the centerpiece.

ENTREE

Lemon-Sherry Chicken Suprème

•

¼ cup flour
1 teaspoon salt
1 teaspoon paprika
6 whole chicken breasts, halved, skinned & boned
¼ cup butter
1 tablespoon cornstarch
2½ cups light cream
¼ cup sherry
½ teaspoon grated lemon peel
1½ tablespoons lemon juice
1½ cups grated Swiss cheese
½ cup chopped parsley

Preheat oven to 350°F.

Combine flour, salt & paprika in flat dish. Coat chicken with flour mixture. Melt butter in a large skillet. Brown chicken on both sides. Arrange chicken in 13x9-inch baking dish.

Mix cornstarch with ½ cup cream. Stir into pan drippings. Cook, stirring, over low heat. Gradually add remaining cream, sherry, lemon peel & juice. Cook & stir until sauce thickens. Pour over chicken. May be refrigerated or frozen at this point.

Bake 30 minutes, covered. Uncover & sprinkle with cheese. Return to oven until cheese melts. Garnish with parsley.

12 servings

VEGETABLES

Dilled Broccoli Salad

•

3 heads broccoli
¼ cup chopped onion
½ cup sliced stuffed olives
3 hard-cooked eggs, chopped
1½ cups sliced celery
1 tablespoon lemon juice
1 teaspoon dill weed
1 cup mayonnaise
1 head Boston lettuce

Cut broccoli into 3-inch spears. Cook broccoli until crisp-tender about 3 minutes. Drain.

Place broccoli in bowl with onion, olives, eggs & celery. Combine lemon juice, dill weed & mayonnaise. Stir dressing into broccoli mixture. Chill 4 hours. Serve in a Boston lettuce cup.

6 servings

DESSERT

Milwaukee Million Dollar Pie

•

Crust:
2 cups crushed chocolate wafer cookies
½ cup butter, melted

Filling:
1¼ cups butter, softened
1⅓ cups sugar
4-ounces unsweetened chocolate, melted
6 large eggs
3 tablespoons Cognac
2 cups finely chopped pecans
1 pint heavy cream, whipped
semi-sweet chocolate curls

Preheat oven to 350°F.

Mix crumbs & melted butter. Press mixture firmly & evenly onto bottom & sides of two 8-inch pie pans or one 10-inch springform pan. Bake 10 minutes & cool.

Cream butter & sugar. Add melted chocolate. Stir. Add eggs, 1 at a time, beating 3 minutes after each addition. Add Cognac & nuts. Pour into crusts. Top each with whipped cream & curls. Chill 3 hours. Freezes well.

12-16 servings

Photographs

Salade St. Simeon, recipe 145
Beth's Sherried Wild Rice Soup, recipe 12
Martini Sole on the Grill, recipe 29
Mustard Ring, recipe 141
Leg of Lamb with Quince Sauce, recipe 78

CONTRASSEGNO I.V.A.
S. PELLEGRINO

tment
POINT HOOKS
e Fly Co.
WIS.
ELLED HOOKS
PATTERNS INSPECTED
TROUT AND BASS
MORE DURABLE
BUCKTAILS
OR GANGS
ERKWILL
ST. CRO
LEADERS
packed 1 dozen
felt pads

ASTORIA
EXTRA

OM AMERICA'S DAIRY

MENU

Cold Strawberry Soup

Creamy Egg Brunch Casserole

Oven Baked Hashbrowns

Fresh Garden Salad

Nana's Banana Bread

California Blush Zinfandel

•

Entertain the Aunts, Uncles & Cousins coming to brunch next Sunday with ease & elegance. Present the Soup in a white tureen & serve in punch cups with a dollop of sour cream & strawberry on top.

Cold Strawberry Soup

•

3 cups Burgundy wine
2 pints strawberries, cleaned, hulled, & sliced
½ cup sugar
1 pint sour cream
extra berries & sour cream for garnish

Simmer burgundy, strawberries & sugar for 30 minutes. Chill. Add sour cream. Purée in blender or processor. Chill. Pour into serving bowls. Garnish with sour cream & a perfect berry.

8 servings

Creamy Egg Brunch Casserole

•

4 slices bacon, chopped
½ pound dried beef, chopped coarsely
½ cup butter, divided
½ pound fresh mushrooms, sliced
½ cup flour
1 quart milk
16 eggs
¼ teaspoon salt
pepper

Preheat oven to 275°F.

Brown bacon in skillet. Remove from pan. Add beef, ¼ cup butter & mushrooms. Reserve a few mushrooms for garnish. Sauté lightly. Sprinkle flour over mixture. Cook 3 minutes. Gradually stir in milk. Cook until sauce is thickened & smooth. Stir constantly. Set aside.

Combine eggs, salt & pepper. Scramble eggs in remaining butter until very soft.

In a 13x9-inch casserole, alternately add a layer of soft scrambled eggs & a layer of sauce. Repeat. Garnish with reserved mushrooms & crumbled bacon. Cover & refrigerate, or bake immediately 30 minutes.

12 servings

Nana's Banana Bread

•

½ cup shortening
1½ cups sugar
2 eggs
3 large ripe, bananas, mashed
1 teaspoon salt
1 tablespoon vanilla
2 cups flour
1 teaspoon baking soda
½ cup buttermilk or sour cream
¾ cup chopped nuts

Preheat oven to 350°F. Butter & flour a 9x5-inch loaf pan.

Cream shortening & sugar. Beat in eggs. Add bananas to creamed mixture with salt & vanilla. Mix until well blended. Sift flour & baking soda. Add alternately to batter with buttermilk. Stir in nuts. Pour into loaf pan. Bake 40-45 minutes.

Recipe makes 22 small cupcakes. Bake 25-30 minutes.

1 loaf

MENU

Poppy Seed Tea Cake

Date Pudding

Croatian Kifle

Watercress, Onion & Cucumber Tea Sandwiches

Pot of Darjeeling Tea

•

Perfect for entertaining lightly with style, tea time has a resurgent popularity. Add 1 level teaspoon tea per cup to a warmed porcelain teapot. Add freshly boiled water. Cover & let steep 3-5 minutes. Gently stir tea. Strain into waiting teacups. Serve with a bit of lemon & sugar.

Poppy Seed Tea Cake

•

⅓ cup poppy seed
1 cup buttermilk
1 cup butter, softened
1½ cups sugar
4 eggs
2½ cups flour
2 teaspoons baking powder
1 teaspoon baking soda
½ teaspoon salt
2 tablespoons grated orange peel
2 tablespoons sugar
1 teaspoon cinnamon

Combine poppy seed & buttermilk. Refrigerate overnight.

Preheat oven to 350°F. Butter & flour a 10-inch tube or bundt pan. Cream butter & sugar. Add eggs, one at a time, beating well after each addition. Combine flour, baking powder, soda & salt. Add to creamed mixture. Add orange peel. Spoon half the batter into prepared pan. Sprinkle with sugar & cinnamon. Top with remaining batter. Bake 1 hour. Cool 10 minutes. Turn out onto rack.

20 servings

Date Pudding

•

1 pound pitted dates, chopped
1½ cups chopped English walnuts
1 cup milk
4 eggs
2 cups sugar
1 cup flour
2 teaspoons baking powder
whipped cream

Preheat oven to 350°F.

Soak dates & nuts in milk until dates are soft. Beat eggs & sugar. Add flour, baking powder & date mixture. Pour into 9-inch square pan. Bake 45-50 minutes. Serve warm with whipped cream.

8 servings

Croatian Kifle

•

2 cups butter, softened
12-ounces cream cheese, softened
4 cups flour
1 can (12 ounces) apricot pastry filling, or thick jam or ¾ cup finely ground almonds
sugar

Combine butter, cream cheese & flour. Use a potato masher to thoroughly mix. Flatten dough. Cover & refrigerate overnight.

Preheat oven to 350°F.

Roll out ⅓ dough onto floured surface to ⅛-inch thick. Cut into 2-inch squares. Place ¼ teaspoon filling in middle of each square. Roll up diagonally. Pinch seam & form into half-moon shape. Place onto baking sheets. Bake 15-20 minutes until lightly browned. Roll immediately in sugar.

12-14 dozen

MENU

Connie's Tomato Quiche

Welsh Leek Pie

Celery Root Coleslaw Salad

Croissants & Nut Breads

Truffles

California Red Gamay

A quiche & pie lunch to delight your most discriminating friends. Mound the Truffles onto a small footed serving dish. Decadence!

ENTREE

Connie's Tomato Quiche

1 9-inch unbaked pie crust
3 tablespoons flour
salt & pepper
2 medium tomatoes, cut into wedges
2 teaspoons olive oil
½ cup pitted Sicilian olives, sliced
1 cup minced scallions
3-ounces Bel Paese cheese, cubed
2 eggs, slightly beaten
1 cup heavy cream
1 cup grated provolone cheese

Preheat oven to 400°F. Pierce pie crust all over with fork. Bake 8 minutes. Set aside.

Combine flour, salt & pepper. Dredge tomato wedges in flour. Heat oil in skillet. Sauté tomatoes 5 minutes. Place in pie crust. Reserve 2 tablespoons scallions. Add olives, scallions & Bel Paese to pie crust.

Combine eggs & cream. Stir in cheese. Pour into pie. Bake 45 minutes until filling is set. Top with reserved scallions. Let stand 5 minutes before serving.

6 servings

ENTREE

Welsh Leek Pie

1 cup flour
¼ cup finely chopped suet or vegetable shortening
pinch salt
1 teaspoon baking powder
4-5 tablespoons water

1½ pounds lean beef stew meat
¼ cup flour
½ teaspoon salt
pepper
2 tablespoons vegetable oil
1½ cups beef stock
2 medium potatoes, cubed
1 medium leek, sliced, including tender greens

To prepare pastry, combine flour, suet, salt & baking powder in processor or with a pastry blender until uniformly pea-size in consistency. Add water. Mix until smooth ball forms. Chill.

Toss beef cubes with flour, salt & pepper. Brown beef in hot oil 2-3 minutes. Add stock. Cover & simmer 1 hour. Add potatoes & leek. Cook 5 minutes. Spoon into 2-quart casserole.

Preheat oven to 375°F.

Roll pastry out ¼-inch thick. Cover casserole with pastry. Trim edges. Cut out decorative pastry designs. Paint top of pastry with water. Apply pastry cutouts. Cut hole in center of pastry for steam to escape. Bake 1 hour until golden brown.

6-8 servings

DESSERT

Truffles

½ cup butter
2 cups powdered sugar
½ cup + 2 tablespoons unsweetened Dutch-process cocoa
3 tablespoons Grand Marnier

Coating:
3 tablespoons powdered sugar
3 tablespoons unsweetened Dutch-process cocoa

Beat butter in large bowl with wooden spoon. Add powdered sugar, ½ cup at a time, beating well after each addition. Add cocoa. Beat well. Add Grand Marnier. Combine. Cover & refrigerate several hours.

Combine coating sugar & cocoa.

Roll truffles by heaping teaspoonfuls into balls. Roll in coating mix. Refrigerate.

2 dozen

MENU

Cobb Salad

Tabouli

Kitchen Sink Pasta Salad

Soft Sesame Bread Sticks

Decorated Sheet Cake

Iced Mint Tea

California White Zinfandel

•

A thank-you luncheon on the lawn for committee members you've worked closely with the past year. Set up card tables with breezy white paper cloths tied at the legs with ribbons. Buffet service allows members to help themselves & return to other jobs.

Cobb Salad

•

1 large head romaine lettuce, torn into bite-size pieces
3 cooked chicken breast halves, skinned, boned & shredded
6 scallions, sliced
6 hard cooked eggs, chopped
3 tomatoes, chopped
½ pound bacon, crisp-cooked & crumbled
½ pound Swiss cheese, grated
2 avocados, peeled, pitted, cubed & tossed in lemon juice
4-ounces blue cheese, crumbled
oil & vinegar dressing

Place romaine on oval serving platter. Arrange remaining ingredients in rows, placing chicken in a strip down the middle. Sprinkle with oil & vinegar, salt & cracked pepper before serving.

6 servings

Tabouli

•

1½ cups bulgar wheat
4 cups boiling water
1¼ cups minced parsley
¾ cup minced mint
3 medium tomatoes, chopped
1 cucumber, peeled, seeded & chopped
1 clove garlic, minced
¾ cup fresh lemon juice
1 teaspoon salt
⅓ cup olive oil

Pour boiling water over bulgar. Let stand 2 hours. Drain excess water. Mix bulgar with remaining ingredients. Chill 4 hours before serving. Serve in hollowed tomatoes, in pita bread, in cocktail-size pita bread, or on bed of lettuce. Serve as a salad, sandwich or appetizer.

8 servings

Kitchen Sink Pasta Salad

•

½ pound linguini, broken into pieces
½ pound bow tie pasta
½ pound vegetable rotini
½ pound vegetable wagon wheel or shell pasta
¾ cup chopped red onion
2 medium green peppers, chopped
2 medium red peppers, chopped
2 large cucumbers, chopped
2 cups chopped celery
1 cup broccoli flowerets
1 cup cauliflowerets
½ pound hard salami, cubed
½ pound boiled ham, julienned
½ pound mozzarella, cubed
1 cup grated Parmesan cheese
½ cup grated romano cheese
1 can (7¾ ounces) pitted black olives, drained
½ cup sunflower seeds
½ cup soy nuts
1 bunch parsley, chopped
2 teaspoons salt
1½ teaspoons pepper

Garlic Herb Vinaigrette:
¾ cup red wine vinegar
2 cups olive oil
2 tablespoons water
2 cloves garlic, minced
2½ teaspoons Italian herbs
1 teaspoon sugar
salt & pepper

3 tomatoes, chopped
3 hard-cooked eggs, chopped

Cook pastas al dente. Rinse under cold water. Drain. Combine pasta & remaining salad ingredients in a very large container. Combine dressing ingredients. Toss 1½ cups dressing with salad. Cover & chill 12 hours or overnight. Before serving, toss with remaining dressing, tomatoes & eggs. Great way to use up bits of this & that from the refrigerator.

20 servings

MENU

Italian Zucchini Pie

Whole Wheat Rolls

Persian Peach Salad

Cherry Date Cake

Italian Chianti Classico
or
Chianti Colli Arentini

•

What to do with all that zucchini? The Pie uses quantities of zucchini & freezes well before baking. Bake 6 Pies for winter meals. Molto grande!!

ENTREE

Italian Zucchini Pie

•

4-5 cups thinly sliced zucchini
1 large onion, chopped
1 clove garlic, minced
1/4 cup butter
1/2 cup chopped fresh parsley
1/2 teaspoon salt
1/2 teaspoon pepper
1/2 teaspoon oregano
2 eggs, slightly beaten
2 cups grated Mozzarella cheese
2 teaspoons Dijon-style mustard
1 unbaked 9-inch pie crust
balsamic vinegar

Preheat oven to 375°F.

Sauté zucchini, onion & garlic in butter until tender. Stir in parsley & seasonings. Combine eggs & cheese. Add vegetables.

Spread mustard on bottom of pie crust. Add vegetable mixture. Bake 40-50 minutes until knife inserted in center comes out clean. Serve each slice with a few drops of balsamic vinegar.

5-6 servings

SALAD

Persian Peach Salad

•

4 fresh peaches, peeled, halved & pitted
lettuce leaves

Dressing:
2 tablespoons Port wine
1 tablespoon apricot jam
1 teaspoon ground ginger
1/2 cup heavy cream, lightly whipped

Arrange peach halves on lettuce leaves.

Heat wine, jam & ginger over low heat until smooth. Strain. Fold into slightly whipped cream. Spoon over peaches.

4 servings

DESSERT

Cherry Date Cake

•

1 1/2 cups flour
1 1/2 cups sugar
1 teaspoon baking powder
1/2 teaspoon salt
4 eggs
3 tablespoons butter, softened
1 cup pitted fresh Bing cherries, halved, or maraschino cherries
2 cups pecan halves
2 cups walnut halves
1 pound pitted dates, sliced lengthwise

Glaze:
1/2 cup butter
1/4 cup water
1 cup sugar
1/2 cup dark rum
whipped cream

Preheat oven to 300°F.

Sift flour, sugar, baking powder & salt. Add eggs, 1 at a time. Beat well. Add remaining ingredients. Stir in gently. Bake in 10-inch tube or Bundt pan 1 hour 30 minutes. Increase temperature to 325°F. Bake 15 minutes.

For the glaze. Boil butter, water & sugar 5 minutes. Add rum. Set cake in pan on rack. Pierce cake with skewer. Slowly pour glaze onto cake. Allow to soak into the cake while cooling. Remove from pan. Store, refrigerated in tightly covered container several weeks. Add fruit juice or rum to moisten. Serve with whipped cream.

20 servings

MENU

White Sangria

Shrimp & Rice Salad

Tina's Tomatoes

Pineapple Cheesecake

Invite your friends for lunch. Serve the Shrimp Salad in red cabbage, halved & hollowed out on bright pink plates. Use plenty of pink & dark red peonies & carnations for the centerpiece.

White Sangria

- 1 bottle (750ml) dry white wine
- ½ cup Curaçao
- 1 lemon, sliced very thin
- 1 orange, sliced very thin
- 1 lime, sliced very thin
- 1 bottle (10 ounces) club soda

Mix wine & Curaçao. Add lemon, orange, & lime slices. Cover & chill at least one hour. Just before serving, add ice cubes & club soda.

To make for a crowd, mix 1 bottle (3 liters) wine, 2 cups Curaçao, with 1 liter plus one 10-ounce bottle club soda.

6 servings

Shrimp & Rice Salad

- ¾ pound fresh shrimp, cooked, peeled & halved
- 1 cup rice, cook according to package directions
- 1 cup vinaigrette dressing
- 1 tablespoon teriyaki sauce
- 1 teaspoon sugar
- 2 cups thin strips of fresh spinach
- ½ cup sliced celery
- ½ cup sliced scallions
- ⅓ cup crumbled crisp-cooked bacon
- 1 can (8 ounces) sliced water chestnuts, drained

Place shrimp & hot rice in bowl. Cool slightly. Combine vinaigrette, teriyaki sauce & sugar. Stir into warm rice. Cover & chill. Fold spinach, celery, scallions, bacon & water chestnuts into rice just before serving.

6-8 servings

Tina's Tomatoes

- 1 tomato, halved
- 2 tablespoons sherry
- salt & pepper
- oregano
- 2 tablespoons mayonnaise
- freshly grated Parmesan

Pierce holes in cut side of tomato. Pour in 1 tablespoon sherry per tomato half. Sprinkle with salt, pepper & oregano. Bake at 350°F. 5-10 minutes. Spread 1 tablespoon mayonnaise on each tomato half. Sprinkle with Parmesan. Broil 2 minutes until lightly browned.

2 servings

MENU

Strawberry Butter

Swedish Pancakes

Buckwheat Yogurt Pancakes

German White Mosel Auslese

•

How about a pancake party on a lazy Sunday morning with the kids??

Strawberry Butter

•

1 cup unsalted butter, softened
2 tablespoon powdered sugar
1 pint fresh strawberries, cleaned & hulled

Put ingredients in blender. Blend until smooth. Mixture may look as though it is separating; continue to blend until smooth. One pint blueberries, apricots or kiwi fruit may be substituted as variations.

2 cups

Swedish Pancakes

•

3 eggs
¾ cup sifted flour
salt
⅛ teaspoon baking powder
¼ teaspoon sugar
1¼ cups milk
1 teaspoon vegetable shortening per pancake

Preheat a 10-inch flat griddle or iron pan over medium heat. Beat eggs. Add flour, salt, baking powder & sugar. Slowly beat in milk until batter is thin.

Melt shortening on griddle. Spread ¼ cup batter quickly to fill entire surface of pan. Use back of large spoon with a very light touch. Pancake should be very thin. Turn when browned. Spread with Strawberry Butter. Or top with syrup, powdered sugar, fresh fruit, jam, even sprinkle with granulated sugar. Roll up, serve & enjoy!!

9 pancakes

PANCAKE

Buckwheat Yogurt Pancakes

•

⅔ cup buckwheat flour
1⅓ cups flour
2 teaspoons baking powder
1 teaspoon baking soda
1 teaspoon salt
2 teaspoons honey or sugar
2 eggs, beaten
¼ cup butter, melted
2 cups yogurt
1¼ cups milk

Mix flours, baking powder, baking soda, salt & sugar. If using honey add it to liquid ingredients. In another bowl combine eggs, butter, yogurt & milk. Add yogurt mixture to dry ingredients. Stir briefly until batter is moist but not smooth. Cook on a hot, lightly-buttered griddle or electric skillet until the edges look dry. Turn to brown other side. Serve with butter & syrup.

4-6 servings

MENU

Bacon & Pasta Omelette

Escarole, Watercress, & Curly Endive Salad with Scallions

Herbed Croutons

Vinaigrette

Amaretto Cherry Bread

Wisconsin Red Chelois

•

A Packer Backer Brunch! Use leftover pasta for the Omelette & toss the Salad with the Herbed Croutons before the game comes on television. The Spicy Salad will really perk up taste buds.

Bacon & Pasta Omelette

•

2 tablespoons butter
1 small onion, finely chopped
½ pound cooked pasta
½ pound crisp-cooked bacon, crumbled
4 eggs, beaten
splash white wine
salt & pepper
Parmesan cheese

Heat butter in large skillet. Sauté onion 5 minutes. Add pasta & bacon. Toss to coat with butter & onion. Combine eggs, wine, salt & pepper. Pour into hot pan. Shake pan to settle ingredients. Cook until golden brown 5 minutes. Turn with spatulas. Cook other side 2 minutes. Invert onto serving plate. Sprinkle with Parmesan. Cut into wedges to serve.

4 servings

Herbed Croutons

•

¼ cup freshly grated Parmesan cheese
2 tablespoons oregano
2 cloves garlic, minced
1 tablespoon basil
½ teaspoon salt
½ teaspoon freshly ground pepper
4-5 cups dry bread cubes, crusts removed
¼ cup olive or salad oil

Preheat oven to 225°F.

In small bowl, mix cheese, oregano, garlic, basil, salt & pepper. In large bowl, toss bread cubes with oil. Toss with cheese-herb mixture until combined. Spread on baking sheets. Bake 1 hour until crisp & light golden, stirring occasionally so all sides toast. Cool. Croutons will keep one month stored in a tightly sealed container.

4-5 cups

Amaretto Cherry Bread

•

1½ cups flour
2 teaspoons baking powder
½ teaspoon salt
½ cup butter, softened
1 cup sugar
3 eggs
½ cup Amaretto liqueur
1 cup chopped walnuts
1 cup sour cherries, pitted, halved & drained

Glaze:
6 tablespoons sugar
6 tablespoons Amaretto liqueur

Preheat oven to 350°F. Butter a 9x5-inch pan.

Sift flour, baking powder & salt. Cream butter & sugar. Add eggs. Fold in dry ingredients, Amaretto, walnuts & cherries. Pour into loaf pan. Bake 1 hour.

For the glaze, mix sugar & Amaretto. While bread is still warm, pierce top of bread with a skewer. Pour glaze over, allowing it to seep into holes. Cool in pan.

1 loaf

MENU

Brother's Punch

California Yogurt Soup

Jack's Chicken Salad

Croissants

Bran Muffins

Lemon Cake with Blueberries

French White
Alsatian Gewürztraminer

•

The menu couldn't be simpler for a gathering of friends or neighbors. The cold Yogurt Soup is refreshing & delightfully different. Serve in dark-colored bowls.

Brother's Punch

•

1-ounce vodka
1-ounce prepared frozen concentrated raspberry juice
2-ounces grapefruit juice
mint sprigs

Pour into tall, ice-filled glasses. Serve with mint sprig garnish.

1 serving

California Yogurt Soup

•

4 cups plain yogurt
1¾ cups chilled chicken stock
4 ice cubes
½ cup golden raisins
2 hard-cooked eggs, chopped
½ cup sliced scallions
1 peeled, seeded cucumber, finely chopped
1 teaspoon salt
½ teaspoon white pepper
finely chopped parsley garnish
finely snipped dill garnish

Combine all ingredients. Chill several hours. Serve sprinkled with parsley & dill.

6-8 servings

Jack's Chicken Salad

•

½ cup mayonnaise
½ cup milk
2 cups cooked, chopped chicken or turkey breast
1 cup chopped celery
1 cup coarsely chopped walnuts
1 large unpeeled Granny Smith apple, chopped
4 scallions, thinly sliced
1 teaspoon tarragon
2 teaspoons finely snipped dill
2 tablespoons poppy seed
2 tablespoons toasted sesame seed
salt & freshly ground pepper

Combine mayonnaise & milk. Mix remaining ingredients in large bowl. Add mayonnaise mixture. Toss to coat. Serve on lettuce, in a split croissant or in melon wedges. Garnish with a few very thin slices of apple.

6 servings

MENU

Cream of Mushroom Soup

Croissant Summer Sandwich

Fresh Lemonade

Raspberry-Walnut "Linzer" Bars

French Beaujolais Morgon, slightly chilled

•

The summer air is warm & vibrant. How about a few friends over for a casual lunch?

Cream of Mushroom Soup

•

½ pound mushrooms, sliced
1 medium onion, chopped
1 cup lightly packed chopped parsley
¼ cup butter
1 tablespoon flour
2 cups beef stock
1 cup sour cream or crème fraîche
fresh chopped parsley, chives or scallions

In a medium saucepan sauté mushrooms, onion, & parsley in butter until mushrooms are limp & liquid has evaporated. Stir in flour. Blend in stock. Bring to boil, stirring. Using blender or processor, whirl broth mixture with cream, a portion at a time, until smooth. Can be made ahead. Cover & chill at this point. Reheat to serve. Garnish with fresh chopped parsley, chives or scallions.

4 servings

Croissant Summer Sandwich

•

Herb Cheese:
1 large clove garlic
1 small onion
1 package (8 ounces) cream cheese, softened
1 cup unsalted butter, softened
¼ cup parsley
¼ cup chives
1 teaspoon salt
½ teaspoon pepper
dash hot pepper

4 croissants, split
4-ounces sprouts: alfalfa, radish or combination
½ pound rare roast beef, thinly sliced
salt & pepper to taste

In a food processor with steel blade inserted, chop garlic & onion. Add cream cheese, butter, parsley, chives, salt, pepper & hot pepper sauce. Mix until blended. Chill overnight.

Spread both sides of croissant with herb cheese. Place sprouts & roast beef on one half. Salt & pepper the other half. Cover & refrigerate one hour or up to 1 day in advance.

4 servings

Raspberry-Walnut "Linzer" Bars

•

1½ cups butter, softened
1 cup powdered sugar
1 egg
salt
½ teaspoon cinnamon
2¾ cups flour
1½ cups finely chopped walnuts or pecans
2 cups raspberry jam
1 tablespoon lemon juice
powdered sugar

In a large bowl cream butter, sugar, egg, salt & cinnamon until fluffy. Gradually fold in flour & nuts. Chill dough 1 hour.

Set aside ⅓ dough. Pat remaining ⅔ dough into a 15x10-inch jelly roll pan.

Stir together jam & lemon juice. Spread evenly over pastry. On a floured surface, pat or roll out remaining dough into a rectangle. Cut into strips ¼-inch wide. Place strips on top of jam in a lattice pattern.

Bake at 375°F. 35-40 minutes, until pastry is lightly browned. Cool. Sprinkle with powdered sugar. Cut into bars.

30 bars

Celebration Gatherings

special occasions, holidays & gifts

VALENTINE'S DINNER FOR TWO

Simple Sole for Two

Pears with Tarragon Cream

Lemon-Broccoli Rice in Heart Mold

Croissants with Herb Butter

Cupid's Kiss Raspberry Cheesecake

French Champagne

•

Victorian is the theme for a small intimate table with a red tablecloth topped by an antique lace coverlet; streamers of burgundy & red ribbons on top; silver candlesticks & crystal tulip glasses chilled by champagne brut; a single red rose in a crystal vase.

ENTREE

Simple Sole for Two

•

1 pound sole fillets
1 tablespoon lemon juice
¼ cup grated Parmesan cheese
2 tablespoons butter, melted
1½ tablespoons mayonnaise
1½ tablespoons chopped onions
chopped parsley & lemon wedges

Preheat broiler.

Place fillets in a flat baking dish. Brush with lemon juice. Let stand 20 minutes. Combine cheese, butter mayonnaise & onion. Broil fillets 6-8 minutes until flaky. Spoon mayonnaise mixture on top of fillets. Broil 3 minutes. Serve garnished with finely chopped parsley & lemon wedges.

2 servings

SALAD

Pears with Tarragon Cream

•

Boston lettuce
4 fresh pears, peeled, cored & halved, rubbed with lemon
pitted Bing cherries
chopped English walnuts

Tarragon Cream Dressing:
2 eggs
4 tablespoons sugar
6 tablespoons tarragon vinegar
salt
white pepper
1 cup heavy cream, whipped

Put pear half, cherries & walnuts on lettuce-lined chilled plates.

In top of double boiler, beat eggs with sugar until light & fluffy. Gradually add vinegar, salt & pepper. Place double boiler over gently boiling water. Continue beating until thickened. Remove from heat. Cool. Fold in cream. Serve on salad.

8 servings

DESSERT

Cupid's Kiss Raspberry Cheesecake

•

1 package (8½ ounces) chocolate wafer cookies, finely crushed
½ cup butter, melted
½ cup sugar

Filling:
2 packages (8 ounces each) cream cheese, softened
¾ cup sugar
3 eggs
¼ cup sour cream
1 tablespoon Grand Marnier
1 teaspoon lemon juice
1 pound red raspberries

Hardening Chocolate Sauce:
2-ounces finest quality milk chocolate
2-ounces finest quality dark chocolate
1 tablespoon vegetable oil

Preheat oven to 350°F.

Combine cookie crumbs, butter & sugar. Press onto bottom & sides of 9-inch springform pan. Bake 10 minutes. Set aside to cool.

Reserve 10-12 whole raspberries. Purée remainder. Measure ⅔ cup raspberry purée for cheesecake. Strain remainder in a sieve. Reserve.

For filling, beat cream cheese, sugar, sour cream, Grand Marnier & lemon juice until very smooth & fluffy. Add the ⅔ cup raspberry purée. Blend well. Pour into prepared crust. Bake 60 minutes. Cool to room temperature.

For sauce, melt chocolates & oil. Frost cheesecake with chocolate sauce. Place reserved whole raspberries in decorative pattern on top of sauce. Refrigerate until sauce hardens. Serve with strained raspberries sweetened with a little Grand Marnier, if desired.

10-12 servings

FRIDAY EVENING
SABBATH CELEBRATION

Bourbon Mustard Chicken

Honey-Baked Carrots & Apples

Whipped Potatoes with Cabbage

Braided Egg Bread

Stellar Lemon Meringue Pie

California White
Sonoma
Johannisberg Riesling

•

A menu for any special occasion, with family & friends to brighten the table & the congenial glow of candlelight.

Bourbon Mustard Chicken

•

¼ cup Dijon-style mustard
¼ cup bourbon
¼ cup dark brown sugar
1 teaspoon Worcestershire sauce
1 teaspoon salt
2 scallions, thinly sliced
4-6 boneless, skinless chicken breast halves, pounded ¼-inch thick
1 tablespoon margarine
1 tablespoon oil

Combine mustard, bourbon, brown sugar, Worcestershire, salt & scallions in non-metal dish. Place chicken in mixture, turning to coat. Cover & marinate one hour. Reserve marinade. Heat margarine & oil in heavy skillet over medium-high heat. Sauté chicken 3-4 minutes each side until golden. Pour off fat. Add marinade. Stir & heat to boiling. Serve over chicken.

4-6 servings

Honey-Baked Carrots & Apples

•

8 medium carrots, sliced
6 medium Granny Smith apples, peeled, cored & sliced
¼ cup honey
⅓ cup brown sugar
2 tablespoons margarine
paprika
watercress, garnish

Preheat oven to 350°F. Butter a 9-inch square pan. Cook carrots in small amount of boiling water 10 minutes until crisp-tender. Drain. Combine carrots, apples & honey. Pour into pan. Dot with margarine. Sprinkle with brown sugar & paprika. Cover & bake 50 minutes. Garnish with watercress sprigs.

8 servings

Stellar Lemon Meringue Pie

•

1 9-inch baked pie crust
1⅓ cups sugar
½ cup cornstarch
¼ teaspoon salt
1¾ cups water
4 egg yolks, beaten
2 tablespoons margarine, melted
1 tablespoon grated lemon peel
½ cup lemon juice

Meringue:
4 egg whites, room temperature
¼ teaspoon cream of tartar
½ cup sugar
lemon slices, garnish

In a saucepan over medium heat, combine sugar, cornstarch & salt. Gradually stir in water with a whisk. Cook, stirring constantly until mixture boils. Boil one minute. Remove from heat. Whisk yolks into saucepan. Return to low heat, stirring constantly. Do not overcook. Remove from heat. Stir in margarine, lemon peel & juice. Pour into pastry shell. Cover with plastic. Refrigerate 3 hours.

For the meringue, preheat oven to 425°F. Butter & flour a baking sheet. Beat egg whites & cream of tartar until soft peaks form. Add sugar by tablespoonfuls. Beat until sugar dissolves & meringue is stiff & glossy. Mound meringue in a 9-inch circle on baking sheet. Bake 5 minutes until golden. Cool 2 minutes. Using 2 large spatulas, lift meringue on top of pie. Garnish with lemon slices.

8 servings

EASTER DINNER

Leg of Lamb with Garlic-Quince Sauce

Pasta Soufflé

Burgundy Onions

Broccoli Bacon Salad

Orange-Cabbage Salad

Silver Dollar Baking Powder Biscuits

Pots of Rum Crème

California Sonoma Pinot Noir

•

Leg of Lamb with Garlic-Quince Sauce

•

6-pound semi-boneless leg of lamb
salt & pepper
3 cloves garlic, slivered
fresh tarragon sprigs
1 cup quince jelly, melted

Sauce:
1 whole head garlic
pan drippings
½ cup water
1 cup quince jelly

Preheat oven to 400°F.

Rub lamb with salt & pepper. With point of sharp knife, make slits in lamb. Insert garlic & tarragon. Place lamb on rack in roasting pan. Place head of garlic for the sauce in pan. Bake 1½ hours or until meat thermometer reads 130°F. for medium-rare, 145°F. medium-well done. Frequently baste with melted jelly. Remove from oven. Tent with foil. Let rest 15 minutes before carving. For sauce, pour off any accumulated fat from roasting pan. Add ½ cup water. Pop each clove garlic from skin. Place in pan juices with jelly over medium heat. Stir up bits of drippings from bottom of pan. Pour into blender. Purée until smooth. Serve with lamb.

8-10 servings

Pictured page 64.

Pasta Soufflé

•

9 tablespoons butter
1 clove garlic, minced
1½ tablespoons Dijon-style mustard
1⅔ cup milk
6-ounces Jarlsberg cheese, grated
¼ pound ham, cut into thin strips
1½ cups quartered, cooked artichoke hearts
¼ teaspoon cayenne
1 teaspoon pepper
6 eggs, separated
½ pound fresh angel hair or other pasta, cooked & drained

Preheat oven to 350°F. Make a wax paper collar to fit a 1½-quart soufflé dish. Butter inside of collar & dish. Dust with Parmesan cheese. Set aside.

In a medium-size saucepan, melt butter. Sauté garlic 1-2 minutes. Stir in mustard. Add milk, cheese, ham, artichokes, cayenne & pepper. Cook, stirring until cheese melts & is hot & bubbly. Remove from heat. Cool. Add egg yolks, 1 at a time, stirring well after each addition. Add pasta. Stir to coat. Beat egg whites until stiff. Stir ⅓ whites into pasta mixture. Blend thoroughly. Gently fold in remaining whites until well blended. Pour into prepared soufflé dish. Bake 40 minutes. Increase heat to 450°F. Bake 10 minutes longer. Remove collar. Serve immediately! Also use as an entrée.

8 servings

Burgundy Onions

•

6 large yellow onions, sliced ¼-inch thick
3 tablespoon butter
1½ cups Burgundy wine
salt & pepper

Separate onions into rings. Melt butter in large skillet. Sauté onions until tender & golden. Add wine, salt & pepper. Cover & simmer over low heat 15 minutes. Remove cover, increase heat & cook until wine reduces to a glaze.

8 servings

Broccoli Bacon Salad

•

2 large heads broccoli, chopped & blanched 1 minute
½ cup raisins
¼ cup chopped scallions or red onion
1 cup mayonnaise
¼ cup sugar
2 tablespoons cider vinegar
12 slices crisp-cooked bacon, crumbled

Combine broccoli, raisins & scallions. Mix mayonnaise, sugar & vinegar. Toss with broccoli. Chill several hours or overnight. Top with bacon before serving.

8-10 servings

Orange-Cabbage Salad

•

1 medium head red cabbage, finely chopped
1 large onion, finely chopped
1 whole orange, finely chopped
½ cup sugar
½ cup champagne vinegar
½ cup vegetable oil
1 tablespoon celery seed
1 cup rendered pork cracklings, optional

Combine cabbage, onion & orange. Mix sugar, vinegar, oil & celery seed. Toss with cabbage mixture. Cover & chill several hours. Toss with cracklings before serving.

12 servings

Pots of Rum Crème

•

1½ envelopes unflavored gelatin
½ cup rum
1½ cups milk
5 eggs, separated
1½ cups sugar
1 teaspoon vanilla
3 cups heavy cream, whipped
fresh cherries or strawberries

Soften gelatin in rum. Heat milk in small pan. Add gelatin-rum mixture. Stir until gelatin completely dissolves. Cool. Beat egg yolks until light & fluffy. Add sugar. Beat until thick. Add vanilla & cooled milk mixture. Fold in whipped cream. Beat egg whites until stiff. Gently fold into mixture. Spoon into little crème pots, demitasse cups or ramekins. Chill. Crème will separate into 2 layers. Garnish with fresh cherries or strawberries.

12 servings

Delight your family & guests with flavor surprises. The Soufflé is a pasta lover's dream! Use a low flowering plant with pastel-colored eggs interspersed among the foliage for the centerpiece. Match pastel colors for linens.

EASTER BRUNCH

Orange Julep

Pear & Poultry Sandwich

Rich Sweet Rolls

Fresh Strawberries in Champagne

Set the table with pastel-colored Easter eggs as accents. Use colored plates & napkins to match the pastel frosting on the Sweet Rolls. Serve Sandwiches & Sweet Rolls in napkin-lined Easter baskets.

Orange Julep

- 1 quart fresh orange juice
- ½ cup minced fresh mint leaves
- ½ cup sugar
- juice of 6 limes
- 2 cups club soda
- mint sprigs, garnish

Mix orange juice, sugar, mint, & lime juice. Chill 1-2 hours. Strain to remove mint. Mix with club soda. Pour into tall glasses filled with chipped ice. Garnish with mint. Refreshing!

8 servings

Pear & Poultry Sandwich

- 4 slices cooked chicken or turkey
- 4 slices buttered toast
- ½ cup mayonnaise
- ⅓ cup finely chopped celery
- 2 tablespoons finely chopped scallions
- ¼ teaspoon salt
- 2 very ripe pears, peeled, cored & thinly sliced
- ½ cup grated cheddar cheese
- paprika

Preheat oven to 350°F.

Arrange chicken or turkey slices on toast on a baking sheet. Combine mayonnaise, celery, scallions & salt. Spread on poultry. Arrange sliced pears on top. Sprinkle with cheese & paprika. Bake 10 minutes. Great for using leftover turkey!

4 servings

Rich Sweet Rolls

- 1 cup butter, softened
- 1 cup sour cream
- 2 cups flour
- ½ cup sugar
- ½ teaspoon cinnamon
- ½ cup chopped pecans

Frosting:

- 1 cup powdered sugar, sifted
- 2 tablespoons butter, softened
- pinch salt
- ½ teaspoon vanilla
- 1-2 tablespoons milk

Combine butter & sour cream. Blend in flour. Form into a ball. Cover & refrigerate 4 hours or overnight. Divide ball into 4 pieces. Keep dough in refrigerator until needed. Roll each piece into 9-inch circle. Cut each circle into 8 triangle-shaped wedges. Mix sugar, cinnamon & pecans. Sprinkle ¼ mixture evenly over wedges. Loosely roll each wedge from wide edge to the point. Place rolls on baking sheet. Repeat for each portion of dough. Preheat oven to 400°F. Bake 15-20 minutes. For frosting, Combine powdered sugar, butter & salt. Add vanilla. Add milk gradually until mixture is spreading consistency. Frost rolls while warm. For Easter, tint frosting with pastel colors.

32 servings

MENU

Father's Day Pork Tenderloin

Green Bean Potato Salad

Corn-on-the-Cob

Mousse au Chocolat Sauce Grand Marnier

French Red Bordeaux Saint-Estèphe

•

A special meal to treat Dads, Grandfathers or Husbands. The Mousse will knock their socks off!

❦

ENTREE

Father's Day Pork Tenderloin

•

Marinade:
¼ cup water
1 tablespoon Worcestershire sauce
1 tablespoon instant coffee
1 large clove garlic, minced

2 pork tenderloins, 2 pounds
2 tablespoons butter
1 cup sour cream
1 tablespoon flour

Prepare marinade by combining water, Worcestershire, coffee & garlic. Cut tenderloins into 6 medallions, 2-inches thick. Flatten with mallet. Place in shallow glass dish. Pour marinade over meat. Turn to coat. Chill several hours or overnight.

Heat butter in skillet. Brown meat. Add marinade. Cover & simmer 20 minutes. Place on serving platter. Keep warm. Combine sour cream & flour. Stir into pan drippings. Cook over medium heat, stirring until thickened. Cook 1 minute. Pour sauce over meat.

6 servings

POTATOES

Green Bean Potato Salad

•

3 pounds tiny new potatoes
1 pound fresh green beans, cut into 1-inch pieces

Dressing:
¾ cup vegetable oil
⅛ cup red wine vinegar
1 teaspoon salt
½ teaspoon pepper
1 tablespoon snipped fresh dill
1 tablespoon Dijon-style mustard
red leaf lettuce
alfalfa or radish sprouts

Peel a strip around the center of each potato. Boil in salted water 10-15 minutes until tender. Drain & cool. Steam beans, partially covered, 10-15 minutes. Rinse under cold water & drain. Combine dressing in blender. Pour over potatoes & beans. Chill. Line a serving platter with lettuce. Spoon salad in center & surround with sprouts.

10 servings

DESSERT

Mousse au Chocolat Sauce Grand Marnier

•

6-ounces semi-sweet chocolate
1-ounce unsweetened chocolate
6 eggs, separated
2 tablespoons dark rum
2 teaspoons vanilla
¼ cup sugar

Sauce Grand Marnier:
½ cup sugar
1 tablespoon cornstarch
¾ cup fresh orange juice
¼ cup Grand Marnier
¼ cup toasted almonds, optional

Melt chocolates in double boiler. Beat yolks until light & thick. Add rum & vanilla. Add chocolate slowly. Beat egg whites to soft peaks. Add sugar & beat until stiff & glossy. Stir ⅓ whites into chocolate mixture. Gently fold in remaining whites. Spoon into dessert dishes or stemmed glasses. Cover & chill several hours or overnight.

For the sauce, mix sugar, cornstarch & orange juice in small saucepan. Bring to boil. Remove from heat. Add Grand Marnier & almonds if desired. Cool & serve over mousse.

8 servings

THANKSGIVING

Roast Turkey

Thanksgiving Apple Stuffing

Autumn Salad

Cranberry-Pineapple Cream Salad

Baked Artichokes & Mushrooms

Hot Cloverleaf Rolls with Butter Curls

Sweet Potato Soufflé with Foamy Sauce

Cranberry Walnut Pie

California Red Merlot

•

Thanksgiving Apple Stuffing

•

¼ cup butter
3 scallions, sliced
3 large mushrooms, sliced
2 Granny Smith or other tart apples, peeled & sliced
3 cups dry bread crumbs
¼ teaspoon each sage, thyme, savory & marjoram
½ cup applesauce
3 tablespoons apple brandy

Preheat oven to 325°F. Butter a 2-quart casserole.

In a medium saucepan, heat butter. Add onions, & mushrooms. Cook until tender. Add apples. Cook 1 minute. Stir in bread crumbs, herbs, applesauce & apple brandy. Add more applesauce if mixture seems dry. Bake, covered, 30 minutes. Make an additional batch to stuff the turkey. Also excellent accompaniment to pork or ham.

4 servings

Autumn Salad

•

Nutmeg-Dill Vinaigrette:
1 tablespoon Dijon-style mustard
¼ cup white wine vinegar
⅛ teaspoon Kosher salt
⅛ teaspoon ground pepper
½ teaspoon dill
½ teaspoon ground nutmeg
½ cup extra-virgin olive oil

3 large unpeeled red delicious apples, very thinly sliced
⅓ cup crumbled Roquefort cheese
4 tablespoons walnuts
1 head romaine, trimmed & cut lengthwise into thirds
1 bunch watercress, trimmed
Kosher salt
cracked pepper
freshly grated nutmeg

For the vinaigrette, combine mustard, vinegar, salt, pepper, dill & nutmeg. Add oil very slowly, whisking constantly. Can be made 3 days in advance. Stir vigorously before using.

In a bowl, combine apple slices, Roquefort, walnuts & 3 tablespoons dressing. Refrigerate, covered, up to 4 hours. At serving time, combine romaine, cress & apple mixture on serving platter. Toss with dressing. Season with salt, pepper & nutmeg to taste.

8 servings

SALAD

Cranberry-Pineapple Cream Salad

•

2 packages (3 ounces each) cream cheese, softened
2 tablespoons mayonnaise
2 tablespoons sugar
1 can (16 ounces) whole berry cranberry sauce
1 can (8 ounces) crushed pineapple, drained
1 cup heavy cream, whipped
Bibb or Boston lettuce
mandarin orange segments
grape clusters

Beat cream cheese, mayonnaise & sugar. Add cranberry sauce & drained pineapple. Blend well. Fold in whipped cream. Pour into a 5-6 cup mold. Freeze overnight. To serve, arrange lettuce on chilled salad plates. Unmold salad. Slice thinly. Garnish with orange segments & grape clusters.

12 servings

Baked Artichokes & Mushrooms

•

½ cup butter
1 clove garlic, minced
1 pound mushrooms, sliced
2 cups quartered artichoke hearts
2 tablespoons lemon juice
½ teaspoon oregano
1 teaspoon basil
1 teaspoon salt
ground pepper
½ cup grated Parmesan cheese
2 tablespoons dry bread crumbs

Preheat oven to 350°F. Lightly butter a 1½-quart casserole.

Melt butter in a large skillet. Sauté garlic & mushrooms 5 minutes. Add lemon juice. Add artichoke hearts. Cook 5 minutes longer. Add oregano, basil, salt & pepper. Cook 1 minute. Pour into casserole. Sprinkle with cheese & bread crumbs. Bake 25-30 minutes.

4 servings

Sweet Potato Soufflé with Foamy Sauce

•

2 cups cooked sweet potatoes or yams
1 cup butter, melted
1½ cups sugar
¼ teaspoon grated nutmeg
1 tablespoon grated lemon or orange peel
¼ cup brandy
6 eggs, well beaten

Foamy Sauce:
3 egg yolks
¾ cup sugar
½ teaspoon vanilla
⅛ teaspoon salt
1 cup heavy cream, whipped

Preheat oven to 350°F. Place 13x9-inch pan with 1-inch boiling water in oven.

In a blender or processor, combine sweet potatoes, butter, sugar, nutmeg, citrus peel & brandy. Combine well. Add eggs. Blend until smooth. Pour mixture into 1½-quart soufflé dish. Put soufflé in pan of water in oven. Bake 1 hour until knife inserted in center comes out clean.

For the foamy sauce, beat yolks. Add sugar gradually. Add vanilla & salt. Beat until thick & pale yellow. Fold in whipped cream. Chill. Makes 1½ cups sauce. Soufflé may be served by itself as a vegetable or topped with foamy sauce as dessert. Sprinkle top of soufflé with extra nutmeg & a pinch of cinnamon for additional flavor.

6-8 servings

DESSERT

Cranberry Walnut Pie

•

1 9-inch unbaked pie crust
2 cups whole cranberries
1 cup whole walnut halves
¼ cup brown sugar
1 egg
½ cup sugar
⅓ cup butter, melted & cooled
½ cup flour

Preheat oven to 325°F.

Place cranberries & walnuts in pie shell. Sprinkle with brown sugar. Combine egg, sugar, butter & flour. Beat well. Spread on top of cranberries. Bake 45-50 minutes.

8 servings

For a buffet-style Thanksgiving dinner, give a simple blessing before guests serve themselves. From that moment on it is understood that guests may begin eating as soon as they are seated. When the last guest is seated, offer toasts to the gathering.

Irish Cream

•

- 1 can (14 ounces) sweetened condensed milk
- 1½ cups heavy cream
- 3 eggs
- 1 cup good Irish whiskey
- ¼ teaspoon coconut extract
- 1½ tablespoons chocolate syrup

Add ingredients to blender or processor. Mix on highest speed 30 seconds. Store in covered container in refrigerator. Keeps several weeks. Stir before serving. Of course, calories & cholesterol left out of the recipe!

Peppermint Brittle

•

- 2 pounds white chocolate
- 30 small candy canes

Line a jelly roll pan with heavy duty foil.

Break up white chocolate. Microwave at medium power 6 minutes. Stir. Microwave 1-2 minutes until melted. Add candy to chocolate. Press into jelly roll pan. Chill until set about 1 hour. Break into small pieces by slamming pan onto counter. Kids can make for teachers!

Cherry-Chip Banana Bread

•

- ½ cup butter, softened
- 1 cup sugar
- 2 eggs
- 2 medium very ripe bananas, mashed
- 2 cups flour, sifted
- 1 teaspoon baking soda
- ¼ cup chopped nuts
- ¼ mini chocolate chips
- ¼ cup chopped maraschino cherries

Preheat oven to 350°F. Butter a 9x5-inch loaf pan.

Cream butter & sugar. Beat until light & fluffy. Add eggs, one at a time. Add bananas. Sift soda with flour. Stir into creamed mixture. Fold in nuts, chips & cherries. Pour into prepared pan. Bake 40-45 minutes. Remove loaf from pan. Cool on wire rack. Makes 15 muffins if desired. Bake 25-30 minutes.

1 loaf

Raspberry Vinegar

•

2½ cups sweetened raspberries
2¼ cups white vinegar
1½ cups sugar

Place raspberries & vinegar in a glass bowl or crock. Set stand 24 hours at room temperature. Strain into saucepan. Stir in sugar. Bring to boil over medium-high heat. Boil 10 minutes. Pour into clean bottles. Give as a gift with the following recipe attached:

Raspberry Vinegar Salad
2-3 parts walnut oil
1 part raspberry vinegar
Boston or bibb lettuce
julienned cucumbers
thinly sliced radishes
salt
pepper
oregano

Mix oil & vinegar. Sprinkle lettuce & vegetables with salt, pepper & oregano. Toss with dressing. Also delicious with pears in the salad.

Half-Hour Apple Butter

•

2 cups unsweetened applesauce
⅓ cup sugar
1 teaspoon cinnamon
¼ teaspoon allspice
⅛ teaspoon ginger
⅛ teaspoon cloves

In a heavy saucepan, combine ingredients. Bring to a boil. Cook ½ hour, stirring often. Flavor improves as it is stored in refrigerator. Spread on buttered English muffins, pancakes, waffles or toasted bread.

1¼ cups

S.K. Caramel Corn

•

1 cup popcorn, popped, about 16 cups
1 cup brown sugar
¼ cup light corn syrup
½ cup butter
½ teaspoon salt
1 teaspoon vanilla
½ teaspoon baking soda
1 cup peanuts

Place popped corn in large doubled brown paper bag. Combine sugar, syrup, butter & salt in bowl. Microwave on high 2 minutes. Stir. Microwave 3 minutes. Stir after each minute. Add vanilla & baking soda. Stir. Pour over popcorn in bag. Shake well. Microwave 1 minute. Repeat. Shake well. Microwave 30 seconds. Add peanuts, if desired. Repeat. Pour on foil or waxed paper to cool. Store in tightly covered containers.

4 quarts

Present these beauties in interesting wrappings, bottles, jars, baskets, packages, a myriad of presentations . . .

CHRISTMAS EVE BUFFET

Ginger Shrimp de Jonghe Miniatures

Baked Holiday Ham

Sautéed Green Beans with Garlic & Cashews

Mustard Glazed Carrots

Cranberry Sauce Grand Marnier

Orange Date Bread

Toffee Rum Cheesecake

After Dinner Eggnog

French Red Beaujolais-Villages Fleurie

•

Ginger Shrimp de Jonghe Miniatures

•

12 cooked shrimp, finely chopped
½ cup butter, softened
1 clove garlic, minced
2 tablespoons minced parsley
1 teaspoon chopped, preserved ginger root
20 bread cutouts, toasted 1 side

Beat butter until light & fluffy. Add garlic, parsley & ginger. Spread shrimp mixture on untoasted side of cutouts. Broil until delicately browned.

20 servings

Mustard Glazed Carrots

•

2 pounds carrots, peeled, sliced diagonally
3 tablespoons butter
3 tablespoons Dijon-style mustard
¼ cup brown sugar
salt
¼ cup chopped fresh parsley

Steam carrots 5 minutes. In small saucepan, melt butter. Add mustard, brown sugar & salt. Cook 3 minutes. Add carrots, turning to coat in sauce. Cook 5 minutes. Sprinkle with parsley.

6 servings

Cranberry Sauce Grand Marnier

•

2 cups sugar
2 cups water
1 pound fresh cranberries
1 envelope unflavored gelatin
3 tablespoons Grand Marnier
grated peel of 1 orange
juice of ½ lemon

In a large saucepan, combine sugar & water. Boil 5 minutes. Add cranberries. Boil 5 minutes longer until skins pop. Soften gelatin in Grand Marnier. Add to hot cranberries. Stir until gelatin is thoroughly dissolved. Cool. Stir in orange peel & lemon juice. Pour into glass serving bowl. Chill. May be frozen.

12 servings

Orange Date Bread

•

½ cup butter, softened
1 cup sugar
2 eggs
⅔ cup buttermilk
2 cups flour
pinch salt
1 tablespoon grated orange peel
1 cup chopped dates
½ cup chopped pecans

Topping:
1 cup sugar
2 tablespoons grated orange peel
½ cup orange juice

Preheat oven to 350°F. Butter & flour a 9x5-inch loaf pan.

Cream butter & sugar. Add eggs one at a time. Alternately add buttermilk & flour. Stir in salt, orange peel, dates & pecans. Bake 1 hour. Combine topping ingredients. Stir until sugar is completely dissolved. Pour over hot bread. Cool in loaf pan.

1 loaf

Toffee Rum Cheesecake

•

½ cup unsalted butter, melted
1 cup ground graham crackers
1 cup ground pecans
2 tablespoons sugar
2 tablespoons brown sugar

Filling:
2 pounds cream cheese, softened
¾ cup sugar
¾ cup brown sugar
3 tablespoons rum
½ cup crushed butter brickle bits
or English toffee
pinch salt
4 eggs

Topping:
2 cups sour cream
¼ cup brown sugar
2 tablespoons rum
½ tablespoon maple sugar
butter brickle bits

Preheat oven to 350°F.

Combine butter, crumbs, nuts & sugars. Blend well. Press mixture on bottom & sides of 10-inch springform pan. Set aside.

For the filling, beat cream cheese & sugars until light & fluffy. Add eggs, one at a time, beating well after each addition. Add rum, butter brickle bits & salt. Blend thoroughly. Pour into crust. Bake 45 minutes. For topping, beat sour cream, brown sugar, rum & maple sugar until sugar dissolves. Spread on top of cheesecake. Sprinkle top with additional butter brickle bits. Continue baking 15 minutes. Remove from oven. Cool on rack. Refrigerate until serving.

10-12 servings

After Dinner Eggnog

•

1 cup frozen custard ice cream
2 cups rich dairy eggnog
1 cup brandy
⅛ cup rum
small scoops ice cream
freshly grated nutmeg

Just before serving, place ice cream, eggnog, brandy & rum in blender. Whirl until frothy. Serve in stemmed glasses. Top with small scoop of ice cream & nutmeg.

12-15 servings

"A Toast! the glistening
holly bough
Which crowns the board
of mirth & pleasure
Sing Noel, Noel!
for 'tis now
Of joy & peace
we have full measure!"
Frank X. Finnegan

CHRISTMAS DINNER
À LA DICKENS

Avocado-Caviar Salad

Christmas Goose with Cumberland Sauce

Pennsylvania-Style Stuffing

Lemon New Potatoes

Frosted Cauliflower

Broccoli Timbales with Ginger-Orange Carrots

Eggnog Mousse with Raspberry Sauce

French White
Alsace Gewürztraminer

•

Gifts & tidings have been exchanged. It is time for serious dining. Place napkins, folded point down, inside the wine glasses. Place a coin or sugared almond in one of the points, bringing the recipient extraordinarily good luck in the year to come. Place thick red gross-grained ribbon down the center & a few across the top of a white cloth for holiday color.

Avocado-Caviar Salad

•

1 head Boston lettuce
2 ripe avocados, peeled, pitted, rubbed with lemon
1 cup sour cream
2-ounces American golden caviar
2-ounces best quality black caviar
lemon slices

On chilled salad plates, arrange several lettuce leaves. Top with ½ avocado, pitted side up. Fill hollow with sour cream. Spoon 1 teaspoon golden caviar on 1 side of the sour cream, 1 teaspoon black on other. Garnish with lemon slice twist dividing the two caviars.

4 servings

Christmas Goose with Cumberland Sauce

•

10-pound goose

Cumberland Sauce:
2 tablespoons red currant jelly
juice of 2 oranges
⅓ of an orange, including peel, finely chopped
½ cup black currants
½ cup light corn syrup
½ cup butter

Stuff goose with Pennsylvania-Style Stuffing. Roast goose 20 minutes at 450°F. Reduce heat to 325°F. Roast at 25 minutes per pound. Let stand, covered, 10 minutes. Carve & serve with Cumberland Sauce.

For the sauce, combine ingredients in saucepan. Bring to boil. Simmer 15 minutes. Serve hot over goose, wild game, duck breasts or other poultry. *(2½ cups)*

8-10 servings

Pennsylvania-Style Stuffing

•

1 pound breakfast sausage links, cut into 1-inch pieces
1 pound bacon, diced
1 large onion, chopped
1 cup finely chopped celery
½ pound mushrooms, sliced
2 Granny Smith apples, cored & sliced
1 cup chopped fresh parsley
1 teaspoon sage
1 teaspoon thyme
1 pound loaf firm white bread, cut into 1-inch cubes
2 cups chicken stock
salt & pepper

Sauté sausage & bacon until crisp & brown. Add onion, celery, mushrooms, apples, parsley & herbs. Sauté, stirring occasionally, 5 minutes. Stir in bread cubes & chicken broth. Season with salt & pepper. Makes enough stuffing for 10-12 pound turkey or goose. Good with other poultry.

8-10 servings

Frosted Cauliflower

•

1 large whole head cauliflower, trimmed of leaves & cored
2 cups peas
1 medium onion, sliced
½ teaspoon Chinese 5-spice seasoning
1 teaspoon salt
¼ cup light cream
¼ cup toasted pine nuts or sesame seed

Steam cauliflower until tender, 15-20 minutes. Drain. Place on heated serving platter. Keep warm. Cook peas & onions until tender. In blender or processor, add peas, onions, 5-spice & salt. Purée until smooth. Frost cauliflower with purée. Sprinkle with pine nuts, sesame seed, crushed flavored croutons or crisp-cooked, crumbled bacon. Surround with cooked baby carrots for another presentation. To serve, cut cauliflower into wedges.

10 servings

VEGETABLE

Broccoli Timbales with Ginger-Orange Carrots

•

1½ pounds broccoli, trimmed into flowerets to fit ramekins
7 eggs
1½ cups heavy cream
½ teaspoon salt
⅜ teaspoon white pepper
freshly ground nutmeg
pinch cayenne

Ginger-Orange Carrots:
36 baby carrots or cut carrots
1¾ cups fresh orange juice
1½ tablespoons peeled, grated, fresh ginger root
fresh cilantro, garnish

Preheat oven to 350°F. Place 13x9-inch pan in oven with 1-inch boiling water. Generously butter 8 ramekins or custard cups.

Blanch broccoli flowerets in boiling salted water 2 minutes. Drain. Combine cream, salt, pepper, nutmeg & cayenne. Beat well. Arrange broccoli in ramekins, stem-side up. Pour egg mixture into ramekins. Set molds in hot water in oven. Bake 40 minutes until knife inserted in center of ramekin comes out clean. For carrots, combine carrots, orange juice & ginger in saucepan. Simmer over medium-low heat until tender, 10-12 minutes. Invert molds onto heated serving platter. Intersperse drained carrots between timbales. Garnish with cilantro leaves.

8 servings

Eggnog Mousse with Raspberry Sauce

•

3 envelopes unflavored gelatin
6 tablespoons cold water
5 cups rich dairy eggnog
⅓ cup sugar
½ teaspoon grated nutmeg
2 cups heavy cream, whipped

Raspberry Sauce:
3 cups sweetened raspberries
2 tablespoons cornstarch
2 tablespoons brandy
chocolate leaves, garnish

In a small bowl, sprinkle gelatin over cold water to soften. Heat 1 cup eggnog. Add sugar. Stir to dissolve. Add gelatin. Stir until gelatin melts completely. Pour into large bowl. Add remaining eggnog & nutmeg. Chill until slightly thickened, about 1 hour. Fold in whipped cream. Pour into 8 cup mold or individual molds. Chill 8 hours or overnight. For the sauce, drain raspberry juices into small saucepan. Dissolve cornstarch & brandy. Add to saucepan. Cook until thickened. Add raspberries. Chill. To serve, unmold mousse onto platter. Drizzle with sauce. Pass remaining sauce.

8 servings

Gifts & tidings have been exchanged. It is time for serious dining. Place napkins, folded point down, inside the wine glasses. Place a coin or sugared almond in one of the points, bringing the recipient extraordinarily good luck in the year to come. Place thick red grosgrain ribbon down the center & a few across the top of a white cloth for holiday color.

NEW YEAR'S EVE

Milwaukee's Bal du Lac Caviar

Mushrooms Stuffed with Chèvre Blue Cheese

Sliced Roast Tenderloin with Horseradish Sauce

Twice Baked Potatoes

Vegetable Gratin

Artichoke Almond Salad

Lemon Cream Ring

Chocolate Whipped Cream Torte

California Cabernet Sauvignon

•

Milwaukee's Bal du Lac Caviar

•

6 hard-cooked, extra large eggs, finely chopped
½ cup finely chopped onion
6 tablespoons butter, melted
½ cup mayonnaise
pinch salt
¼ teaspoon pepper
1 pint sour cream
1 jar (4.6 ounces) black caviar
curly endive
poppy seed or other favorite crackers

Combine eggs & onions. Stir in butter, mayonnaise, salt & pepper. Put into plastic-lined 7-inch mold. Chill at least 4 hours. Unmold onto large serving plate. Remove plastic. Frost with sour cream. Gently cover with caviar using the tip of a small spoon. Surround with small leaves of curly endive. Place crackers around endive.

14 servings

Mushrooms Stuffed with Chèvre Blue Cheese

•

24 large mushrooms, stems removed
2 teaspoons grated onion
⅓ cup butter
1¼ cups fine, fresh bread crumbs
2 tablespoons minced parsley
1 tablespoon lemon juice
½ teaspoon salt
¼ cup crumbled goat's milk blue cheese (chèvre)
melted butter

Arrange mushroom caps in baking dish. Chop stems very fine. Sauté stems & onions in butter over medium heat. Remove from heat. Add bread crumbs, parsley, lemon juice & salt. Combine well. When mixture cools, add crumbled cheese. Spoon stuffing into caps. Brush mushroom tops with melted butter. May be frozen at this point. Bake 5 minutes at 450°F. (increase baking time if frozen). Broil until delicately browned.

8 servings

Vegetable Gratin

•

1½ cups cauliflowerets
1½ cups baby peas
1½ cups baby or sliced carrots
1½ cups broccoli flowerets
1 can (9 ounces) sliced waterchestnuts
1½ cups heavy cream
1 tablespoon fresh chopped basil
salt & pepper
1 cup fresh bread crumbs
butter

Preheat oven to 375°F. Butter an oval 2-quart casserole.

Steam vegetables until crisp-tender. Drain.

In a small saucepan, cook cream over medium heat until reduced by half. Add basil. Toss with vegetables. Season with salt & pepper. Pour vegetable mixture into casserole. Sprinkle with bread crumbs. Dot with butter. Bake 30 minutes until hot & bubbly.

8 servings

Artichoke Almond Salad

•

12 cooked artichoke hearts, halved
⅓ pound fresh snow peas, cut into ½-inch pieces
⅓ pound fresh mushrooms, sliced
lettuce leaves

Dressing:
¼ cup red wine vinegar
¼ cup vegetable oil
2 teaspoons Dijon-style mustard
1 teaspoon each: salt, pepper, dill, finely chopped garlic
1 cup light cream

½ cup toasted sliced almonds, or crushed honey-roasted almonds

Combine vegetables. Mix dressing ingredients. Toss vegetables with enough dressing to coat. Serve on lettuce lined platter topped with almonds. Add shredded cooked chicken for a hearty luncheon salad.

8 servings

Lemon Cream Ring

•

1 package unflavored gelatin
⅔ cup water
½ cup sugar
⅛ teaspoon salt
grated peel of 1 lemon
juice of 1 lemon
1 can (6 ounces) frozen lemonade concentrate
1 cup heavy cream, whipped
fresh fruit

In a saucepan over medium-low heat, dissolve gelatin. Stir in sugar & salt. Stir to dissolve. Remove from heat. Add lemon peel, juice & concentrate. Chill to jelly-like consistency. Fold in cream. Pour into 4-cup mold. Chill until firm. Unmold onto serving platter. Decorate with assorted fresh fruits.

8 servings

Chocolate Whipped Cream Torte

•

3-ounces semi-sweet baking chocolate
⅓ cup butter
1¾ cup flour, sifted
1½ cups sugar
1½ teaspoons baking soda
1 teaspoon salt
1½ cups buttermilk or sour cream
1 teaspoon vanilla
2 eggs, slightly beaten
½ cup chopped walnuts, optional

Frosting:
2 pints heavy cream, whipped
1-2 tablespoons unsweetened cocoa
2 tablespoons powdered sugar

Preheat oven to 350°F. Butter & flour 2 9-inch round cake pans lined with waxed paper circles.

Melt chocolate & butter in small saucepan over low heat. Cool slightly. Pour into large bowl. Sift flour, sugar, soda & salt. Combine with chocolate mixture. Add buttermilk, vanilla & eggs. Beat well. Add walnuts. Pour into prepared pans. Bake 30-35 minutes. Cool 10 minutes. Remove cakes from pans. Remove paper. Cool on racks.

For frosting, combine whipped cream, cocoa & powdered sugar. Divide each cake into 2 layers. Spread filling between each layer. Frost top & sides. Decorate with sifted cocoa or pipe additional cream rosettes on top of cake. Decorate with candied violets & candied coffee beans. Prepare 1 day in advance.

10 servings

Hang colorful paper streamers from the chandelier to the tabletop. Keep the lights subdued & put a stack of all-time favorite music on the stereo for a nostalgic New Year's Eve fête. Serve champagne at the appointed hour with the Torte. Roll up the carpet for wee hours dancing.

❦

CELEBRATION

Potted Pâté
with
Toast Points

Herbed Salmon Steaks

Asparagus Romano on Tomato Fettucini

Roquette
Vinaigrette

Irresistible Chocolate Mint Demitasse Cream

California Red Zinfandel

•

When there is an occasion to celebrate above & beyond the norm, this is sure to top the expectations of your guests. The Salmon & Pasta are pictured on page 4. Conviviality & sharing the event are terrific rewards.

❦

Herbed Salmon Steaks

•

Herb Sauce:
½ cup fresh lemon juice
2 tablespoons butter, melted
1 tablespoon fresh chopped tarragon or 1 teaspoon dried
1 tablespoon finely chopped shallots
½ teaspoon freshly ground pepper

4 salmon steaks, 1-inch thick

Preheat broiler or prepare grill.

Combine lemon juice, butter, tarragon, shallots & pepper. Mix well. Set aside. Place salmon on rack in a shallow pan. Pour several tablespoons sauce over steaks. Broil or grill 6 inches from heat 7 minutes. Turn steaks. Top with more sauce. Return to heat 5 minutes until fish flakes easily. Serve with any remaining sauce.

4 servings

Pictured page 4.

Asparagus Romano on Tomato Fettucini

•

¼ cup butter
1 large onion finely chopped
2 cloves garlic, finely chopped
1 tablespoon flour
¼ cup dry white wine
½ teaspoon tarragon leaves
½ teaspoon thyme leaves
2½ cups chicken stock
3 pounds asparagus, cleaned, tips only (reserve tender stems for soups)
2 large egg yolks, slightly beaten
½ cup freshly grated romano cheese
salt & freshly ground pepper

1 pound tomato fettucini or pappardelle, cooked & drained
extra grated romano cheese

In a large sauce pan melt butter over medium heat. Sauté onions 5 minutes. Add garlic. Cook 2 minutes. Add flour, stir. Add wine. Simmer 3 minutes. Add herbs & stock. Ten minutes before serving add asparagus tips. Cook 3 minutes. Off heat, beat in egg yolks. Return pan to medium-low heat, stirring constantly. Cook 5 minutes. Add romano, salt & pepper to taste. On a heated platter toss fettucini with asparagus sauce. Sprinkle with additional cheese. Serve immediately.

6 Servings

Pictured page 4.

Irresistible Chocolate Mint Demitasse Cream

•

6-ounces semi-sweet chocolate, melted
pinch salt
1 egg
1 teaspoon vanilla
2 tablespoons sugar
3 tablespoons peppermint schnapps
¾ cup milk
whipped cream & strawberries, garnish

Combine chocolate & other ingredients in blender or processor. Whirl until smooth. Pour into demitasse cups. Chill. Serve with a dollop of whipped cream topped with a perfect strawberry. Serve with demitasse spoons.

6 servings

Elegant Gatherings

sophisticated dining experiences

MENU

Pork Tenderloin in Puff Pastry

Asparagus

Beets in Orange Sauce

Blue Cheese Flan with Dried Apricots & Figs

German White Rheingau Spätlese

•

An elegant meal to serve to friends or family. Blanch baby spring asparagus quickly to retain crispness & color. Potted primroses are the perfect centerpiece. Coordinate short candles to match.

❦

ENTREE

Pork Tenderloin in Puff Pastry

•

3 pork tenderloins
¾ cup finely minced scallions
1 cup apple cider or juice
3 tablespoons olive oil
¾ teaspoon salt
½ pound mushrooms, sliced
¾ teaspoon thyme, crushed
2 large stalks celery, chopped
20 peppercorns
10 parsley sprigs
1½ pounds puff pastry sheets (3 sheets)
2 egg whites, slightly beaten
1 cup chicken stock
¼ cup butter, softened
¼ cup flour

Place pork in shallow dish. Combine scallions, cider, oil, salt, mushrooms, thyme, celery, peppercorns & parsley sprigs. Pour over pork. Marinate at least 12 hours, turning occasionally.

Preheat oven to 350°F.

Remove tenderloins & mushrooms from marinade & drain well. Reserve marinade. Cut each tenderloin in half. Roll out each pastry ⅛-inch thick. Divide pastry in half. Place mushrooms down center of each piece of pastry. Place pork on top. Bring ends of pastry over pork, then bring sides up & seal well. Place pork, seam side down, on a jelly roll pan. Bake 1 hour & 45 minutes. Remove from oven. Brush crust generously with beaten egg whites. Bake 5 minutes longer, until crust is golden. Remove from oven. Let stand 5-10 minutes.

Pour reserved marinade into blender & process until smooth. Pour into saucepan. Add chicken stock. Cook over medium heat. Combine soft butter & flour. Drop mixture by teaspoonfuls into sauce & cook until thickened. Pour sauce over baked tenderloin & serve.

6 servings

VEGETABLE

Beets in Orange Sauce

•

½ cup sugar
1½ tablespoons cornstarch
⅛ teaspoon salt
grated peel of 1 orange, slice fruit for garnish
1 cup water
¾ cup orange juice
4 cups whole baby beets

Mix sugar, cornstarch, salt & grated orange peel in sauce pan. Add water. Stir & cook until thickened. Add orange juice & heat. Pour over hot beets & serve. Garnish with thin slices of orange which have been glazed in sauce.

8 servings

DESSERT

Blue Cheese Flan with Dried Apricots & Figs

•

¾ cup crushed, rich, round crackers
2 tablespoons butter, melted

Filling:
2 packages (8 ounces each) cream cheese, softened
8-ounces blue cheese, crumbled
1⅔ cup sour cream, divided
3 eggs
⅛ teaspoon pepper
dried apricots, figs, etc.

Combine crushed crackers & butter. Press onto bottom of lightly buttered 9-inch springform pan. Bake at 350°F. 10 minutes.

Combine cheeses at medium speed until blended. Add ⅔ cup sour cream, eggs & pepper. Beat until fluffy. Pour into crust, bake at 300°F. 45 minutes. Stir remaining sour cream until smooth. Spread carefully over top. Return to oven for 10 minutes. Cool on rack. Refrigerate several hours. May be prepared 1-2 days before serving. Loosen sides from springform with sharp knife & remove. Garnish with dried fruits.

18 servings

MENU

Almond Turkey Cutlets

Ginger Orange Rice

Sautéed Water Chestnuts with Bacon & Spinach

Upside Down Lemon Meringue Pie

French Red Burgundy Côte de Beaune

•

If a big turkey on Thanksgiving doesn't fit into your lifestyle, try this recipe. Add a side dish of stuffing if desired.

Almond Turkey Cutlets

•

- ¾ cup ground, toasted almonds
- ⅓ cup chopped parsley
- ¾ cup bread crumbs
- 2 egg whites, beaten with 1 teaspoon water until frothy
- 6 turkey cutlets
- 4 tablespoons butter, divided
- 6 tablespoons Parmesan cheese
- 3 tablespoons slivered almonds
- 1 clove garlic, lightly crushed
- ¼ cup white wine
- juice of ½ lemon
- ½ cup heavy cream

Combine ground almonds, parsley & bread crumbs. Dip cutlets into egg white mixture, then into parsley mixture, coating well on both sides. Chill several hours to set coating.

Melt 2 tablespoons butter in skillet. Quickly sauté cutlets until brown & crisp on each side. Sprinkle each cutlet with 1 tablespoon cheese. Remove to warm platter.

In same pan, melt 2 tablespoons butter. Add slivered almonds, & garlic. Sauté until almonds are light brown. Add wine & lemon juice. Cook until reduced by ½. Add cream. Whisk until slightly thickened. Remove garlic clove. Pour sauce over cutlets. Serve immediately.

4-6 servings

Ginger-Orange Rice

•

- 3 tablespoons butter
- 2 tablespoons finely chopped onion
- 2 teaspoons grated orange peel
- ½ teaspoon ground ginger
- ⅛ teaspoon poultry seasoning
- ⅛ teaspoon ground pepper
- ½ cup orange juice
- 2 cups chicken stock
- 1 tablespoon chopped parsley
- 1 cup long grain rice

Melt butter. Cook onion in butter until soft. Blend in orange peel, ginger, poultry seasoning & pepper. Add orange juice & stock. Bring to boil. Add parsley & rice. Stir with fork. Cover tightly. Simmer over low heat 25 minutes until rice is tender & liquid absorbed. Stir with fork before serving. Best to prepare close to serving time as possible.

4-6 servings

Upside Down Lemon Meringue Pie

•

- 4 eggs, separated
- ¼ teaspoon cream of tartar
- 1½ cups plus 2 teaspoons sugar, divided
- grated peel & juice of 1 lemon
- 2 cups heavy cream, divided
- ¼ teaspoon vanilla

Preheat oven to 275°F. Butter a 10-inch glass pie plate.

Beat egg whites until soft peaks form. Gradually add cream of tartar & 1 cup sugar. Beat until stiff & glossy. Spread in pie plate fully over the edge. Bake 1 hour until golden. Turn off oven. Open door slightly & let rest inside oven 1 hour.

Beat egg yolks in top of double boiler 5 minutes until thick & lemon-colored. Over medium heat, gradually add ½ cup sugar, juice & grated peel of lemon. Beat & heat until very thick. Cool, stirring occasionally.

Whip 1 cup cream. Gently fold into cooled lemon mixture. Pour into shell & refrigerate 24 hours, covered.

4 hours before serving, whip remaining cream with vanilla & 2 teaspoons sugar. Pipe or swirl over top of dessert.

8 servings

MENU

Fruited Sangria

Surprise Dip

Green Pepper Dip

Shrimp & Couscous Salad

Taiwan Chicken Salad

Ginger Muffins

White Chocolate Cake

Fruited Sangria

- 2 cups orange juice
- 2 cups pineapple juice
- 1 cup sweet-sour soda
- ½ cup cherry juice
- ½ cup brandy
- ½ cup triple sec
- ½ gallon Burgundy or white wine
- orange slices & lime wedges, garnish

Blend ingredients together. Serve in tall, ice-filled glasses. Garnish with orange slices & a lime wedge.

20 servings

Surprise Dip

- 1 cup packed, grated carrots
- 1 cup mayonnaise
- 1 cup Parmesan cheese

Mix ingredients together. Bake at 350°F. 30 minutes. Serve hot with assorted crackers.

2-3 cups

Green Pepper Dip

- 1 green pepper
- water
- 1 large onion
- 2 packages (8 ounces each) cream cheese, softened
- 5 tablespoons sugar
- 5 tablespoons vinegar

Cut up pepper & onion & place in blender. Cover with cold water & blend. Put pulp in strainer & squeeze out liquid. Return pulp to blender & add remaining ingredients. Blend until smooth. Pour into serving container. Chill. May be frozen. Defrost to serve. Surround with fresh summer squash, zucchini, cauliflower, broccoli, etc. to be used as dippers. May also be used as a salad dressing.

3 cups

Shrimp & Couscous Salad

•

½ cup chicken stock
½ teaspoon salt
1 tablespoon butter
⅓ cup couscous
1 cup small shelled, cooked, shrimp
1 cup raw cauliflower &/or broccoli flowerets
8 black olives, sliced
1 tablespoon snipped fresh chives

Dressing:
2 tablespoons wine vinegar
½ teaspoon Dijon-style mustard
½ teaspoon anchovy paste
salt to taste
2 tablespoons olive oil
2 tablespoons sour cream

3 hours before serving, combine stock, salt, butter & couscous in a saucepan. Heat to boiling. Cover & remove from heat. Let stand five minutes. Fluff with fork. Turn into a bowl & chill, covered.

In a small bowl combine vinegar, mustard, anchovy paste & salt with a fork. Add olive oil & beat until well blended. Stir in sour cream. Chill.

Shortly before serving, combine couscous, shrimp, cauliflower &/or broccoli, olives & chives. Toss with dressing.

2-3 servings

Taiwan Chicken Salad

•

2 whole chicken breasts, skinned & boned
2 cups chicken stock
¾-inch piece fresh, peeled ginger root
4-ounces Chinese rice sticks (MAIFUN), broken into 3-inch pieces
oil for deep-frying
4 cups torn lettuce
1 bunch scallions, sliced including green tops
2 tablespoons slivered almonds, toasted

Dressing:
¼ cup sugar
¼ cup vinegar
¼ cup vegetable oil
1½ teaspoons salt
1 teaspoon sesame oil
2 tablespoons toasted sesame seed

Slowly simmer chicken breasts in stock with ginger root until chicken is no longer pink, about 30 minutes. Shred meat & set aside.

In a large saucepan, heat vegetable oil, 2-inches deep, to 350°F. Test one rice stick to make sure oil is hot enough; the rice stick should puff immediately. Cook sticks by small handfuls until very lightly browned. Drain on paper towels.

Combine dressing ingredients. Blend until sugar is dissolved.

Just before serving, combine chicken, rice sticks, lettuce & scallions in large salad bowl. Toss gently with dressing & garnish with almonds. Serve immediately.

6-8 servings

White Chocolate Cake

•

⅓ cup grated white chocolate
½ cup boiling water
1 cup butter, softened
2 cups sugar
4 eggs, separated
1 teaspoon vanilla
2½ cups sifted cake flour
1 teaspoon baking soda
1 cup buttermilk
1 cup coconut
1 cup chopped pecans or walnuts

Frosting:
1 package (8 ounces) cream cheese, softened
½ cup vegetable shortening
2 cups powdered sugar
1 teaspoon vanilla

Preheat oven to 350°F. Butter & flour 3 9-inch paper-lined cake pans.

Melt chocolate in boiling water. Set aside to cool. Cream butter & sugar until fluffy. Mix in egg yolks, one at a time, beating well after each addition. Add melted chocolate & vanilla.

Sift cake flour & soda. Add to creamed mixture with buttermilk. Do not over mix. Beat egg whites until stiff. Fold in gently. Stir in coconut & pecans or walnuts. Divide batter between three layer pans. Bake 25 minutes. Cool 10 minutes. Remove from pans. Remove paper.

For frosting, mix cream cheese, shortening, powdered sugar & vanilla. Spread between layers, top & sides.

12-14 servings

A delicious, different-flavor dinner party. Hang Chinese lanterns filled with little Christmas tree lights. If possible remove legs from your table, place top on floor & sit on pillows!!

❦

MENU

Mustard-Curry Spinach Salad

Chicken Wellington with Port-Currant Sauce

Basil Garden Beans & Mushrooms

Chocolate Ice Cream with Walnut Fudge Sauce

German Mosel Auslese
or
California Port

•

Invite friends over for an evening of cards. Have dinner, then retire to the "card" room. Enjoy dessert while playing.

Mustard-Curry Spinach Salad

•

- 2/3 cup vegetable oil
- 1/4 cup California wine vinegar
- 2 tablespoons Chablis
- 2 teaspoons soy sauce
- 1 teaspoon sugar
- 1 teaspoon dry mustard
- 1/4 teaspoon curry powder
- 1/2 teaspoon salt
- 1 clove garlic, minced
- 1 teaspoon cracked pepper
- 1 pound bacon, crisp-cooked, crumbled
- 4 hard cooked eggs, finely chopped
- 3 bunches spinach, cleaned, dried, & chilled

Combine oil, vinegar, Chablis, soy sauce, sugar, dry mustard, curry powder, salt, garlic & pepper. Mix well. Combine bacon, eggs & spinach. Toss with dressing when ready to serve.

6 servings

Chicken Wellington with Port-Currant Sauce

•

- 6 whole chicken breasts, skinned & boned, halved
- salt & pepper
- 6-ounces wild rice
- 1/4 cup grated orange peel
- 2 eggs, separated
- 3 sheets (8 ounces each) puff pastry
- 1 tablespoon water
- 1 jar (10 ounces) red currant jelly
- 1 tablespoon prepared mustard
- 3 tablespoons port wine
- 1/4 cup lemon juice

Preheat oven to 375°F.

Season chicken with salt & pepper. Cook wild rice according to package directions. Stir in orange peel. Beat 2 egg whites until stiff. Fold into rice. Set aside.

Roll out each sheet puff pastry 1/8-inch thick. Divide pastry into 1/4's. Place chicken breast on each pastry 1/4. Spoon 1/4 cup rice on top. Roll up. Place seam side down on jelly roll pan. Beat 2 egg yolks & water. Brush on dough. Bake 50 minutes.

Heat currant jelly, mustard, wine & lemon juice. Serve sauce warm with chicken.

8-12 servings

Basil Garden Beans & Mushrooms

•

- 1 1/2 pounds fresh green or yellow wax beans, trimmed
- 1/4 cup vegetable oil
- 3/4 pound fresh mushrooms, sliced
- 2 tablespoons chopped onions
- 1 clove garlic, minced
- 1 green pepper, chopped
- 1/4 cup boiling water
- 1 teaspoon salt
- 1 tablespoon fresh chopped basil
- 1/2 cup grated Parmesan cheese

Heat oil in pan. Add mushrooms, onion, garlic & green pepper. Cook slowly 5 minutes. Add beans, water, salt & basil. Cover & cook 10-15 minutes. Stir in several tablespoons cheese. Sprinkle remaining cheese on top.

6 servings

MENU

Spicy Marinated Brussels Sprouts

Muenster Cheese Cubes

Pork Tenderloin with Vegetable-Caper Sauce

Späetzle

Baked Apples in Apples Brandy

Mary Newton Cake

Sliced Peaches

French Red Bordeaux Saint Estèphe

•

This typical German combination of foods, pork with apples, is particularly satisfying when surrounded by family on a late Sunday afternoon. The menu is elegant for company also!

Pork Tenderloin with Vegetable-Caper Sauce

•

2 pounds whole pork tenderloins
¼ cup butter, melted
1 small onion, chopped
1 small carrot, chopped
½ cup beef stock
1½ tablespoons lemon juice
1 teaspoon grated lemon peel
¾ teaspoon thyme leaves
½ bay leaf
salt & pepper to taste
½ cup light cream
2 tablespoons flour
2 tablespoons capers

Preheat oven to 400°F.

Place tenderloins in 2-quart casserole with butter, onion & carrot. Roast at 400°F. 10 minutes. Reduce heat to 350°F. Add stock, lemon juice, lemon peel, thyme, bay leaf, salt & pepper. Braise, covered, 30-40 minutes until meat is tender. Remove tenderloins from pan & keep warm. Remove bay leaf. Combine cream & flour until smooth. Stir into pan juices. Cook over medium heat, stirring constantly, until thickened. Add capers. Slice tenderloins & serve with sauce. Good with noodles or späetzle & a fruit garnish, such as spiced apple rings or cranberries.

4-6 servings

Baked Apples in Apple Brandy

•

10 large baking apples
1 cup dried currants
1⅔ cups apple brandy, divided
1⅔ cups ground, toasted hazelnuts
⅔ cup packed brown sugar
⅔ cup heavy cream
½ teaspoon ground cinnamon
¼ teaspoon freshly ground nutmeg
1 cup apple cider
⅓ cup honey
1 cup whole cranberries
watercress

Preheat oven to 350°F.

Combine currants & ⅔ cup brandy in large bowl. Let stand ½ hour. Stir in nuts, sugar, cream, cinnamon & nutmeg. Cut ¼-inch slice from tops of apples. Remove cores to ½-inch from bottom, making a 1-inch wide hollow. Arrange apples ½-inch apart in shallow baking dish. Spoon currant mixture into centers of apples. Pour 1 cup brandy & 1 cup cider around apples. Spoon honey over apples. Bake 30 minutes, basting frequently with pan juices until apples are tender. Arrange on serving platter. Garnish with watercress & cranberries. Serve with pan juices.

10 servings

Mary Newton Cake

•

2 eggs
1 cup sugar
salt
1 cup flour
1 teaspoon baking powder
½ cup milk
2 tablespoons butter

Preheat oven to 350°F. Butter & flour a 11x7-inch pan.

Beat eggs until light & fluffy. Gradually add sugar & salt. Sift together flour & baking powder. Gradually add to eggs & sugar. Mixture will be thick. Scald milk with butter. Add to batter slowly beating until smooth & creamy. Pour into cake pan. Bake 20-25 minutes until springy to the touch in center of cake. Cake may be served plain like tea cake, dusted with powdered sugar or ice cream. Another favorite combination is with sugared peaches or strawberries like a shortcake.

6-8 servings

MENU

Fancy Scampi

Saffron Rice Balls

Raspberry Carrots

Crème Brûlée

Coffee with Chicory

French White Vouvray

•

Set the table with a bright yellow cloth & napkins & plenty of blue iris. Blue plates would make the light menu even more special!

Fancy Scampi

•

1 pound fresh mushrooms, sliced
2 small onions, finely chopped
½ green pepper, chopped
2 tablespoons butter
3 medium tomatoes, peeled & chopped
2 tablespoons flour
1 cup cream
½ teaspoon white wine-Worcestershire sauce
1½ teaspoons sherry-pepper sauce
½ cup dry sherry
3 pounds scampi, cleaned & cooked

Preheat oven to 375°F. Butter a 2-quart casserole dish.

Sauté mushrooms, onion & green pepper in butter. Add tomatoes & cook gently 8-10 minutes. Stir in flour. Slowly add cream, stirring until thickened. Add Worcestershire sauce, sherry-pepper sauce, sherry & scampi. Simmer 2 minutes. Transfer to casserole dish & bake 10 minutes.

6 servings

Raspberry Carrots

•

1½ pounds carrots, peeled & sliced thin
⅓ cup raspberry vinegar
½ cup olive oil
¼ cup chopped fresh mint
salt & pepper

In small amount of boiling water, cook carrots 3-4 minutes until nearly tender. Drain. Place carrots in a bowl. Sprinkle immediately with vinegar. Add olive oil & toss well. Sprinkle with chopped fresh mint. Season to taste. Toss again. Refrigerate at least overnight. Keeps several days. Bring to room temperature before serving.

6 servings

Crème Brûlée

•

4 cups heavy cream
¼ cup sugar
8 egg yolks
¼ teaspoon salt
2 teaspoons vanilla
½ cup brown sugar

Preheat oven to 350°F. Put large pan with 1-inch boiling water in oven.

Heat cream & sugar in top of double boiler until sugar dissolves. Put egg yolks, salt & vanilla in a bowl. Beat slightly. Combine cream & egg mixtures. Pour into glass 12x8-inch pan. Place inside pan of water in oven. Bake 45 minutes. Cool. Sprinkle brown sugar evenly over top of brûlée. Place under broiler to melt & carmelize sugar. Do not burn! Chill. If dessert is chilled more than several hours before serving, the brown sugar will weep.

8 servings

MENU

Salted Almonds

Grilled Ginger Lamb

Creamy Lemon Spinach Noodles

Strawberry Cake Roll

French Red Burgundy Chalonnais

•

The lamb looks beautiful served on a bed of hot sautéed cabbage. Try a salad of snow pea pods, water chestnuts, celery & sesame seed dressing. Ahhhh! The delights of summer entertaining.

ENTREE

Grilled Ginger Lamb

•

1 leg of lamb, butterflied
1/4 cup soy sauce
1/2 cup Burgundy
1/2 cup vegetable oil
1/3 cup peeled, grated ginger root
juice of one fresh lemon
1/4 cup minced onion
1 1/2 tablespoons honey
2 cloves fresh garlic, minced
1 1/2 teaspoons salt
1/2 teaspoon fresh ground pepper
1/8 teaspoon cayenne
1 cup beef stock

Pat lamb dry with toweling. Place in large glass pan. Combine soy sauce, Burgundy, oil, ginger, lemon juice, onion, honey, garlic, salt, pepper & cayenne in blender. Whirl 2 minutes. Pour over lamb. Marinate, covered, overnight or at least 6 hours, turning occasionally. Reserve marinade.

Grill lamb 15-20 minutes each side until medium rare. Baste with marinade while cooking. Can be oven broiled.

Add marinade to beef stock. Heat in small saucepan. Pass sauce with sliced lamb.

10 servings

PASTA

Creamy Lemon Spinach Noodles

•

2 tablespoons butter
3 tablespoons flour
1 teaspoon salt
white pepper
2 cups light cream
1/3 cup sliced pimiento-stuffed olives
1/2 pound spinach or herbed pasta, cooked & drained
1/4-1/3 cup grated Parmesan cheese
2 teaspoons grated lemon peel

In a saucepan, melt butter. Blend in flour, salt & pepper. Heat until bubbly. Add cream gradually, stirring constantly. Bring to a boil & cook 1-2 minutes. Add olives. Toss noodles with sauce in a warm serving dish. Sprinkle Parmesan cheese & lemon peel evenly over top.

6 servings

DESSERT

Strawberry Cake Roll

•

4 eggs
3/4 cup sugar
1 teaspoon vanilla
3/4 cup sifted flour
3/4 teaspoon baking powder
1/4 teaspoon salt
powdered sugar

Strawberry Butter Cream:
1 1/4 cups unsalted butter, softened
2 cups powdered sugar
4 egg yolks
1/2 cup puréed fresh strawberries
3 tablespoons strawberry preserves

Whipped Cream Filling:
1 pint fresh strawberries, chopped
1 pint heavy cream
1/2 cup powdered sugar
1 teaspoon vanilla

Preheat oven to 400°F. Line a 15x10-inch jelly roll pan with waxed paper. Butter lightly.

Beat eggs until light. Add sugar gradually. Beat until thick & lemon colored. Add vanilla. Sift flour, baking powder & salt. Fold into egg mixture. Pour into pan. Bake 10 minutes. Invert pan onto towel sifted with powdered sugar. Remove pan & paper. Roll cake inside towel starting at 10-inch side. Cool.

For the butter cream, beat butter & sugar until light & fluffy. Beat in yolks. Add berries & preserves. May be made in advance. Cover & chill. Soften to room temperature. For the cream filling, whip cream, vanilla & powdered sugar until stiff. Fold in berries.

To assemble: Unroll cake. Spread with cream filling. Reroll. Place seam-side down on serving plate. Frost with butter cream. Chill several hours.

10-12 servings

MENU

Fennel Soup

Cider Simmered Pork with Hazelnuts

Egg Noodles

Brussel Sprouts

Persimmon Cookies

California Zinfandel

•

Serve the soup in hollowed out red cabbage bowls. Do not hollow out too much! Top with a sprig from the fennel bulb.

Fennel Soup

•

- 4 large fennel bulbs, trimmed & thinly sliced
- 2-3 large yellow onions, thinly sliced
- 5 tablespoons butter
- salt & pepper
- 6½ cups chicken stock
- 1 tablespoon lemon juice
- 1 cup heavy cream
- ¼ cup dry sherry
- ½ cup chopped fresh parsley
- ¼ cup finely chopped red pepper

Sauté fennel & onions in butter until soft. Add salt & pepper. Transfer to a blender or food processor. Purée. Return to large pot. Add stock, lemon juice, cream, sherry & parsley. Heat, but do not boil. Serve immediately topped with a sprinkle of red pepper.

10 servings

Pictured page 113.

Cider-Simmered Pork with Hazelnuts

•

- 1½ pounds boneless pork chops
- ½ teaspoon salt
- ½ teaspoon dried thyme
- ½ tablespoon vegetable oil
- 1 medium onion, chopped
- ⅓ cup hazelnuts (filberts)
- ¾ cup cider
- 2 tablespoons hazelnut liqueur
- salt & pepper
- 1 tablespoon butter
- 1 large unpeeled Delicious apple, cut into ¾-inch cubes

Rub pork with salt & thyme. Heat oil in a 10-inch skillet. Brown pork chops over medium-high heat until golden, 3-5 minutes per side. Remove pork & set aside. Add onion & hazelnuts. Sauté 2 minutes. Add cider & loosen brown bits from bottom of pan. Return pork to pan. Cover & simmer until tender, 30-45 minutes depending on thickness. Remove pork to serving platter & keep warm. Purée pan juices, hazelnuts, etc. in processor or blender. Briefly return to pan to heat. Stir in liqueur.

In small skillet melt butter until bubbly over medium heat. Add apple & cook five minutes, stirring frequently until crisp-tender. Place sautéed apples on serving platter with pork. Pass warmed sauce separately.

4 servings

Persimmon Cookies

•

- 1 cup persimmon pulp
- ½ teaspoon lemon juice
- ½ teaspoon baking soda
- ½ cup butter
- 1 cup sugar
- 1 egg
- ½ teaspoon cinnamon
- ½ teaspoon cloves
- ½ teaspoon nutmeg
- 2 cups sifted flour
- 1 cup white or black raisins
- 1 cup chopped, mixed walnuts & pecans

Preheat oven to 350°F.

Add lemon juice & baking soda to persimmon pulp in a small bowl. Stir. Set aside. Cream butter & sugar. Add egg. Beat until light & fluffy. Add persimmon pulp. Stir. Add flour, cinnamon, cloves & nutmeg. Mix well. Stir in raisins & nuts. Drop by tablespoonfuls onto baking sheet. Bake 15 minutes.

3 dozen

MENU

Shrimp Delight on Toast Points

Herbal Leg of Lamb

Vidalia Onion Relish

Mushroom-Pistachio Baked Barley

Broccoli Salad

Cranberry Ice with Lemon Cookies

Oregon State Red Pinot Noir

•

Spring & lamb are definitely simpatico! Remember to serve lamb rare to medium-rare. The menu is easy on hosting chores & long on color.

❦

Shrimp Delight on Toast Points

•

- 1 cup butter, softened
- 1 cup fresh parsley, chopped
- ½ teaspoon fresh basil
- ½ teaspoon fresh thyme
- ½ teaspoon fresh oregano
- 2 cloves garlic, crushed
- salt & pepper
- 1½ pounds medium shrimp, peeled
- 3 cups artichokes, chopped
- 1 pound Danish Fontina cheese, grated

Preheat oven to 350°F.

Mix butter, parsley, basil, thyme, oregano, garlic, salt & pepper. May be prepared 2-3 days in advance. Sauté shrimp in ½ the butter mix. Discard any liquid. Place cooked shrimp & artichokes in shallow baking pan. Dot with remaining butter mixture. Sprinkle cheese on top of mixture. Bake 10 minutes or until cheese melts. Serve hot over toast points.

6 servings

Herbal Leg of Lamb

•

- ½ cup Dijon-style mustard
- 2 tablespoons soy sauce
- 1 clove garlic, minced
- 1 teaspoon ground rosemary
- ¼ teaspoon ground ginger
- 2 tablespoons olive oil
- 6 pound leg of lamb
- watercress & mint garnish

Blend mustard, soy, garlic, rosemary & ginger. Beat in olive oil by drops to make a creamy sauce.

Dry lamb well with toweling. Using a pastry brush, spread sauce over lamb. Place on roasting rack. Let rest several hours before cooking. Roast at 350°F. 1¼ hours for medium. Place lamb on HOT platter. Garnish with watercress & mint leaves.

8 servings

Mushroom-Pistachio Baked Barley

•

- 1 large onion, chopped
- 1 pound mushrooms, sliced
- 1 cup pearl barley
- 7 tablespoons butter, divided
- 2 cups chicken stock, divided
- ½ cup coarsely chopped pistachios
- salt & pepper

Preheat oven to 350°F. Butter a 1½-quart casserole.

Sauté onion & ½ the mushrooms in 5 tablespoons butter until soft. Add barley. Sauté until barley browns slightly. Turn into casserole. Pour 1 cup chicken stock over barley mixture. Bake, covered, 25 minutes. Add additional 1 cup stock & cook until liquid is absorbed & barley is tender, about ½ hour.

Sauté remaining mushrooms in 2 tablespoons butter. Cook, over low heat until mushrooms become very dry & almost black in color, but not burned. Mix pistachios with mushrooms. Sprinkle on top of barley before serving.

8-10 servings

MENU

Baked
Wisconsin Brie
with Herbs

**Perfect
Prime Rib**

**Linguini
Con Tuto Mare**

Italian
Sesame Twist
Bread

**Bourbon-Pecan
Mocha
Tart**

*California
Red Merlot*

•

The best of surf & turf for an occasion of merit, a promotion, engagement, or anniversary. Lay the table with your finest wares. Use a flowering plant for the centerpiece with small party balloons tied to wooden skewers stuck in the plant or a copy of an announcement with ribbons tied to the skewers. Congratulations!

Perfect Prime Rib

•

Any size prime rib roast, room temperature
garlic clove
sesame oil
salt & pepper

Preheat oven to 375°F. Rub roast all over with cut garlic clove. Rub with sesame oil. Season with salt & pepper. Place roast on rack in middle of oven. Roast 1 hour. Turn oven off. Do not open oven at any time. May be held in oven for several hours. Turn oven on again to 375°F. 30 minutes before serving for rare, 40 minutes for medium rare. Works for any size prime rib roast. Ask butcher for a roast to serve the number of guests.

Linguini Con Tuto Mare

•

1 cup butter
2 cloves garlic, minced
1/3 pound mushrooms, chopped
1/2 cup chopped parsley
2 cups chicken or clam stock
2 cups chopped clams
2 cups crab meat
1/2 pound shelled shrimp
1 1/2 pounds linguini, cooked & drained

In a large saucepan, melt butter. Sauté garlic, mushrooms & parsley 5 minutes. Add chicken broth, bring to a boil. Reduce heat. Add clams, crab & shrimp. Cook 5-7 minutes. Toss linguini with sauce on large heated platter. Serve immediately.

6-8 servings

Bourbon-Pecan Mocha Tart

•

1/2 cup butter, softened
2 1/2 tablespoons sugar
1 egg, beaten
1/2 cup ground pecans
1 1/3 cups flour

Filling:

3-ounces unsweetened chocolate
3 tablespoons butter
2/3 cup sugar
3 tablespoons bourbon
1 teaspoon instant coffee
4 eggs, room temperature
1 cup light corn syrup
1 teaspoon vanilla
2 cups coarsely chopped pecans
16 large pecan halves
whipped cream or ice cream, if desired

Preheat oven to 350°F. Butter an 11-inch tart pan.

Cream butter & sugar. Add egg. Beat well. Add pecans & flour. Mix well. Press onto bottom & sides of tart pan. Refrigerate 30 minutes. Bake 15 minutes. Remove from oven. Set aside.

For the filling, add chocolate, butter & sugar in top of double boiler over low heat. Dissolve coffee in bourbon. Add to chocolate. Stir until smooth. Remove from heat. Cool slightly. In a bowl, beat eggs, corn syrup, & vanilla. Stir in chocolate mixture & chopped pecans. Increase oven temperature to 400°F. Pour chocolate mixture into pastry. Top with pecan halves. Bake 25 minutes. Serve warm with ice cream or whipped cream if desired.

10-12 servings

MENU

Shrimp & Kiwi Supreme

Chicken with Juniper Berries

Artichoke Rice

Green Beans with Toasted Pine Nuts

Chocolate Cinnamon Torte

California Gewürztraminer

•

Invited your boss & her husband over for dinner? Here is an elegant way to entertain. Throw a starched cloth & napkins on the table, soft candlelight & wine glasses.

SALAD

Shrimp & Kiwi Supreme

•

½ cup white wine vinegar
½ teaspoon Dijon-style mustard
¼ cup sugar
¼ teaspoon salt
1 cup vegetable oil
6 kiwi fruit, peeled & wedged
40 cooked, shelled medium shrimp
2 oranges, peeled & sectioned
red leaf lettuce

Combine vinegar, mustard, sugar, & salt in blender or food processor. Mix well. With machine running, slowly add oil. Add 2 of the kiwi fruit. Strain dressing to remove seeds.

Arrange cooked shrimp, remaining kiwi wedges & orange sections pinwheel-fashion on a bed of red leaf lettuce. Carefully pour kiwi dressing over shrimp & fruit to lightly coat. Serve chilled as a first course or salad.

8 servings

ENTREE

Chicken with Juniper Berries

•

6 tablespoons butter, divided
2 tablespoons flour
2 cups chicken stock
1 tablespoon juniper berries
1 medium onion, chopped
1 stalk celery, chopped
8 peppercorns, crushed
1 teaspoon salt
2 cups sour cream
2 teaspoons brandy
2 teaspoons gin
3 whole chicken breasts, skinned, boned, & halved
2 tablespoons vegetable oil

Melt 2 tablespoons butter in a 2-quart saucepan. Add flour. Cook 2 minutes. Slowly add chicken stock. Add juniper berries, onion, celery, crushed peppercorns & salt. Simmer mixture 30 minutes until fairly thick, stirring frequently. Remove from heat. Blend in sour cream. Return to low heat. Simmer gently ten minutes. Strain sauce through a fine sieve. Add brandy & gin. Stir. Keep warm.

In large sauté pan, over medium heat, melt 4 tablespoons butter & oil. Sauté chicken, 3-5 minutes each side, until done. Place chicken breasts on a heated platter. Spoon some sauce over breasts. Pass remaining sauce. Garnish with tiny evergreen sprigs.

6 servings

DESSERT

Chocolate Cinnamon Torte

•

2 cups sugar
1½ cups butter, softened
2 eggs
2 tablespoons ground cinnamon
2⅔ cups flour, divided
3-4 ounce block of semi-sweet chocolate
5 cups heavy cream
1 cup cocoa

Tear 14 sheets waxed paper, 9½-inches long. Trace bottom of 9-inch cake pan on one sheet. Cut out circles.

Preheat oven to 375°F. Beat sugar, butter, eggs, cinnamon & 2 cups flour at low speed until combined. Increase speed to medium. Beat 3 minutes. Stir in remaining flour. Do not overmix. With damp cloth, moisten BACK of a baking sheet. Place 1 or 2 circles on back. Spread a scant ⅓ cup dough in thin layer on each circle. Bake 8-10 minutes until lightly browned. Remove from oven. Cool 5 minutes. Remove cookie to wire rack. Repeat. Stack cooled cookies. Cover with plastic. Prepare 1-3 days in advance.

For chocolate curls, soften chocolate bar in hands. With vegetable peeler, scrape along side of chocolate. Place curls on plate & chill.

Whip cream & cocoa until soft peaks form. To assemble, peel off paper. Place cookie on serving platter. Spread ½ cup cocoa-cream to edges. Repeat. Spread remaining cocoa-cream on top. Garnish with mound of chocolate curls. Chill at least 4 hours or overnight.

16 servings

Pictured page 172.

MENU

Palm Salad

Seafood Chili

Wild Pecan Rice

Cornbread Sticks

The Best Chocolate Sauce

Mint Ice Cream

French White Burgundy Chablis

•

A rich special "Chili" to delight a seafood lover's palate. Serve the ice cream in green glass sherbet dishes & garnish with mint sprigs & whole strawberries. Stick a profiterole cookie or two on the side.

Palm Salad

•

- 1 can (14 ounces) hearts of palm, cut into julienne strips
- 1 bunch radishes, thinly sliced
- 2 bunches watercress, well trimmed
- 2 heads Belgian endive, cut into ¼-inch pieces
- ⅓ cup chopped parsley

Dressing:

- ¾ cup vegetable oil
- ¼ cup tarragon vinegar
- 1 egg yolk
- 1 tablespoon Dijon-style mustard
- 1 shallot, minced
- 1 teaspoon salt
- ¼ teaspoon ground pepper

Blend dressing ingredients together. Chill. To serve, toss salad ingredients lightly with dressing.

8 servings

Seafood Chili

•

- 3 tablespoons olive oil
- 1 bunch scallions, sliced
- 1 cup chopped celery
- 1 green pepper, chopped
- 2 large potatoes, chopped
- 3 cloves garlic, minced
- 2 cups chopped, peeled tomatoes
- 1 can (15 ounces) tomato sauce
- 1 cup white wine or chicken stock
- 1 teaspoon thyme
- salt & pepper
- 1 tablespoon pesto sauce
- 1 tablespoon oyster sauce
- 1 tablespoon green peppercorns, mashed
- 2 cans (10 ounces each) whole baby clams
- 1½-2 pounds firm white fish, Haddock, Pollack, Ocean perch, chopped
- 1 pound shrimp, crab, scallops or combination, chopped

Sauté scallions, celery, green pepper, potatoes & garlic gently in olive oil. Add tomatoes, tomato sauce, wine, thyme, basil pesto, oyster sauce & peppercorns. Simmer 30 minutes. Five minutes before serving add clams & selected seafood.

6 servings

The Best Chocolate Sauce

•

- 5-ounces bittersweet chocolate
- 3 tablespoons butter
- 1⅓ cups sugar
- ¼ cup cornstarch
- ¼ cup light corn syrup
- ¾ cup evaporated milk

Melt chocolate & butter in double boiler. Mix remaining ingredients. Add to chocolate. Cook, stirring constantly until sugar is dissolved & mixture is smooth, 10 minutes. Store in refrigerator. Heat to serve. May be flavored with brandy, schnapps, mocha, nuts, etc.

2 cups

MENU

Broiled Herbed Shrimp

Madagascar Green Peppercorn Steak

Braised Cherry Tomatoes

Polenta with Parmesan

Poached Pears with Sauce Anglaise

California Chenin Blanc with Shrimp

California Cabernet Sauvignon with Entrée

•

Green peppercorns are delightful & add zip to any recipe. The impressive menu could be pared down to suit your entertaining mood.

APPETIZER

Broiled Herbed Shrimp

•

1½ pounds fresh shrimp, peeled
½ cup butter, melted
2 cloves garlic, pressed
2 tablespoons fresh lemon juice
1 tablespoon chopped fresh parsley
1 teaspoon dried oregano
1 teaspoon dried basil
½ teaspoon salt
½ teaspoon freshly ground pepper
3 cups cooked rice
parsley, garnish

Preheat oven to 450°F.

Place shrimp in single layer in shallow baking dish. Combine butter, garlic, lemon juice, parsley, oregano, basil, salt & pepper. Pour over shrimp. Bake 5 minutes, then broil 4-inches from heat 5 minutes. Serve over rice. Garnish with parsley.

6 servings

ENTREE

Madagascar Green Peppercorn Steak

•

4 slices beef tenderloin, 1-inch thick
4 tablespoons green peppercorns, mashed

Marinade:
⅔ teaspoon green peppercorns, mashed
1 tablespoon soy sauce
1 teaspoon sugar
2 teaspoons vegetable oil
1 tablespoon Worcestershire sauce

1 tablespoon butter
1 tablespoon vegetable oil
½ cup brandy
1 teaspoon cornstarch
2 tablespoons water
½ cup heavy cream

Flatten steaks with rolling pin to ½-inch thick. Spread green peppercorns on each steak. Set aside.

For the marinade, mix peppercorns, soy sauce, sugar, vegetable oil & Worcestershire sauce. Pour over steaks. Marinate one hour.

Scrape peppercorns & marinade off steaks & reserve.

Over high heat in a large skillet, add butter & oil.

Sauté steaks 2 minutes each side for medium rare. Add brandy & flambé 1 minute. Remove steaks to heated platter. Combine cornstarch with water. Add to pan juices. Stir. Add cream & reserved marinade. Stir until bubbly. Serve sauce over steaks.

4 servings

DESSERT

Poached Pears with Sauce Anglaise

•

Sauce Anglaise:
1 cup milk
½ cup heavy cream
6 tablespoons sugar
4 egg yolks
2 teaspoons cornstarch
1 teaspoon vanilla

Pears:
8 pears, slightly underripe, peeled, leave stems on
1 tablespoon lemon juice
4 cups water
2 cups sugar
3 whole cloves
1 cinnamon stick
1 tablespoon grated lemon peel

For Sauce, combine milk & cream. Bring just to a boil. Beat sugar into egg yolks until pale & creamy. Add cornstarch. Stir cream into egg yolks, beating vigorously. Return to low heat & cook 15 minutes, until mixture is creamy. Remove from heat. Add vanilla. Chill, covered, overnight.

For the pears, slice a piece off the bottom of each pear so it will stand upright. Place in cold water & 1 tablespoon juice. Set aside.

Add sugar to 4 cups water & bring to a boil. Add cloves, cinnamon stick & lemon peel. Add pears. Keep at rolling boil until pears are tender & easily pierced with a fork, about 30 minutes. Put pears in individual serving dishes. Pour a little cooking syrup over each to glaze. Chill at least 4 hours. Serve with Sauce Anglaise spooned over top.

8 servings

MENU

Sole Caledonia

Brown Rice

Tipsy Carrots

Chocolate Loaf

California Napa Chardonnay

•

There is understated elegance when presenting this menu & wine at your next dinner party. Pale blue cloth, napkins & candles with peach & blue carnations in the centerpiece & you will delight the eye as well as the palate.

ENTREE

Sole Caledonia

•

1 pound fillets of sole
½ cup dry white wine
1 cup asparagus tips
½ cup halved cherry tomatoes
½ cup sliced mushrooms
2 tablespoons butter
2 tablespoons flour
salt & white pepper
1¼ cups hot milk
1 egg yolk
½ cup fresh bread crumbs
¼ cup freshly grated Parmesan cheese

In a large skillet, poach fillets in wine 2-3 minutes. Remove fillets to buttered baking dish. Reserve poaching liquid. Top fillets with asparagus, tomatoes & mushrooms. In small saucepan, heat butter. Stir in flour, salt & pepper. Add heated milk. Stir until thickened. Add a little hot milk mixture to egg yolk. Return to pan. Bring to boil. Add poaching liquid. Stir until blended & smooth. Pour evenly over fillets & vegetables. Combine bread crumbs & cheese. Sprinkle evenly over sauce. Bake at 350°F. 30 minutes until browned & bubbly.

4 servings

VEGETABLE

Tipsy Carrots

•

24 baby carrots or equivalent sliced carrots
2 tablespoons orange-flavored liqueur
¼ cup brandy
¼ cup honey
juice of 1 lemon
2 tablespoons chopped Italian parsley

Cook carrots until crisp-tender in small amount of salted water 10 minutes. Arrange in buttered 1-quart baking dish. Combine liqueur, brandy, honey & lemon in small saucepan. Bring to boil. Reduce by ⅓. Pour over carrots & marinate overnight. Reheat in 350°F. oven 20 minutes or microwave. Sprinkle with parsley.

6-8 servings

DESSERT

Chocolate Loaf

•

1½ cups ground walnuts, divided
12-ounces semi-sweet chocolate pieces
¾ cup unsalted butter
3 tablespoons unsweetened cocoa powder
⅓ cup sugar
4 egg yolks
5 egg whites
pinch salt

Vanilla Mousseline:

1 cup milk
1 teaspoon vanilla
3 egg yolks
3 tablespoons sugar
1 cup heavy cream
¼ cup powdered sugar

Line bottom of 1-quart loaf pan with waxed paper. Liberally butter inside of pan. Sprinkle 1 cup walnuts over inside of pan. Gently press into place. Set aside.

Combine chocolate, butter & cocoa in 1-quart saucepan. Cook over low heat until melted. Remove from heat. Cool. With mixer, add sugar & beat 3 minutes. Beat in yolks one at a time. Beat egg whites & salt until stiff & glossy. Stir ⅓ whites into chocolate mixture. Gently fold in remaining whites. Turn into prepared pan. Cover with plastic. Refrigerate. May be frozen 3 weeks. Defrost in refrigerator.

For mousseline, scald milk. Set aside. Combine yolks & sugar. Beat until thick & lemon-colored. Whisk milk into eggs. Return to saucepan. Cook over low heat, stirring, until mixture thickens & coats spoon. Do Not Boil. Strain custard into bowl. Cover & refrigerate. May be made 3 days in advance. Before serving, whip cream & powdered sugar until stiff. Fold cream into custard. Turn out loaf onto serving plate. Remove paper. Press remaining walnuts onto loaf. Slice & serve with sauce.

10 servings

Notable Gatherings

presented by Wisconsin Chefs, Cooks & Caterers

Escargot Bon Maman

•

24 large mushrooms, stems removed
3 tablespoons butter
pinch salt
½ teaspoon finely chopped shallots
24 escargots
⅓ cup dry red wine
1 cup brown sauce, recipe follows
½ teaspoon chopped garlic
1 teaspoon chopped parsley

Brown Sauce:
1 tablespoon clarified butter
1 tablespoon flour
½ cup beef stock

Sauté mushroom caps in butter in sauté pan over medium heat. Add salt. Remove caps from pan. Divide caps between six escargot dishes. Keep warm. Sauté shallots in same pan 20 seconds. Add escargots. Increase heat. Add wine. Cook 30 seconds. Add brown sauce. Remove escargots & place in mushroom caps. Keep warm. Reduce sauce over high heat 1 minute. Reduce heat to medium. Add garlic & parsley. Lightly spoon sauce over escargots.

For the sauce, heat butter in saucepan. Add flour. Cook over low heat, stirring occasionally, until flour & butter are blended & turn the color of brown wrapping paper. Add stock. Blend with whisk until slightly thickened.

6 servings

Veal Tenderloin Robert

•

1½ pounds (16 1½-ounce slices) veal tenderloin
salt & pepper
2 thin slices prosciutto ham, finely chopped
8-ounces Brie cheese, peeled & softened
¼ cup flour
1 cup unsalted butter
4-ounces morels or other mushrooms
3 shallots, finely chopped
1 cup cream
1 cup chopped parsley
fresh lemon juice

Pound veal. Season lightly with salt & pepper. Combine prosciutto & Brie. Spread mixture on veal slices. Roll up. Dust veal with flour. Melt butter over medium-high heat in large skillet. Sauté veal rolls until brown on all sides & cooked through. Remove to a warm covered plate.

In same pan sauté mushrooms & shallots in remaining butter. Add cream. Bring to boil. Reduce sauce to desired consistency. Add parsley. Season to taste with lemon juice & salt. Spoon sauce over veal.

6-8 servings

MENU

Escargot Bon Maman

Veal Tenderloin Robert

Vegetable Sauté

Very Fine Pasta

Lightly Dressed Cactus, Celeriac, & Mushroom Salad

Israeli Date Dessert

California Merlot

•

Grenadier's
Milwaukee, Wisconsin

Grenadier's has been open since the mid-'70s. Chef Knut Apitz believes the principle of quickly prepared, lightly sauced, low-fat food can apply to anything. Grenadier's offers continental cooking in the true sense of the word, from French, German, Italian, American to almost anywhere else—Chinese, Indian, or South American.

MENU

Bibb & Romaine Salad with Herbed Mayonnaise Dressing

Pheasant Périgourdine

Forcemeat

Wild Rice

Sautéed Provençale Vegetables

Crêpes Flambées Forêt Noire

French Red
Bordeaux Margaux

•

The English Room
Milwaukee, Wisconsin

French Chef Edouard Charles Becker brings a light & colorful touch in menu design to the restaurant that consistently wins acclaim for its continental food. The extensive menu is complemented by more than 400 wine offerings from their cellar. Expert maître d' Frank Bonfiglio's attention is famous.

Pheasant Périgourdine

•

2-2½ pound pheasant
salt & pepper
1 recipe forcemeat, recipe follows
4-ounces salt pork
cheesecloth
1 cup butter, melted
½ large onion, diced
1 medium carrot, diced
2 stalks celery, diced
2 shallots, quartered
1 teaspoon thyme
½ bay leaf
½ tablespoon flour
1½ cups water
1½ cups chicken stock
¼ cup Madeira
2 medium mushrooms, finely chopped
½-ounce truffles, finely chopped
2 round toasts

Preheat oven to 350°F.

Season pheasant inside & out with salt & pepper. Stuff with forcemeat. Cut salt pork into 4 slices. Lay on the pheasant breast. Place pheasant in roasting pan. Cut a piece of cheesecloth to cover bird completely. Soak in melted butter. Lay on top of bird. Roast 50-65 minutes, basting with melted butter & twice with a sprinkle of water. Transfer to warm platter.

Place roasting pan over medium heat. Add onions, carrots, celery, shallots, thyme & bay leaf to drippings. Cook until brown. Add flour. Cook until flour is browned. Add water & stock. Boil rapidly until mixture is reduced by half. Strain through a sieve into a small pan. Over medium heat, add Madeira, mushrooms & truffles. Stir & simmer a few minutes. Season to taste. Serve pheasant on toast. Coat with sauce. Pass remaining sauce.

2 servings

Forcemeat

•

1 thick slice bacon, ground
¼ pound chicken livers, chopped
⅓ teaspoon finely chopped shallot
1 tablespoon finely chopped mushrooms
⅓ teaspoon finely chopped truffles
½ teaspoon parsley
2 tablespoons butter
⅓ cup brown sauce
1 egg yolk
salt, pepper, nutmeg
bread crumbs

Sauté bacon, livers, shallot, mushrooms, truffles & parsley in butter. Add brown sauce, yolk, salt, pepper & nutmeg. Stir until liquid is incorporated. Press mixture through a sieve. Add bread crumbs until liquid is completely absorbed.

2 servings

Crêpes Flambées Forêt Noire

•

4 crepes
½ pint excellent ice cream
⅔ cup sugar
¾ cup red wine
2-inch piece orange peel
2 whole cloves, stuck into orange peel
1 stick cinnamon
1 cup lightly crushed raspberries
1-ounce Himbeergeist, or eau de vie de framboise
2 tablespoons sliced almonds

Roll each crepe around ¼ cup ice cream. Freeze. May prepare in advance.

In heavy sauté pan over medium heat, stir sugar until melted & light brown. Add wine, orange peel & spices. Increase heat. Boil, stirring, until mixture is reduced to a bubbly texture. Add raspberries & 3-4 tablespoons of their juice. Cook until mixture is smooth & glazed. Remove spices & orange peel. Heat Himbeergeist & ignite. Add to sauce. Spoon flaming sauce over crepe. Sprinkle with almonds.

2 servings

MENU

Chilled Cantaloupe Soup in Melon Baskets

Phyllo Vegetable Strudel with Hollandaise

Green Salad with Fresh Fruit & Papaya Seed Dressing

Dilly Yeast Muffins

Sawmill Toffee

California Sauvignon Blanc

•

Karen Maihofer
Creative Cuisine

Karen is accredited by the International Association of Cooking Professionals. Currently teaching for MATC & the Grand Gourmet School, she also operates her own cooking school & catering business, Creative Cuisine. Karen's menus & food are known for their simplicity, elegance, ease of preparation & beautiful garnishes.

Chilled Cantaloupe Soup in Melon Baskets

•

4 medium cantalopes
1½ cups apple juice
⅔ cup sugar
½ cup dry sherry
1 tablespoon fresh lemon juice
¾ teaspoon ground ginger
¾ teaspoon vanilla
mint sprigs

To prepare baskets, draw a light circle around circumference of melon. With a V-cutter or knife, make zig-zag cuts around melon on top of line. Pull melon halves apart. Remove seeds. Scoop out pulp. Reserve shells. Cut a tiny slice off bottom of each melon half to sit flat.

In large bowl, combine pulp, apple juice, sugar, sherry, lemon juice, ginger & vanilla. In blender, whirl 2 cups mixture at a time until smooth. Pour into covered container. Chill overnight. Stir before serving. Pour into melon baskets. Garnish with mint sprigs. Serve with a straw or spoon.

8 servings

Green Salad with Fresh Fruit & Papaya Seed Dressing

•

1 large head romaine lettuce, torn into bite-size pieces
1 head leaf lettuce, torn into bite-size pieces
2 papayas, peeled, cut into 1-inch dice, reserve seeds
2 avocados, peeled, pitted, sliced, sprinkle with lemon juice
1 pint strawberries, halved
2 kiwi fruit, peeled, sliced ¼-inch thick

Papaya Seed Dressing:
½ cup sugar
½ cup white wine vinegar
¼ cup minced onion
½ teaspoon dry mustard
1 teaspoon salt
½ cup vegetable oil
3 tablespoons papaya seeds

Arrange greens on 14-inch platter. Place mound of papaya in center of greens. Arrange avocado slices spoke-fashion around papaya. Alternate kiwi & strawberries around outside of platter.

For dressing, place ingredients except oil & papaya seeds in blender. Blend smooth. With machine running slowly add oil. Add papaya seeds. Blend until they resemble coarsely ground pepper. Chill up to 3 days in advance. Drizzle dressing onto salad just before serving.

10 servings

Dilly Yeast Muffins

•

3½ cups unbleached flour
¼ cup sugar
1 teaspoon salt
1 package quick rise yeast
1½ cups milk
⅓ cup butter
1 jumbo egg
2-3 tablespoons snipped fresh dill or 1-1½ teaspoons dried

Lightly butter 18 muffin cups.

In food processor, combine 1½ cups flour, sugar, salt, & yeast. In saucepan, heat milk & butter to 130°F. Pulse processor to blend dry ingredients. With machine running, add milk mixture. Let machine run 30 seconds. Add egg & dill. Run 1 minute. Add enough additional flour to make a stiff, but still sticky dough. Batter is very soft. Cover work bowl with plastic. Put in warm place to rise until double in volume, 30 minutes. Stir down.

Preheat oven to 400°F. Fill muffin cups 2/3-full. Cover & let rise 15 minutes until dough almost fills tin. Bake 12-15 minutes. Do not overbake. Should be served warm. May be frozen.

18 muffins

Photographs

Fennel Soup, recipe 102
California Ham, recipe 148
Hungarian Nut Torte, recipe 145
Picante Crab Fondue, recipe 142
Monte's Beef Tenderloin, recipe 165

Camembert Normand
fabriqué à la louche avec des laits crus.

Mary E Wood
No.1
1844

MENU

Dilled Leek Soup

Armenian Lamb Shanks

Brown & Wild Rice

Seasonal Vegetables

Kourabiedes Greek Shortbread Cookies

Dilled Leek Soup

- 1 pound zucchini, coarsely chopped
- 1 large leek, washed & chopped
- 4 tablespoons bacon fat
- 2 tablespoons snipped fresh dill
- 5½ cups chicken stock
- salt & pepper
- 1 cup cream

In a large saucepan, cook zucchini & leek in fat over medium heat 10 minutes until soft, not brown. Add dill, stock, salt & pepper. Cover & simmer 20 minutes. Remove from heat. Cool slightly. In a blender or processor, purée in batches. When ready to serve, reheat. Add cream. Ladle into heated bowls.

4-6 servings

Kourabiedes Greek Shortbread Cookies

- 2 cups flour
- 1 cup powdered sugar
- 1 cup butter, softened
- powdered sugar

Preheat oven to 300°F.

Sift flour & sugar. Add to butter. Thoroughly work with fingers. Form into balls the size of a walnut. Place on baking sheet. Flatten with the bottom of a glass dipped in powdered sugar. Bake 20-30 minutes. Do not let them get brown! Dust with powdered sugar.

3 dozen

The Painted Lady
Newburg, Wisconsin

Originally called the "Max Weinand Saloon," the Painted Lady has served as a tavern since its construction in 1875. The varied menu features homemade hot breads, soups, dressings, desserts & entrées in a dining style described as "haute cuisine à la Newburg."

MENU

Curried Carrot Soup

Tomato Herbed Fish Fillets

Lemon Fromage

French White Muscadet

•

Tomato Herbed Fish Fillets

•

2 pounds any fish fillets, cut into serving pieces
½ cup bread crumbs
2 cups peeled, seeded & chopped tomatoes
½ cup sliced scallions
2 teaspoons oregano
2 teaspoons basil
1 cup mayonnaise
1 cup grated cheddar cheese

Preheat oven to 400°F.

Dredge fillets in bread crumbs. Arrange in buttered shallow casserole or individual ramekins. In a small bowl, combine tomatoes, scallions, oregano & basil. Spoon over fillets. Mix together mayonnaise & cheddar cheese. Spread over fillets. Bake 20 minutes.

6-8 servings

Lemon Fromage

•

3 eggs
2 egg yolks
½ cup sugar
grated peel of 1 lemon
1 package unflavored gelatin
juice of 2 lemons
2 cups heavy cream, whipped
1 pint fresh strawberries

Beat eggs & yolks until light & frothy. Add sugar gradually. Continue beating until mixture is thick & light colored. Add lemon peel. Soften gelatin in lemon juice. Melt over hot water. When dissolved, add to egg mixture. Beat well. Fold cream into mixture. Pour into 1-quart melon mold or another 1-quart mold. Chill 4 hours. Unmold & garnish with strawberries.

6-8 servings

Naomi Arbit
The Gourmet Touch

Naomi Arbit is a cooking teacher, home economist, food consultant & co-author of 7 cookbooks distributed nationally & internationally. She is the weekly food columnist for Community Newspapers in Wisconsin & Illinois under the title, The Gourmet Touch.

MENU

Mushrooms in Sour Cream

Cream of Artichoke Soup

Caesar Salad

Arroz con Pollo

Southern Butter & Nut Cake

Oregon State Pinot Noir

•

Marcia's Gourmet House
Racine, Wisconsin

"Food with Taste" is the motto of this popular catering & gourmet-to-go specialty store featuring daily take-out soups, stews, quiche, salads, entrées & bakery specialties. Marcia's Gourmet House was featured on ABC-TV's 20/20 program.

APPETIZER

Mushrooms in Sour Cream

•

1 pound mushrooms, sliced
2/3 cup scallions, sliced
2 tablespoons butter
1 tablespoon lemon juice
1 tablespoon flour
1 cup sour cream
2 tablespoons snipped fresh dill
1/4 teaspoon salt
freshly ground pepper
toasted French bread slices

Sauté mushrooms & scallions in butter & lemon juice 4 minutes. Stir in flour. Cook slowly 1 minute. Add sour cream, dill, salt & pepper. Cook 1 minute. Serve immediately over toasts.

4 servings

SOUP

Cream of Artichoke Soup

•

3 tablespoons diced onion
3 tablespoons diced carrot
3 tablespoons diced celery
1/4 cup butter
2 cups chopped cabbage
1/2 cup chopped onion
2 cloves garlic, minced
1 can (14 ounces) artichoke bottoms, drained & rinsed
4 cups chicken stock, divided
2 teaspoons chervil
2 tablespoons finely chopped parsley
1 teaspoon salt
1/2 teaspoon paprika
1/4 cup dry sherry
1/8 teaspoon hot pepper sauce
fresh ground pepper
1 tablespoon cornstarch
2 tablespoons cold water
2 cups light cream

In large kettle, sauté onion, carrot & celery in butter 5 minutes. Remove from pan. Set aside. In same butter, sauté cabbage, remaining onion & garlic 5 minutes. Spoon cabbage mixture into blender or processor. Add artichokes & 2 cups stock. Purée. Return to kettle. Add remaining stock, diced vegetables, chervil, parsley, salt, paprika, sherry, hot pepper sauce & pepper. Simmer 10 minutes. Combine cornstarch & water. Add to soup, stirring until slightly thickened. Add cream. Heat gently without boiling.

6-8 servings

ENTREE

Arroz con Pollo

•

3 1/2 pound frying chicken, cut into serving pieces
1/4 cup olive oil
seasoned salt
pepper
2 cups chopped onion
2 cloves garlic, minced
1 cup chopped celery
1 cup chopped green pepper
4 cups water, divided
2 teaspoons salt
1/4 teaspoon powdered saffron
2 bay leaves
2 cups chopped tomatoes
2 cups long grain rice
1 cup petite peas, cooked
pimiento strips
olive oil

In large skillet, brown chicken over medium high heat in olive oil. Sprinkle with seasoned salt & pepper. Remove to dutch oven or roasting pan. Pour off all but 1/4 cup fat. Add onion, garlic, celery & peppers. Cook 5 minutes. Add to chicken. Add 2 cups water to frying pan to deglaze. Pour over chicken. Add remaining water, salt, saffron, bay leaves, tomatoes & rice. Bring to boil. Stir well. Cover & simmer 30 minutes, or bake at 325°F. 30 minutes. Garnish with peas, pimiento & a drizzle of olive oil before serving.

4 servings

MENU

Cured Norwegian Salmon with Mustard Sauce

Herb Stuffed Lamb Leg with Garlic Butter Sauce

Toasted Coconut Flan

French Red Burgundy Côtes du Nuits

•

Claus on Juneau Milwaukee, Wisconsin

Norwegian chef Claus Bierek offers gourmet French & Scandinavian food in the style of "Cuisine Nouvelle" in his contemporary dining room.

APPETIZER

Cured Norwegian Salmon with Mustard Sauce

•

2 pounds fresh salmon fillet, tail portion
1 cup Kosher salt
1 tablespoon freshly ground white peppercorns
1½ cups sugar
1 bunch fresh dill, chopped, about 1½ cups
½ cup sweet sherry
¼ cup Cognac
poached eggs

Mustard Sauce:
1 cup mayonnaise
2 tablespoons Pommard mustard
juice from salmon marinade, about 2 tablespoons
2 tablespoons fresh chopped dill

Place salmon fillet in shallow pan. Combine salt, peppercorns, sugar & dill. Evenly spread over fillets. Pour sherry & Cognac over fillets. Cover. Refrigerate 24 hours.

For the sauce, combine ingredients. Serve the salmon very thinly sliced with mustard sauce ladled over a poached egg.

16-20 servings

ENTREE

Herb Stuffed Lamb Leg with Garlic Butter Sauce

•

4-5 pound Wisconsin boneless leg of lamb, butterflied
salt
freshly ground pepper
½ cup coarse brown mustard
2 tablespoons coarsely chopped garlic
½ cup chopped fresh parsley
1 tablespoon each chopped fresh dill, thyme, tarragon & marjoram, or any fresh aromatic herbs

Garlic Butter Sauce:
2 whole heads garlic, peeled
½ cup water
½ cup butter
1 teaspoon lemon juice

Preheat oven to 350°F.

Rub interior of leg with salt & pepper. Spread mustard evenly over meat. Place garlic & herbs down center of leg. Roll up roast. Secure with butcher's twine. Roast until thermometer reads 130-145°F. depending on preference. Remove from oven. Cover with foil.

For the sauce, in a 1-quart saucepan, bring garlic & water to boil. Reduce liquid to ¼ cup. Add butter. Over low heat, whisk until blended. Add lemon juice. Strain sauce through sieve. Serve lamb sliced on Garlic Butter Sauce.

8-12 servings

DESSERT

Toasted Coconut Flan

•

Caramel Coating:
1 cup sugar
¼ cup water

6 egg yolks
6 eggs
2 cups heavy cream
2 cups milk
1 cup sugar
1 teaspoon vanilla
2 cups toasted flaked coconut

Preheat oven to 275°F. Place a 13x9-inch pan with 1-inch boiling water into oven.

In a small saucepan over medium heat combine 1 cup sugar & water. Cook until sugar is rich caramel color. Pour hot caramel into a 2-3 quart soufflé dish, turning the dish to coat the sides & bottom with caramel. Set aside to cool. In a medium size saucepan, heat cream, milk, sugar & vanilla near the boiling point. In top of double boiler whisk yolks & eggs. Add cream mixture to beaten eggs. Heat in double boiler until hot to touch. Do not boil. Sieve mixture into a bowl. Add toasted coconut. Pour flan mixture into prepared soufflé dish. Place soufflé dish into heated pan of water in oven. Bake 65-75 minutes until completely firm. Chill completely. Invert onto serving tray. Serve with poached peaches or pears if desired.

8-10 servings

MENU

Brandied Corn Chowder in Mini Pumpkins

Roast Loin of Pork with Peanut Sauce

Dilled New Potatoes

Candied Julienne of Sweet Potatoes & Zucchini

Cream Cheese Apple Pie

French Red Rhône Côte Rôtie

•

Citrus Chicken Spinach Salad

Fresh Cinnamon Apple Bread

Homemade Pecan Walnut Pie

The Vintage House Wisconsin Rapids, Wisconsin

This talented cook, Ellen Jensen, offers a Fall Dinner Menu as well as a Country Luncheon. Her theory as a caterer is to specialize each menu she creates, coordinating theme, client style & party setting. Creative presentation of food is the key to her success.

ENTREE

Roast Loin of Pork with Peanut Sauce

•

5 pound loin of pork

Peanut Sauce:
3 tablespoons peanut oil
1 yellow onion, chopped
½ teaspoon crushed garlic
½ teaspoon crushed red pepper
6 tablespoons soy sauce
4 tablespoons sherry
pinch ground ginger
¾ cup creamy-style peanut butter
1 cup chicken stock
1 cup heavy cream

Roast the loin of pork at 350°F. until meat thermometer reads 175°F.

For the sauce, sauté onions & garlic in oil with red pepper. Add soy, sherry, ginger, peanut butter & stock. Simmer 30 minutes. Strain mixture. Add cream. Serve sliced loin with sauce.

8 servings

SALAD

Citrus Chicken Spinach Salad

•

1 chicken breast, sliced into ¼-inch strips
1 teaspoon Worcestershire sauce
1 teaspoon honey
1 tablespoon orange juice
2 tablespoons beef stock
½ cup hot bacon dressing
⅛ cup sliced mushrooms
2 tablespoons chopped scallions
2 tablespoons chopped fresh parsley
¼ cup cold water
1 tablespoon cornstarch
fresh spinach leaves
⅛ cup sliced toasted almonds

In medium sauté pan, cook chicken strips with Worcestershire, honey, orange juice, stock, dressing, mushrooms, parsley & green onions. Simmer 5-7 minutes until bubbling. Dissolve cornstarch in water. Add to pan. Cook until thickened. Serve on top of fresh spinach. Top with almonds.

1 serving

Pictured page 169.

DESSERT

Homemade Pecan Walnut Pie

•

1¼ cups dark corn syrup
1 cup packed light brown sugar
4 tablespoons butter
½ cup chopped pecans
½ cup chopped walnuts
4 eggs
1 teaspoon vanilla
1 9-inch unbaked pie crust

Preheat oven to 350°F.

Combine corn syrup & brown sugar in saucepan. Bring to boil. Stir until sugar is dissolved. Add butter, pecan & walnuts. Remove from heat. Beat eggs in bowl. Add vanilla. Pour eggs into syrup. Stir well. Pour into pie crust. Bake 45-50 minutes.

8 servings

MENU

Shrimp Denise

Sautéed Oriental Vegetables

Cherries Jubilee

French Red Beaujolais Moulin-à-Vent

•

Frenchy's

A fascinating legacy of great restaurants is that they live long after their demise in the hearts & minds of former patrons.

Shrimp Denise

•

½ cup butter, softened
2 cloves garlic, finely minced
2 teaspoons Worcestershire sauce
2 teaspoons steak sauce
½ teaspoon seasoned salt
12 jumbo shrimp, cooked & peeled
12 5-inch pieces bacon
1½ cups cooked wild rice

Combine butter, garlic, sauces & salt. Shape into a loaf. Wrap in plastic. Chill until very firm.

Split shrimp down the back halfway through. Stuff with seasoned butter. Wrap with bacon, fastened with a toothpick. Broil 2 minutes.

Spoon rice evenly into shallow serving casserole. Arrange shrimp attractively on rice. Dot with remaining butter mixture. Bake 375°F. 10 minutes.

2-3 servings

MENU

Hamming It Up

Kaiser Rolls

Baked Beans

Salads

California Johannisberg Riesling

•

Paulus Foods Cedarburg, Wisconsin

Mark Paulus offers the ham recipe deemed, "truly nectar of the gods," from his butcher shop.

Hamming It Up

•

1 large sheet heavy-duty foil
6-10 pound boneless ham
ground cloves
brown sugar
2 cups apricot nectar

Preheat oven to 325°F.

Place ham on foil. Rub with ground cloves. Pack ½-inch brown sugar on top of ham. Pour apricot nectar over ham. Seal foil. Place in baking pan. Bake 2 hours. Remove ham, reserve juices. Slice for sandwiches. Return to pan juices. Cover leftovers with juices in glass container. Can be frozen & reheated in microwave for easy meals.

15-18 sandwiches (6-pound ham)

MENU

Refreshing Grapefruit
&
Cucumber Salad

Fresh Tuna with Soy & Ginger

Spicy Mayonnaise Sauce

Boiled New Potatoes with Parsley

Aunt Grace's All American Three Layer Fudge Cake

California Red Zinfandel

ENTREE

Fresh Tuna with Soy & Ginger

- 3 tablespoons soy sauce
- 1 tablespoon lemon juice
- 1 clove garlic, minced
- ½ teaspoon peeled, grated fresh ginger root
- salt & pepper
- 2 tuna steaks, ½-¾ pound each

In glass dish, mix soy, lemon, garlic, ginger, salt & pepper. Add tuna, turning to coat. Cover & refrigerate at least 2 hours, turning occasionally. Remove steaks from dish. Reserve marinade. Broil tuna 4-inches from heat, 6-8 minutes, turning once. Or, grill tuna 6-inches from coals, 8-10 minutes, turning once. Heat marinade to boiling. Serve tuna with marinade.

2 servings

DESSERT

Aunt Grace's All American Three Layer Fudge Cake

- 2 cups sifted cake flour
- 2 cups sugar
- 1 teaspoon salt
- 1½ teaspoons baking soda
- ½ cup unsalted butter, softened
- 3-ounces unsweetened chocolate, melted
- 1¼ cups milk, divided
- 1 teaspoon vanilla
- ½ teaspoon baking powder
- 3 eggs

Mocha Butter Frosting:

- ⅓ cup unsalted butter, softened
- 3 cups powdered sugar, divided
- pinch salt
- ¼ cup milk or light cream
- 1½-ounces unsweetened chocolate, melted
- ½ teaspoon instant coffee powder
- 1½ teaspoons vanilla

Preheat oven to 350°F. Butter 3 8-inch round waxed paper-lined cake pans.

In large bowl, sift together flour, sugar, salt & baking soda. Add butter, 1 tablespoon at a time. Beat at medium speed until blended. Gradually add chocolate, ¾ cup milk & vanilla. Beat 2 minutes. Add baking powder, remaining milk & eggs. Beat 2 minutes. Divide batter evenly among pans. Tap pan on counter. Bake 35-40 minutes. Cool pans on racks 10 minutes. Remove layers from pans. Carefully peel off paper. Cool completely.

For frosting, beat butter, salt & 1 cup sugar at medium speed until light & fluffy, 2 minutes. Alternately add remaining sugar & milk beating until smooth. Add chocolate, coffee powder & vanilla. Beat 3 minutes, until spreading consistency. Spread between cake layers. Frost sides & top of cake.

8-10 servings

Myra Dorros
Modern Gourmet of Milwaukee

Accredited chef & teacher, Myra is a graduate of Madeleine Kamman's Cooking School in Boston & Annecy, France & is certified by the International Association of Cooking Professionals. She writes a weekly food column for the Milwaukee Journal, The Chef's Hat. As a food consultant, she coordinates a program that educates & trains Milwaukee High School students in food-related jobs.

MENU

Bibb, Red Cabbage & Scallion Salad with Duck Cracklings

Angel Hair Pasta with Black Truffle Sauce

Veal with Green Olives, Prosciutto & Spinach

California White Napa Valley Chardonnay

•

John Byron's Milwaukee, Wisconsin

Since opening in 1978, John Byron's has a reputation for serving creative unique specialties. All ingredients are the freshest & highest quality obtainable depending on seasonal availability. Chef Sanford D'Amato changes menus completely 3-4 times a year. The wine list, primarily with a California bent from smaller producers, has twice received the Wine Spectator's Top 100 Award.

SALAD

Bibb, Red Cabbage & Scallion Salad with Duck Cracklings

•

3 cups diced duck skin, from neck, etc.
4 heads bibb lettuce
¼ cup peanut oil
2 pounds red cabbage, finely shredded
2 bunches scallions, cut on bias into 1-inch pieces
1 tablespoon honey
¼ cup balsamic vinegar
1 teaspoon lemon juice
salt & pepper

Render duck skin until crispy & browned. Strain. Reserve ¼ cup fat. Arrange bibb lettuce on 6 plates. Heat duck fat & oil in large sauté pan. Add cabbage. Sauté 15 seconds. Add scallions, honey, vinegar, lemon juice, salt & pepper. Toss 30 seconds. Serve on lettuce beds. Garnish with cracklings.

6 servings

PASTA

Angel Hair Pasta with Black Truffle Sauce

•

1-ounce black truffles, julienned, reserve juice
¾ cup Madeira
1 cup veal stock
½ cup heavy cream
8-10 ounces fresh angel hair pasta, cooked & drained
salt & freshly ground pepper

Add truffle juice, Madeira & stock to sauté pan. Reduce by ½. Add cream. Boil until reduced to 1 cup. Add all but 4 strips truffle. Divide pasta onto 4 plates. Cover with sauce. Garnish with remaining truffle strips.

4 servings

ENTREE

Veal with Green Olives, Prosciutto & Spinach

•

3 2-ounce slices veal loin
salt & pepper
flour for dusting
2 tablespoons clarified butter
1 teaspoon chopped shallot
juice of ½ lemon
¾ cup white wine
3 brine-cured, pitted, Sicilian green olives
6 spinach leaves, blanched
4 tablespoons cold butter
1 tablespoon finely julienned prosciutto ham

Slightly flatten veal. Season with salt & pepper. Dust with flour. Heat butter in sauté pan. When hot, add veal. Sauté 15-25 seconds each side. Remove to plate. Keep warm.

Add shallots. Sauté 5 seconds. Add lemon, white wine & olives. Remove olives when hot. Add spinach leaves. Heat & remove from pan. Arrange on plate in circle. Reduce sauce by ⅔. Add cold butter using whisk over medium heat. Do not boil. Add veal & prosciutto to sauce. Remove & arrange on plate. Pour sauce over veal. Garnish with olives.

1 serving

MENU

Cream of Autumn Squash Soup

Garden Lettuce Salad with Cranberry Blossom Honey Vinaigrette

Shredded Veal with Zucchini & Mushrooms

Egg Noodles

Hazelnut Torte

French White Burgundy
Mâcon Pouilly-Fuissé

•

Nick Spinelli, Jr.

Nick graduated with honors from Culinary Institute of America & has worked in New York, Palm Beach, San Francisco, Quebec & Munich. He currently is Executive Chef for the First Wisconsin National Bank. Nick is a well-known teacher of gourmet cooking & the art of garnishing in Chicago & Milwaukee areas.

Cream of Autumn Squash Soup

•

- 1 small acorn squash, cleaned & cut into 1/8's
- 1 small buttercup squash, cleaned & cut into 1/8's
- 1 small pie pumpkin, cleaned & cut into 1/8's
- 1 large Bermuda onion, chopped
- 3 quarts chicken stock
- 1/4 cup butter
- 1/4 cup flour
- salt & white pepper
- 3/4 cup milk
- herbed croutons

Place squashes & onion in large pot with stock. Bring to boil. Simmer until squashes are tender. Remove squashes & onion. Reserve stock. Scoop out pulp from squashes. Purée onion & pulp in blender or processor.

Melt butter in saucepan. Add flour. Cook 2-3 minutes. Gradually add stock. Add purée. Stir to blend. Cook 5-10 minutes. Add milk. Cook 5 minutes. Season to taste. Serve in small carved-out pumpkins. Garnish with herbed croutons.

16 servings

Shredded Veal with Zucchini & Mushrooms

•

- 5 pounds sliced veal, cut into julienne strips
- 1½ cups flour seasoned with salt & black pepper
- ½ cup olive oil
- 1 cup salad oil
- 5 pounds small zucchini, halved & sliced
- 3 pounds mushrooms, sliced
- 2 cups veal or chicken stock
- 1 cup dry white wine
- 2 cups lemon juice
- 1½ cups finely chopped parsley
- 2 tablespoons cornstarch
- ½ cup water

Dredge veal strips in flour. Spread out to rest 5 minutes. Combine the 2 oils. In a large skillet, use oil as needed to sauté veal in batches. Remove to plate. Sauté zucchini & mushrooms until crisp-tender. Remove to plate with veal.

In a 2-quart saucepan combine stock, wine & lemon juice. Bring to boil. Simmer 30 minutes. Combine cornstarch & water. Add to sauce. Stir. Add parsley. Remove from heat. Fold in veal, zucchini & mushrooms. Reheat to boil. Serve with pilaf, noodles or boiled potatoes.

16 servings

Hazelnut Torte

•

- 1½ cups toasted, skinned hazelnuts, finely ground
- 4 egg whites
- 1⅓ cups superfine sugar
- 3 teaspoons vanilla, divided
- 1 teaspoon fresh lemon juice
- 1 cup heavy cream
- 2 tablespoons sugar
- powdered sugar

Preheat oven to 300°F. Butter & flour 2 9-inch paper-lined cake pans.

Beat egg whites until stiff. Gradually add sugar. Beat 2 minutes. Add 2 teaspoons vanilla & lemon juice. Beat 2 minutes. Carefully fold in ¾'s of nuts. Spread mixture evenly into pans. Bake 1 hour until layers are set but not brown. Turn out onto wire racks. Remove paper. Cool thoroughly.

Beat cream with sugar & remaining vanilla until stiff. Add additional powdered sugar for sweeter cream. Fold in remaining hazelnuts. Frost layers, sides & top of torte with cream. Chill several hours.

8 servings

MENU

Spinach Linguini with Port Wine & Scallops

Chicken Diane

Sugar Snap Peas

French White Alsace Riesling

•

Spinach Linguini with Port Wine & Scallops

•

4 tablespoons butter
2 pounds bay or sea scallops
2 shallots, chopped
2 tablespoons tomato paste
¼ teaspoon seasoned salt
1½ cups heavy cream
¼ cup port wine
1 pound fresh spinach linguine, cooked & drained

In large skillet, melt butter. Sauté scallops & shallots 2-4 minutes. Do not overcook. Remove scallops to warm platter. Add tomato paste, salt, cream & port. Bring to boil. Reduce sauce until slightly thickened. Return scallops to pan. Add linguine. Toss to coat. Serve immediately.

4 servings

Chicken Diane

•

3 tablespoons butter
4 skinless, boneless chicken breast halves
½ pound mushrooms, sliced
2 tablespoons flour
1 cup chicken stock
3 scallions, sliced
1 teaspoon Cajun spice blend
pinch oregano
¼ cup heavy cream

Sauté chicken breasts in butter 5 minutes over medium-high heat. Add mushrooms. Sauté several minutes. Remove chicken to warm plate. Sprinkle flour over mushrooms. Stir to coat. Cook 2 minutes over low heat. Add stock, scallions & spices. Return chicken to pan. Cook 10-15 minutes until sauce is slightly thickened & chicken is tender. Blend cream into sauce. Heat through. Serve with noodles or rice.

4 servings

The Boulevard Inn
Milwaukee, Wisconsin

The Boulevard Inn has long been known for their outstanding Continental & American cuisine emphasizing fresh seafood & an impressive California wine list.

MENU

Shrimp à la Greque

Pasta with Broccoli & Anchovy Sauce

Boule de Neige

Italian White Soave

•

Shrimp à la Greque

•

¼ pound sun dried tomatoes in oil, finely chopped, reserve oil
2 cloves garlic, finely chopped
3 tablespoons capers, drained
½ teaspoon oregano
2 pounds shrimp, peeled & cleaned
2 cups crumbled feta cheese

Preheat oven to 450°F.

Place tomatoes & oil in bowl. Add garlic, capers, oregano & shrimp. Toss. Arrange equal portions shrimp mixture in individual ramekins. Sprinkle with feta. Bake 10 minutes.

6-8 servings

Pasta with Broccoli & Anchovy Sauce

•

2 cups broccoli flowerets
3 tablespoons olive oil
3 tablespoons butter
8 anchovy fillets
1 clove garlic, minced
1 pound pasta, cooked & drained
1 cup freshly grated Parmesan cheese

Blanch broccoli in boiling salted water 2-3 minutes until crisp-tender. Drain. Rinse with cold water. Drain.

Heat oil & butter in large sauté pan. Sauté anchovies & garlic, mashing with wooden spoon. Add broccoli. Cook & stir 3-5 minutes until broccoli is well coated with sauce. Spoon mixture into a serving bowl. Add pasta to bowl. Toss with broccoli mixture until well combined. If sauce is too thick, add more butter & 2-3 tablespoons hot water. Sprinkle with Parmesan. Serve immediately.

4-6 servings

Jill Heavenrich

Well known in Milwaukee for her culinary arts, she operated the Jill Heavenrich Cooking School specializing in the fundamentals of continental cuisine & entertaining menus.

MENU

Salmon with Shallot Agresto Sauce & Mixed Peppercorns

Angel Hair Pasta with Cauliflower & Raw Tomato-Basil Sauces

Chicken Breasts, Artichokes & Oysters with Vernaccia Wine

Italian White Vernaccia di San Gimignano

•

Marangelli's Milwaukee, Wisconsin

Italian Chef John Marangelli is a master in presenting "the pinnacle of Italian cuisine." He is considered by some to be a culinary treasure. John's artistic combinations of flavors & textures make the palate & memory sing.

Angel Hair Pasta with Cauliflower & Raw Tomato-Basil Sauces

•

Cauliflower Sauce:
- 1½ cups chicken stock
- ½ milk
- ½ cup heavy cream
- 2 cups caulifIowerets
- ½ cup peeled, chopped celery
- 6-8 white celery leaves
- 2 tablespoons freshly grated Parmesan cheese

Raw Tomato-Basil Sauce:
- ¼ cup extra virgin olive oil
- 2 cloves garlic, mashed to paste
- 1 tablespoon finely chopped Italian parsley
- 1 pound ripe plum tomatoes, peeled, seeded, drained & finely chopped
- 3 tablespoons coarsely chopped fresh basil

- ¼ cup butter, softened
- 1 tablespoon extra virgin olive oil
- 1 teaspoon fresh lemon juice
- 8-ounces fresh angel hair pasta, cooked al dente & drained
- 2 tablespoons freshly grated Parmesan cheese

For the cauliflower sauce, bring stock & milk to boil in medium saucepan. Add cauliflower, celery & leaves. Cook 10-15 minutes. Strain stock into another saucepan. Purée vegetables in blender or processor. Add cream to stock. Bring to boil. Add puréed vegetables. Simmer a few minutes. Off heat, stir in cheese. Set aside.

For raw tomato basil sauce, add oil to saucepan over medium heat. Sauté garlic. Do not brown. Add parsley. Add tomatoes. Stir. Bring just to the boil. Remove from heat. Add basil. Stir. Set aside.

To serve, in a large flat bowl, whip together butter, oil & lemon juice. Add hot pasta. Toss until evenly coated. Add ½ cauliflower sauce & Parmesan. Toss. Divide remaining cauliflower sauce onto 4 plates. Use long-tined fork to make 4 rolls of pasta. Set each roll on top of cauliflower sauce. Enlarge center hole of each roll with 2 forks. Fill each hole with raw tomato-basil sauce.

4 servings

Pictured page 170.

Chicken Breast, Artichokes & Oysters with Vernaccia Wine

•

- 4 skinless, boneless chicken breast halves
- 4 medium-large artichokes
- 2 quarts ice water
- 2 tablespoons lemon juice
- 12 large fresh oysters, shucked, covered in own juices in bowl
- 2 tablespoons extra virgin olive oil
- ¼ cup clarified butter
- 1 clove garlic, lightly crushed
- 2 tablespoons finely chopped Italian parsley
- 1 tablespoon finely chopped mint
- ¼ cup Vernaccia wine
- ⅜ cup reserved oyster juice
- ½ cup heavy cream
- flour
- 1 cup extra virgin olive oil, divided
- 2 large bunches fresh sage leaves
- ¼ cup Vernaccia wine
- salt & freshly ground pepper

Separate loins from breasts. Remove membrane from loins. Cut each remaining breast into 3 strips the size of the loin. Pat dry. Set aside.

Trim stem from artichokes to 1-inch from bottoms. Remove tough outer leaves. Cut tops off artichokes, leaving 2-inch thick base. Remove inner choke. Evenly trim exterior of woody skin. Place in ice water with lemon juice. Set aside.

Carefully lift oysters from their juice. Gently pat dry. Set aside. Strain juice through cheesecloth. Set aside.

In a medium sauté pan over medium-high heat, allow pan to get hot 5-6 minutes. Add olive oil. Drop in oysters. Cook 1 minute until edges curl. Outside will be crisped, inside slightly warm. Transfer to plate.

Reduce heat to medium, add butter, garlic, parsley & mint. Add wine. Reduce by ½. Add strained oyster juice. Bring to boil. Add cream. Lower heat. Reduce by half several minutes.

Cut each artichoke into 8 wedges. Pat dry. Set aside.

Lightly dredge chicken strips in flour. In a large sauté pan over medium-low heat, add ¼ cup olive oil. Cook chicken a few strips at a time until light golden & very soft in center. Do not overcook. Remove chicken to plate. Set aside.

Return pan to high heat add remaining oil. When hot, carefully add artichokes all at once. *Be Careful Of Hot Oil.* Lightly brown artichokes several minutes. Drain off oil. Return pan to high heat. Add sage & wine. Reduce by ½. Add chicken strips. Mix together. Stir in oyster-cream sauce. Bring up to boil. Remove from heat. Correct seasoning.

On each plate, arrange chicken strips & artichokes in ray pattern. Reheat oysters in very hot oven or broil a few seconds. Place in center of ray. Pour sauce on top.

4 servings

MENU

Zucchini
with
Basil Soup

Quiche

Garden Vegetable Salad
with
Tarragon Vinaigrette

**Rhubarb
Tart**

Rhubarb Tart

•

½ cup butter
1 cup flour
½ cup powdered sugar

Filling:
2 eggs, beaten
1 cup sugar
¼ cup flour
1 teaspoon baking powder
¼ teaspoon salt
1 tablespoon grated orange peel
½ teaspoon cinnamon
3 cups diced rhubarb
whipped cream
cinnamon-sugar

Preheat oven to 350°F.

Combine butter, flour & powdered sugar. Pat onto bottom & ½-inch up the sides of a 12x8-inch pan. Bake 15 minutes. Cool.

For the filling, combine all ingredients. Spread over crust. Bake 40 minutes until rhubarb is tender. Top with whipped cream & sprinkle with cinnamon sugar.

12 servings

*Monches Mill House
Hartland, Wisconsin*

Owner Elaine D. Taylor offers this typical luncheon menu. The chilled Soup is sprinkled with chopped radishes & cucumbers. The Garden Salad is a combination of marinated carrots, beans, broccoli, brussel sprouts, button squash & cherry tomatoes.

❦

Shrimp & Artichoke Linguini with Casino & Provençale Sauces

•

MENU

Shrimp & Artichoke Linguini with Casino & Provençale Sauces

Chocolate Decadence

California Petite Sirah

•

Casino Sauce:
2 cups butter, softened
4 cloves garlic, chopped
1 cup finely chopped parsley
1/8 cup finely chopped green pepper
1/8 cup chopped pimiento, drained
salt
1 teaspoon pepper
1/4 cup dry white wine
1-ounce anchovy paste

Provençale Sauce:
1/4 cup olive oil
1/4 cup halved garlic cloves, crushed
1 large onion, chopped
1/2 teaspoon basil
1/2 teaspoon oregano
2 tablespoons finely chopped celery
2 tablespoons finely chopped parsley
4 cups peeled, chopped plum tomatoes
1/2 cup dry white wine
3 tablespoons concentrated clam base

12 large peeled, butterflied fresh shrimp
tempura flour
1/4 cup olive oil
2-3 tablespoons white wine
1 cup Casino Sauce
1 recipe Provençale Sauce
12 cooked artichoke hearts, halved
1 pound linguini, cooked & drained

For Casino Sauce, place ingredients in processor. Whirl until blended & smooth. Chill. Use as topping for fish, vegetables, steaks or whenever a full-flavored butter is required.

For Provençale Sauce, heat oil in small saucepan. Add garlic. Cook until golden but not burned. Strain oil into sauté pan. Discard garlic. Over medium heat, sauté onion in oil until limp. Add herbs. Cook 2 minutes. Add celery. Sauté 5 minutes. Add parsley, tomatoes, wine & clam base. Stir. Bring to boil. Simmer 10 minutes. Use for any recipe requiring a rich tomato sauce.

To serve, dust shrimp with tempura flour. Heat oil in 10-inch sauté pan. Add shrimp & wine to pan. Simmer 1 minute. Add Casino & Provençale Sauces. Cover & bring to boil. Uncover pan, add artichokes. On heated platter, toss linguini with sauce. Serve immediately.

6-8 servings

The Anchorage Restaurant
Milwaukee, Wisconsin

Seafood specialties have been perfected at the restaurant situated on the banks of the Milwaukee River. The Sauces are wonderfully versatile.

Buffet Gatherings
brunches, cocktail parties, dinners

MENU

Molly Hogans

Brandied Chicken Liver Pâté

Eggs Fantastic

Toasted English Muffins with Herb Butter

Bars & Cookies

Cinnamon Coffee

Before or after tobogganing on a sunny winter day, have guests help themselves to Molly Hogans & a terrific brunch for hearty souls.

BEVERAGE

Molly Hogans

6 eggs
1 cup sugar
1 tablespoon vanilla
1 can (12 ounces) frozen orange juice
1 can (6 ounces) frozen limeade
1 quart gin or vodka
2 bottles (2 liters each) lemon-lime soda
2 oranges, sliced
maraschino cherries

Add eggs to blender. Mix. Slowly add sugar, vanilla & juices. Blend well. Pour into large container. Add gin or vodka. Refrigerate at least one hour.

Fill tall glasses with ice. Add 2 ounces juice-gin or vodka mixture. Top with lemon-lime soda. Garnish with orange slice & cherry.

25 servings

APPETIZER

Brandied Chicken Liver Pâté

½ cup butter
1 pound chicken livers
½ cup sliced onion
1 small bay leaf
½ teaspoon dry mustard
¼ teaspoon curry powder
1 teaspoon salt
¼ cup excellent brandy

Melt butter in skillet. Add chicken livers, onion, bay, mustard, curry & salt. Cover & cook 8 to 10 minutes. Remove bay leaf & add brandy. Cool 5 minutes.

Whirl smooth in a food processor or blender. Pack into a buttered crock. Cover & chill several hours or store in freezer.

Serve with assorted breads, crackers or raw mushrooms.

12 servings

ENTREE

Eggs Fantastic

12 eggs
⅓ cup sour cream
1 pound sausage, any type
1 medium onion, chopped
¼ pound fresh mushrooms, sliced
½ pound cheddar cheese, grated
½ pound mozzarella cheese, grated
½ pound Swiss cheese, grated
salt & pepper

Beat eggs & sour cream. Pour into buttered 13x9-inch casserole. Bake 400°F. 10 minutes until eggs are set.

Sauté sausage, onion & mushrooms. Season with salt & pepper. Drain fat. Spread meat mixture over eggs & top with grated cheeses. Bake 325°F. 30 minutes until cheese melts.

Can be served with picante or salsa sauce over eggs.

8-12 servings

MENU

Camembert Puffs

Guacamole Shrimp Tortilla Chips

Three Pepper Prize Spread

California Gamay Beaujolais

•

Curtain time is 8 pm, but there is time for a pre-theater cocktail party. Pass trays to keep the party lively. Don't worry about leftovers!

Camembert Puffs

•

½ pound puff pastry or patty shells
½ cup Dijon-style mustard
⅓ cup sesame seed
6-8 ounces Camembert cheese, cubed
hot vegetable oil

Roll puff pastry ⅛-inch thick. Cut into 3-inch squares. With a pastry brush, spread a thin layer of mustard in center, not on edges of pastry. Sprinkle sesame seed over mustard. Place a cube of cheese on sesame seed. Moisten edge of pastry with water. Seal in a triangle shape. Chill in refrigerator 30 minutes or more.

Fry puffs in 375°F. oil about 1 minute until golden brown. Salt if desired. Serve piping hot.

Puffs may be frozen before cooking. Freeze on baking sheet. Place in plastic bag. Fry puffs a few seconds longer if frozen.

18-24 servings

Guacamole Shrimp Tortilla Chips

•

1 pound medium shrimp (about 25), cooked, cleaned & halved
2 ripe avocados
1 teaspoon salt
2½ tablespoons lemon juice
1 clove garlic, minced
2 tablespoons chopped scallions
dash chili powder & cayenne
50 round tortilla chips
50 cilantro leaves or flat leaf parsley

Chill shrimp. Mash avocados with fork. Add salt, lemon juice, garlic, scallions, chili powder & cayenne. Mix well. Just before serving spread tortilla chips with guacamole & top with half a shrimp. Garnish with cilantro or parsley.

50 servings

Pictured page 6.

Three Pepper Prize Spread

•

1 package (8 ounces) cream cheese or Neufchâtel, softened
½ cup grated parmesan cheese
1 medium sweet red pepper, finely diced
1 medium sweet green pepper, finely diced
1 medium sweet yellow pepper, finely diced
1 small onion, finely chopped
1 tablespoon fresh chopped basil

Beat cream cheese until light & fluffy. Fold in remaining ingredients. Chill until serving. Bake 350°F. 15 minutes. Spread on toast points, muffin halves, crackers, etc.

2 cups

MENU

Korean Bulgogi

Beef & Ginger Dim Sum

Grilled Rock Shrimps

Mélange of Oriental Melons

Almond Crisps

Light Dry Sherry or Jasmine Tea

•

Present these Far Eastern morsels as a tea-time alternative to the cocktail party. Set a table in your garden and let Mother Nature provide the backdrop.

Korean Bulgogi

•

Marinade:
½ cup soy sauce
1½ cups water
1 teaspoon sesame seed
1 teaspoon vegetable oil
1 carrot, grated
3 cloves garlic, minced

1½ pounds sirloin tip roast, sliced into very thin strips
vegetable oil
Silver dollar cocktail buns

Combine soy, water, sesame seed, oil, carrot & garlic. Marinate beef strips overnight. Remove beef from marinade. Heat small amount of vegetable oil in wok over medium-high heat. Stir-fry beef a few seconds. Add marinade. Remove to chafing dish. Serve with tiny cocktail buns.

8-12 servings

Beef & Ginger Dim Sum

•

Filling.
1 pound lean ground beef or pork
2 slices fresh peeled ginger, finely chopped
1 cup cooked, chopped spinach
1 tablespoon soy sauce
2 teaspoons rice wine or dry sherry
1 tablespoon cornstarch
½ teaspoon sesame oil

1 package (16 ounces) round wonton skins, or square skins with corners cut off

Dipping Sauce:
⅓ cup beef stock
⅓ cup soy sauce
⅓ cup rice vinegar or dry sherry
2-3 slices fresh peeled ginger, finely chopped
2-3 cloves garlic, finely chopped
2 teaspoons sesame oil
2 teaspoons sugar

Combine filling ingredients. Let stand 20 minutes. Put about 1 teaspoon filling in center of each skin. Bring skin up around filling. Pinch skin together so filling is enclosed. Finished dim sum should look like a miniature draw string purse. The dim sum may be frozen on baking sheets before cooking. Store in plastic bag. Combine sauce ingredients. Let stand 10 minutes to blend flavors.

Steaming dim sum: Place dim sum on a lightly oiled steamer rack in a pot or wok filled with 1-inch water. Cover pot. Steam over boiling water 15 minutes. *Pan frying dim sum:* Put 2 tablespoons peanut oil in bottom of skillet or wok over medium-high heat. Add dim sum in 1 layer. Reduce heat to low. Cook 5 minutes or until browned. Add ⅓ cup beef stock. Cover & cook 5 minutes or until liquid has evaporated.

Serve with dipping sauce.

8-10 servings

Almond Crisps

•

2 egg whites
½ cup sugar
¼ teaspoon vanilla
⅓ cup flour
4 tablespoons butter, melted
½ cup sliced almonds, toasted

Preheat oven to 375°F. Lightly butter baking sheet.

In a medium bowl combine egg whites with sugar. Beat until stiff. Add vanilla. Fold in flour, butter & almonds. Blend well. Drop batter by teaspoonfuls onto baking sheet several inches apart. Bake 5-6 minutes, until lightly browned. Cool 2 minutes. Remove from pan while still slightly warm.

5 dozen

MENU

Onion Mushroom Olive Salad

Wedges of Round Greek Bread

Feta Mint Tart

Pocket Gyros with Yogurt Sauce

Butter Cookies

Fresh Fruit

California Petite Sirah

•

The menu stirs up thoughts of the Aegean Sea & balmy evenings dining al fresco. Place fat glass shades over the candles & a colorful cloth on a table for two or twelve. Serve gyros in napkin lined baskets. Yasou!!

Onion Mushroom Olive Salad

•

1 pound whole mushrooms
1½ cups pitted black olives
1½ cups pitted green olives
1 large red onion, sliced & separated into rings
1½ cups artichoke bottoms

Dressing:
½ cup olive oil
½ cup red wine vinegar
½ cup white vinegar
1 tablespoon dill
1 clove garlic, minced
1 teaspoon oregano
1 teaspoon salt
½ teaspoon pepper

Place mushrooms, olives, onions & artichokes in large covered container. Blend dressing ingredients. Cover mushroom mixture with dressing. Seal container tightly. Refrigerate at least 4 hours. Keeps several weeks. Serve as an appetizer or as a salad atop spinach leaves.

8 servings

Feta Mint Tart

•

1 9-inch unbaked tart shell
1 package (8 ounces) cream cheese, softened
5-ounces feta cheese, room temperature
2 tablespoons butter, softened
¼ cup heavy cream
3 eggs
2 tablespoons chopped fresh mint
fresh ground pepper
mint sprigs

red & green grape clusters

Preheat oven to 375°F.

Beat cream cheese until fluffy. Add crumbled feta. Beat until blended. Add butter, cream, eggs, mint & pepper. Pour into prepared, pastry-lined tart pan. Bake 40-45 minutes, until tart is puffy & brown. Cool 5 minutes on wire rack. Remove tart from pan. Garnish with mint sprigs & grape clusters.

8-12 servings

Pocket Gyros with Yogurt Sauce

•

1¼ pounds lean ground beef
1¼ pounds lean ground lamb
¼ cup chopped fresh oregano
1 tablespoon fresh thyme leaves
1 medium onion, finely chopped
2 large cloves garlic, finely chopped
¾ teaspoon salt
¾ tablespoon ground pepper

8-10 pita breads
3 tomatoes, chopped
1 large onion, thinly sliced

Yogurt Sauce:
1 cup plain yogurt
¼ cup finely chopped cucumbers
¼ cup finely chopped onion
1 clove garlic, minced
2 teaspoons olive oil
¼ teaspoon salt
¼ teaspoon pepper

Preheat oven to 325°F.

Combine beef, lamb, oregano, thyme, onion, garlic, salt & pepper. Pack into 9x5-inch loaf pan. Bake 1 hour & 15 minutes. Cool. Slice meat ¼-⅜-inch thick.

Combine sauce ingredients. Chill. Serve meat in split pita pockets with tomatoes, onions & yogurt sauce.

8-10 servings

MENU

Breakfast Fruit Kebobs

Eggs Florentine

English Muffins with Mushrooms & Canadian Bacon

Mustard Ring

Cherry Tomato Halves

Blueberry Coffee Cake

Glazed Chocolate Chip Cheesecake

Mint Juleps

FRUIT

Breakfast Fruit Kebobs

•

4 cups mixed fruits: seedless grapes, papaya, melon, pineapple, guava, strawberries, mango, etc.
1 lime, thinly sliced
½ cup vanilla yogurt
1 teaspoon honey
¼ teaspoon freshly grated nutmeg
2 teaspoons lime juice
watercress sprigs

Toss fruit in bowl with lime slices. Thread on 6-inch skewers. Arrange on platter. Combine yogurt, honey, nutmeg & lime juice. Drizzle over kebobs. Garnish with lime slices & watercress sprigs.

4-6 servings

ENTREE

Eggs Florentine

•

9 eggs
½ cup butter, softened
1 pound cottage cheese
½ pound Swiss cheese, grated
½ pound feta cheese, crumbled
4 cups chopped, cooked spinach
½ teaspoon grated nutmeg

Preheat oven to 350°F. Butter a 13x9-inch casserole.

Beat eggs slightly. Add butter & cheeses. Mix well. Add spinach & nutmeg. Pour into prepared casserole. Bake 1 hour until knife inserted in center comes out clean.

8 servings

ENTREE

English Muffins with Mushrooms & Canadian Bacon

•

6 tablespoons butter, divided
1 pound Canadian bacon, sliced ¼-inch thick
½ pound mushrooms, sliced
2 medium potatoes, peeled & sliced very thin
2 cups light cream
½ teaspoon summer savory
ground pepper
Toasted, buttered English muffins

In a large pan, sauté bacon in 2 tablespoons butter over medium heat, 2-3 minutes. Remove to platter. To same pan, add 2 tablespoons butter. Sauté mushrooms a few minutes. Remove to platter. Sauté potatoes in remaining butter, about 5 minutes. Return bacon & mushrooms to pan. Add cream, savory & several grinds of pepper. Simmer, covered, 10 minutes until potatoes are tender. Remove cover. Simmer several minutes to reduce sauce slightly. Serve over muffins.

4 servings

Mustard Ring

•

4 eggs
¾ cup sugar
1½ envelopes unflavored gelatin
1½ tablespoons dry mustard
½ teaspoon turmeric
¼ teaspoon salt
1 cup water
½ cup flavored white vinegar, tarragon, champagne, dill, etc.
1 cup heavy cream

Beat eggs in top of double boiler over medium-low heat. Mix sugar & gelatin. Add to eggs. Add mustard, turmeric, salt, water & vinegar. Cook until thick. Cool. Stir in unwhipped cream. Pour into 4 cup ring mold. Chill. To serve fill center with fruit, steamed vegetables or cherry tomatoes.

8-10 servings

Pictured page 62.

Blueberry Coffee Cake

•

½ cup butter, softened
1 cup sugar
2 eggs
2 cups flour, sifted
2 teaspoons baking powder
½ teaspoon baking soda
½ teaspoon salt
½ cup buttermilk
½ teaspoon vanilla
1 cup fresh blueberries
1 tablespoon sugar
1 teaspoon cinnamon

Preheat oven to 375°F. Butter 9x5-inch loaf pan.

Cream butter & sugar. Add eggs. Mix well. Add flour, baking powder, baking soda & salt alternately with the buttermilk. Add vanilla. Beat until smooth. Fold in blueberries. Combine sugar & cinnamon. Sprinkle on top of batter. Bake 55 minutes. Let rest 10 minutes. Remove from pan. Cool. Slice & serve with butter if desired.

1 9x5-inch loaf

Glazed Chocolate Chip Cheesecake

•

1¼ cups chocolate wafer cookie crumbs
⅓ cup butter, melted
3 packages (8-ounces each) cream cheese, softened
¾ cup sugar
3 eggs
1 teaspoon vanilla
1 cup semi-sweet chocolate chips, coarsely chopped in blender or processor

Glaze:
½ cup unsweetened cocoa powder
½ cup sugar
½ cup heavy cream
¼ cup unsalted butter, cut into pieces

chocolate leaves or other garnish

Preheat oven to 450°F.

Mix crumbs & butter. Press into bottom of 8 or 9-inch springform pan. Set aside.

Beat cream cheese & sugar at medium speed until blended. Add eggs one at a time, mixing well after each addition. Add chocolate chips & vanilla. Pour into prepared pan. Bake 10 minutes. Reduce heat to 250°F. Continue baking 35 minutes. Loosen cake from edges of pan. Cool before removing sides. Chill.

Combine glaze ingredients in top of double boiler over simmering water. Stir until smooth & shiny, 5 minutes. Cool 5 minutes, stirring occasionally. Pour over cake, tilting to cover evenly. Use spatula to spread over top and sides. Refrigerate several hours. Decorate with chocolate leaves.

10-12 servings

What a great Saturday in May to celebrate with a Derby Party Brunch. Start with Mimosas & end on the eloquent note of a traditional Mint Julep. Spring bouquets of flowers & bright napkins coordinated with jockey-colors set the tempo. Fashion the Mustard Ring into a horse-shoe shape. The do-ahead menu combined with buffet service makes entertaining a breeze.

MENU

Spiced Cranberry Apple Glögg

Crispy Green Salad

Picante Crab Fondue

Sausage Fondue

Crusty French or Italian Bread

Fruit & Cheese Platter

Designed to warm up guests post-ice skating or cross-country skiing. Dust off the fondue pot & gather 'round the fireplace for an informal, one-table, help-yourself, food fest. Don't forget the long-handled forks to spear bread cubes.

Spiced Cranberry Apple Glögg

- 2 quarts cranberry apple juice
- 6-7 cups Burgundy wine
- 1½ cups water
- ½ cup sugar
- 2 cinnamon sticks
- 8 whole cloves
- raisins, almonds, & orange slices, garnish

Combine ingredients in large dutch oven. Heat gently 1 hour. Do not boil. Keeps on low heat several hours. Garnish each mug before serving.

25-30 servings

Picante Crab Fondue

- ⅓ pound sharp cheddar cheese, grated
- 1 package (8 ounces) cream cheese
- 1 cup cooked king crab
- ¼ cup light cream
- ½ teaspoon white wine Worcestershire sauce
- 1 small clove garlic, finely chopped
- ⅛ teaspoon cayenne pepper or crushed red pepper
- French bread

In double boiler, over medium-low heat, combine cheeses. Stir constantly until blended & smooth. Add remaining ingredients. Stir occasionally. Serve hot from fondue pot. If fondue thickens, add a little cream. Serve with French bread cubes.

6 servings

Pictured page 118.

Sausage Fondue

- ½ pound bulk Italian sausage
- 1 small onion, chopped
- 1 clove garlic, minced
- 1 can (8 ounces) tomato sauce
- 2 tablespoons cornstarch
- ¼ cup water
- ¼ teaspoon salt
- ⅛ teaspoon pepper
- 1¾ teaspoons oregano, crushed
- ¾ pound sharp cheddar cheese, grated
- ½ pound mozzarella cheese, grated
- Italian bread

Brown sausage, onion & garlic. Drain fat. Mix cornstarch & water. Add to meat with tomato sauce, oregano, salt & pepper. Stir. As mixture thickens, add cheese, ½ cup at a time, stirring after each addition. Serve from a fondue pot with cubes of Italian bread.

6 servings

MENU

Bountiful Antipasto Platter

Serbian Cheese & Pepper Canapés

Seafood Manicotti

Double Pizza Puff

Poached Peaches in Wine

Italian Red Valpolicella

•

A simple robust menu for any season. Dress the occasion up or down to fit your mood. Adjust the seafood in the Manicotti & filling for the Puff to fit your budget. The Puff can be an appetizer, side dish or main course, depending how you slice it.

Serbian Cheese & Pepper Canapés

•

1 cup butter, softened
4-ounces feta cheese, crumbled
1½-ounces cream cheese, softened
2 large green peppers
1 large red pepper
2 tablespoons vinegar & oil dressing
2 cloves garlic, minced
1 teaspoon salt
½ teaspoon sugar
⅛ teaspoon crushed red pepper
thinly sliced firm bread, cut into canapés

Beat butter & cheeses until light & fluffy. Cover & refrigerate up to 1 week.

Place whole peppers on oven rack closest to broiler. Broil 10-15 minutes, turning every 3-4 minutes. Blisters will appear on outer skin. Plunge peppers into cold water. Remove outer skins, seeds & stems. Chop peppers finely. Mix dressing, garlic, salt, sugar & crushed red pepper. Add peppers. Cover & refrigerate at least 1 hour, no longer than 24 hours.

To serve, bring cheese to room temperature. Spread cheese on bread canapés, crusty French bread or rye crackers. Top with pepper mixture.

12-15 servings

Seafood Manicotti

•

1 tablespoon olive oil
1 pound mixed seafood, shellfish & fish fillets

Sauce:
2 cloves garlic
1 can (15 ounces) tomato sauce
1 can (6 ounces) tomato paste
1¼ cups water
2 teaspoons basil
1 teaspoon oregano
1 tablespoon chopped parsley
salt & pepper

½ pound mozzarella cheese, grated
½ cup cottage cheese
4 tablespoons grated Parmesan cheese
2 eggs, slightly beaten
2 tablespoons butter, softened
½ teaspoon salt
½ teaspoon pepper
14 manicotti noodles, uncooked
extra grated Parmesan cheese

Lightly sauté a selection of seafood in olive oil. Remove from pan. Set aside.

Add garlic, tomato sauce, tomato paste, water, basil, oregano, parsley, salt & pepper to pan. Simmer 20-30 minutes. Set aside.

Combine cheeses, eggs, butter, salt & pepper. Add sautéed seafood. Stuff noodles with mixture. Arrange in bottom of buttered 13x9-inch pan. Cover with sauce. Sprinkle with additional Parmesan cheese. Cover tightly with foil. Bake at 350°F. 45 minutes.

May be assembled in advance & frozen. Bake, if frozen, 10 minutes longer.

6 servings

ENTREE

Double Pizza Puff

•

½ pound puff pastry sheets
1 can (11 ounces) pizza sauce
sliced ham or prosciutto
mushrooms
olives
capers
pepperoni
onions, etc.
grated provolone cheese
grated mozzarella cheese
1 egg, beaten

Roll out each pastry sheet to twice its length & width. Spread one-third of the sauce on the lower half of the pastry within ½ inch of the edge.

Be creative, cover sauce with layers of your favorite pizza ingredients. Brush edges of pastry with egg. Fold top over ingredients. Seal. Use fork to pierce holes in top. Bake 425°F. 15-20 minutes until golden brown. Cool 5 minutes. Cut into desired serving portions. Smaller pieces for hors d'oeuvres, larger wedges for entrée servings or side dishes.

6 servings per puff

MENU

Assorted Pickled Peppers, Olives & Relishes

Cocktail Pita Bread with Feta-Cream Cheese

Borscht

Irish Soda Bread

Apple Brownies

French Côtes-du-Rhône Châteauneuf-du-Pape

•

Winter picnics are terrific after a few miles have slid under your skis. Port the Borscht in a 1-gallon thermos. Serve in hot cups. Wrap the warm Soda Bread in newspapers & foil.

Borscht

•

3 pounds chuck steak, cut in large pieces
water
1½ cups cocktail vegetable juice
2 bay leaves
¼ teaspoon basil
1 large clove garlic, crushed
1 tablespoon salt
6 peppercorns
6 cups water
4 carrots, chopped
4 stalks celery, chopped
1 medium onion, chopped
1 large leek, chopped
1 small green pepper, chopped
1 can (16 ounces) stewed tomatoes
½ cup lemon juice
2 tablespoons sugar
1 small cabbage, shredded
2 large potatoes, peeled & chopped
2 pounds cooked, chopped beets, reserve liquid
½ cup minced fresh parsley
3 tablespoons minced fresh dill
1 pint sour cream

Put meat in a large kettle. Cover with water. Bring to a boil. Skim surface. Add vegetable juice, basil, bay leaves, garlic, salt, peppercorns & remaining water. Bring to boil. Add carrots, celery, onion & leek. Cover. Simmer 1¼ hours. Add green pepper, tomatoes, lemon juice & sugar. Cook 30 minutes. Add cabbage & potatoes. Cook 25 minutes. Add beets & juice, parsley & dill. Simmer 20 minutes. Serve hot with a dollop of sour cream.

12-15 servings

Irish Soda Bread

•

4 cups flour
¾ cup sugar
1 tablespoon baking powder
1 teaspoon salt
1 teaspoon baking soda
⅛ teaspoon cream of tartar
½ cup butter, melted
1 cup raisins
1 teaspoon caraway seed
1½ cups buttermilk
2 eggs

Preheat oven to 325°F. Butter a 9-inch round pan or casserole.

Sift flour, sugar, baking powder, salt, baking soda & cream of tartar into a large bowl. Add butter. Blend until mixture crumbles. Add raisins & caraway seeds. Mix buttermilk & eggs. Combine with dry ingredients. Mix well. Form into a round loaf. Place in prepared pan. Bake 1 hour & 15 minutes. Remove from pan. Cool on wire rack.

1 loaf

Apple Brownies

•

1 cup butter
½ teaspoon salt
2 cups sugar
2 eggs, beaten
2 cups flour
1 teaspoon baking powder
1 teaspoon baking soda
1 teaspoon cinnamon
2 cups peeled, sliced tart apples
½ cup chopped walnuts
ice cream

Preheat oven to 325°F. Butter a 9x9-inch pan.

Cream butter, salt, sugar & eggs. Add flour, baking powder, baking soda & cinnamon. Mix in apples & nuts. Spread in pan. Bake 45 minutes. Serve warm, à la mode.

12 servings

MENU

Salade St. Simeon

Shrimp & Wild Rice en Cocotte

Garden Green-Vegetable Gratin

Cornbread Hearts

Hungarian Nut Torte

California Sauvignon Blanc or French White Bordeaux Graves

•

Entertaining in style, from salad to torte. Polish your finery & set the table with elegance, for an intimate dinner, hosting the boss, or a gathering of favorite friends. Write the menu with guests' names on stiff white stock to use as place cards.

SALAD

Salade St. Simeon

•

2 small heads bibb lettuce, torn into bite-size pieces
1 head radicchio, torn into bite-size pieces
1 bunch watercress, stems removed

Dressing:
4 tablespoons extra-virgin olive oil
4 tablespoons balsamic vinegar
salt & pepper

8-12 slices (1/4-inch thick) French bread, toasted
8-12 slices goat cheese (chèvre)

Combine greens in bowl. Chill. Mix dressing ingredients. Just before serving, melt goat cheese on top of toasted bread under broiler. Toss greens with dressing. Serve on individual salad plates topped with toasts.

4-6 servings

Pictured page 57.

ENTREE

Shrimp & Wild Rice en Cocotte

•

1 cup wild rice
5 1/4 cups chicken stock, divided
1/4 cup butter
1 onion, chopped
1 pound mushrooms, sliced
1 clove garlic, minced
2 tablespoons flour
1/2 cup dry white wine
1/2 teaspoon salt
fresh ground pepper
1 teaspoon tarragon, crushed
1 1/2 pounds cooked, shelled shrimp

Place rice & 4 cups stock in pan. Bring to boil. Simmer, covered, 45-50 minutes. Uncover. Fluff with fork. Simmer 5 minutes. Pour off any excess stock.

Sauté onion, mushrooms & garlic in butter 5 minutes. Add flour. Stir over medium heat 3 minutes. Add remaining stock & wine gradually. Stir until slightly thickened. Add salt, pepper & tarragon. Combine rice, mushroom mixture & shrimp. Pour into 2-quart casserole. Bake, covered, 350°F. 20-30 minutes until heated through. Do not overbake.

6 servings

DESSERT

Hungarian Nut Torte

•

2/3 cup ground walnuts
1/3 cup ground almonds
1/3 cup toasted, ground hazelnuts
1/4 cup sugar
6 tablespoons unsalted butter, melted

Filling:
1 1/4 cups packed brown sugar
2 eggs
1 egg yolk
3/4 teaspoon baking powder
1 3/4 cups ground walnuts
1 cup flaked coconut
1/2 cup flour
3 tablespoons raspberry, hazelnut, or almond liqueur, divided
whipped cream, optional

Preheat oven to 350°F. Butter a 9-inch springform pan & dust with ground almonds.

In a bowl, combine walnuts, almonds, hazelnuts, sugar & butter. Press into prepared pan. Set aside.

In same bowl, beat brown sugar, eggs, the yolk, & baking powder. Stir in walnuts, coconut & flour. Add 1 tablespoon liqueur of your choice. Pour filling into crust. Bake torte 30-35 minutes until set & dark golden brown. Brush top of hot torte with remaining liqueur. Let cool in pan on rack. Garnish with whipped cream, if desired.

10-12 servings

Pictured page 116.

Bermuda Triangles

•

1 package (8 ounces) cream cheese, softened
2 teaspoons milk
½ teaspoon prepared horseradish
¼ teaspoon salt
¼ teaspoon pepper
1 cup cooked, flaked crab
1 cup small cooked shrimp
2 scallions, finely chopped
4 tablespoons ground almonds
1 package frozen phyllo pastry, thawed
½ cup butter, melted

Combine cream cheese, milk, horseradish, salt & pepper. Fold in crab, shrimp, scallions & almonds.

Keep phyllo sheets covered with damp towel as you work. Brush 1 sheet with melted butter. Top with another sheet. Brush with butter. Top with a third sheet. Divide into 6 strips & cut in half. Place 1 teaspoon filling at one end of each strip. Fold into triangles as for a flag. Repeat with remaining sheets & filling. Place triangles on baking sheet. Butter the tops. Bake at 400°F. 10-12 minutes until golden. May be frozen before baking. Store triangles in plastic bags until needed.

30 triangles

APPETIZER

Green Chili Gougère

•

¾ cup water
6 tablespoons butter
¾ cup flour, sifted
3 eggs
grated Parmesan cheese

Filling:
1 package (8 ounces) cream cheese, softened
2 tablespoons minced onion
1 can (4 ounces) chopped ripe olives
1 can (4 ounces) chopped green chilies

Preheat oven to 400°F.

In a saucepan heat water & butter to boiling. Add flour all at once. Cook, stirring until mixture forms a ball that leaves the sides of the pan. Remove from heat. Add eggs, one at a time, beating vigorously after each addition. Drop by teaspoonfuls onto baking sheet. Sprinkle each with Parmesan cheese. Bake 35-40 minutes until puffy & dry.

Beat cream cheese until light & fluffy. Stir in onion, olives & chilies. Just before serving, split puffs in half. Fill with 1 teaspoon filling. Puffs can be baked in advance & frozen in airtight bags.

3 dozen

APPETIZER

Lime Marinated Shrimp

•

¾ cup mayonnaise
2 tablespoons fresh lime juice
1 small onion, sliced very thinly
dash white wine Worcestershire sauce
1 pound cooked, peeled shrimp
snipped chives & minced parsley
lime slices

Combine mayonnaise, lime juice, onion, & Worcestershire. Gently stir in shrimp. Chill at least 24 hours. Serve garnished with chives, parsley & lime slices.

4-6 servings

Avocado Stuffed Tomatoes

•

- 1 pint red or yellow cherry tomatoes
- 1 large ripe avocado
- 2 scallions, minced including greens
- 1 tablespoon lemon juice
- ½ teaspoon ground cumin
- hot pepper sauce
- 4 slices crisp-cooked bacon, crumbled

Remove a thin slice from top of each tomato. Scoop out pulp. Drain, upside down on paper toweling 30 minutes. Mash avocado coarsely with fork. Stir in scallions, lemon juice, cumin, & hot pepper sauce. Add more or less lemon, cumin & hot pepper sauce to taste. Fill tomatoes with avocado mixture. Top with bacon pieces.

24 servings

Sesame Wafers

•

- 2 cups butter, softened
- 1½ cups sugar
- 3 cups flour
- 1 cup toasted sesame seed
- 2 cups shredded coconut
- ½ cup finely chopped almonds

In large bowl, cream butter & sugar until light & fluffy. Beat in flour. Stir in sesame seed, coconut & almonds until well mixed. Dough will be very stiff. Divide dough into thirds. Place on long sheet of wax paper. Shape into roll. Wrap & refrigerate until firm. Cut into ¼-inch slices. Place on baking sheets. Bake at 300°F. 30 minutes until slightly brown. Remove immediately.

14 dozen

Three-Step Dark Chocolate Truffles

•

- 1 package (6 ounces) semi-sweet chocolate chips
- ½ cup orange juice
- 3 tablespoons light rum
- 1 package (8½ ounces) chocolate wafer cookies, crushed
- 3 cups sifted powdered sugar, divided
- 1 cup finely chopped walnuts
- 1 container (4 ounces) chocolate jimmies
- 1-1½ tablespoons water
- unsweetened cocoa, optional

Melt chocolate chips in top of double boiler. Remove from heat. Add orange juice & rum. Stir. Add crushed chocolate wafers. Stir in 2 cups powdered sugar & nuts. Blend well. Cover. Chill 2 hours.

Roll pieces of dough into 1-inch balls. Roll ball in jimmies, pressing firmly as you roll. Place on baking sheet. Chill overnight. Blend remaining powdered sugar & 1-1½ tablespoons water to make glaze. Add cocoa to taste, if desired. Dip chilled chocolate balls halfway into glaze to coat top.

4 dozen

This menu is bound to be a hit With-or-Without-the-Pool for a summer cocktail buffet party. Start early to enjoy the sunset. Enjoy dreamy Latin music borrowed from the library.

❦

MENU

Beef Bacon-Wrapped Water Chestnuts

Hot & Spicy Shrimp Dip

Marinated Beef Cocktail Sandwiches

California Ham

Cornbread Muffins

Lima-Green Bean Bake

Romaine Salad with Brewers Dressing

Mocha Fudge Cake

Special Draft Beer & California Mountain Zinfandel

•

Hot & Spicy Shrimp Dip

•

2 packages (8 ounces each) cream cheese
¼ pound chopped, cooked shrimp
¼ cup chopped onion
1 tomato, peeled, seeded & chopped
3 pickled banana peppers, seeded & chopped
1-2 cloves garlic, finely chopped

Gently heat ingredients in top of double boiler. When hot, pour into chafing dish. Serve with tortilla chips or garlic melba rounds.

3½ cups

Marinated Beef Cocktail Sandwiches

•

Marinade:
1 cup soy sauce
½ cup dry sherry
⅓ cup olive oil
3 cloves garlic, minced
1 tablespoon grated, peeled fresh ginger root, or 2 teaspoons ground ginger

3-4 pounds beef top round or sirloin tip roast

Combine marinade ingredients. Place meat in heavy-duty plastic bag. Pour marinade into bag. Seal bag & place in bowl. Marinate beef, refrigerated, 48 hours. Turn bag several times each day. Remove from refrigerator 1 hour before roasting. Place beef in roasting pan. Bake 325°F. 1-2 hours to desired doneness. Baste with marinade 3-4 times while roasting. Cool. Refrigerate several hours. Slice or shave meat. Serve cold on cocktail buns.

40 servings

California Ham

•

1 whole or boneless ham, any size or variety

Marinade:
2 large oranges, quartered
2 cups dry white wine
6 dried hot chili peppers, crushed
20 peppercorns
1 cup chopped celery leaves
2 carrots, sliced
½ cup chopped parsley

Pierce ham all over with skewer. Place in heavy-duty plastic bag. Squeeze juice from oranges into the bag. Add the squeezed quarters & remaining marinade ingredients to the bag. Seal. Place in bowl. Refrigerate several days, turning occasionally. Score ham & place in roasting pan. Bake at 325°F. until heated through. Baste with marinade several times. Have guests slice their own to put in ham buns or in tiny cornbread muffins. Spicy & delicious. Number of servings varies according to ham size. Ask the butcher.

Pictured page 114.

Lima-Green Bean Bake

•

Sauce:
6 tablespoons butter
2 tablespoons flour
1 teaspoon salt
¼ teaspoon pepper
dash cayenne
¼ teaspoon Worcestershire sauce
1 cup light cream
½ cup grated Parmesan cheese

1½ cups french-cut green beans
1½ cups baby lima beans

Preheat oven to 300°F. Butter a 1½-quart casserole.

Melt butter in saucepan. Add flour, salt, pepper, cayenne, & Worcestershire. Cook 3 minutes. Add cream. When sauce thickens, add Parmesan. Stir until melted. Alternate layers of vegetables & sauce in casserole. Bake, uncovered, 1 hour. Best thing anyone did to a lima.

4-6 servings

Romaine Salad with Brewers Dressing

•

Dressing:
⅔ cup beer
⅔ cup vegetable oil
1 teaspoon paprika
¼ teaspoon salt
1 clove garlic, minced
1 tablespoon celery seed
1 tablespoon mustard seed
1 tablespoon stone-ground mustard
dash hot pepper sauce
2 tablespoons brown sugar
2 tablespoons Dijon-style mustard

romaine lettuce, grated cheddar cheese, sunflower seeds & finely shredded red onions

Combine dressing ingredients in a jar. Shake vigorously. Use dressing within 3 days. Serve with salad ingredients according to number of guests.

1¾ cups

Mocha Fudge Cake

•

½ cup strong coffee or espresso
8-ounces sweet chocolate
1 cup sugar
1 cup unsalted butter
4 eggs

¼ cup red currant jelly, melted

Frosting:
1 cup heavy cream
¼ cup powdered sugar
¼ teaspoon vanilla

Preheat oven to 350°F. Line a 1-quart soufflé dish or charlotte mold with well-buttered foil.

In a heavy saucepan heat coffee, chocolate, sugar & butter until chocolate melts. Beat in eggs, one at a time, incorporating well after each addition. Pour into prepared pan. Bake 30 minutes until top is crisp & center does not look set. Cool & refrigerate at least 24 hours. Before serving invert cake onto decorative plate. Remove foil. Brush with currant jelly. Refrigerate 15 minutes. Whip cream with powdered sugar & vanilla. Frost cake. Do not worry about leftovers.

8-10 servings

A New Year's All-Day Football Party couldn't be more delectable. Spread the table with this bountiful array of crowd pleasing offerings & root on your favorite teams.

❦

MENU

Broccoli Stuffed Game Hens

Wild Rice Pilaf

Tomato Onion Summer Salad

Parmesan Monkey Bread

Chocolate Fudge Cake & Strawberries

California Red Sonoma Pinot Noir

•

Game hens are the perfect entrée for buffets. Make extra wild rice for the stuffing when making the Pilaf. Seating can be a problem for large groups. Set up card tables anywhere there is space & cover with tablecloths, a single candle & a bud vase.

Broccoli Stuffed Game Hens

•

1 small bunch broccoli, trimmed into small flowerets
1 cup cooked wild rice
½ cup grated Swiss cheese
salt & pepper
4 game hens
2 tablespoons butter, melted

Preheat oven to 375°F.

Steam broccoli 5 minutes until crisp-tender. Drain & cool slightly. Combine broccoli & cheese. Salt & pepper inside of hens. Stuff with broccoli mixture. Brush hens with butter. Bake on a rack in baking pan 1¼-1½ hours. For a variation, chop giblets & add to broccoli with ½ teaspoon thyme.

4 servings

Wild Rice Pilaf

•

½ cup wild rice, cook according to package directions
1 cup long grain rice, cook according to package directions
1 bunch scallions, thinly sliced
½ pound mushrooms, sliced
2 tablespoons butter
¼ cup light soy sauce

Preheat oven to 350°F. Butter a 1½-quart casserole.

Sauté onions & mushrooms in butter 5-7 minutes. Add soy sauce & rices. Mix well. Place in casserole. Bake 20 minutes.

8 servings

Tomato & Onion Summer Salad

•

1 clove garlic
4 ripe tomatoes, thinly sliced
1 Bermuda onion, thinly sliced
1 tablespoon fresh oregano leaves
salt & pepper
4 tablespoons vegetable oil
1 tablespoon tarragon vinegar
freshly grated asiago cheese

Rub salad bowl with garlic clove. Mince the garlic & add to tomatoes, onions, oregano, salt & pepper. Toss with oil & vinegar. Chill 2 hours. Sprinkle with cheese before serving. For variation, add fresh salad pepper strips, sliced cucumbers, zucchini &/or summer squash & dress with balsamic vinegar & oil. Refreshing & crunchy.

4 servings

Ethnic Gatherings

heritage themes & American regional

MENU

Grapefruit Margaritas

"Gringo" Chile Relleno Casserole

Tex-Mex Fajitas

Seasoned Rice Salad

Texas Sesquicentennial Praline Pound Cake

Serve Fajitas in heated, little enamelware frying pans with bright bandana napkins tied on the handles.

"Gringo" Chile Relleno Casserole

1 pound cheddar cheese, grated
16-ounces chopped green chilies
1 pound Monterey Jack cheese, grated
3 cups light cream
4 eggs, beaten
¼ cup cornmeal
1 teaspoon salt
1 teaspoon Worcestershire sauce
1 cup red picante sauce cooked & thickened with 1 tablespoon cornstarch & 1 tablespoon water

Preheat oven to 350°F. Butter a 13x9-inch pan.

Layer cheddar cheese, green chilies, & Jack cheese, in order, into prepared pan. Blend cream, eggs, cornmeal, salt & Worcestershire sauce. Pour over layers of cheese & chilies. Top with picante sauce. Bake 40 minutes. Cut into squares. Ole!

10-12 Servings

Tex-Mex Fajitas

2 pounds flank or skirt steaks

Marinade:
½ cup olive oil
¼ cup red wine vinegar
⅓ cup fresh lime juice
⅓ cup chopped onion
1 teaspoon sugar
1 teaspoon Mexican oregano
salt & pepper
¼ teaspoon cumin
3 cloves garlic, minced

6 large flour tortillas

Toppings:
Onion slices
Green & red pepper strips
Chopped tomatoes
Shredded lettuce
Guacamole
Sour cream
Picante sauce

Tenderize the steak. Combine marinade ingredients. Add steaks, coat evenly. Cover & refrigerate overnight. When ready to serve, grill steak over hot coals, preferably mesquite, 4-5 minutes each side. Remove steaks. In a large skillet, grill fresh onion & pepper slices. Slice steaks into thin strips. Fill warm tortillas with steak, onions, peppers, tomatoes, lettuce, guacamole, sour cream, & picante sauce. Wrap tortilla around filling. Serve in skillets. May also be made with chicken breast. Mamacita—Que Bueno!

6 servings

Texas Sesquicentennial Praline Pound Cake

1 cup butter, softened
½ cup vegetable shortening
1 pound dark brown sugar
5 eggs
3 cups flour, divided
½ teaspoon baking powder
¼ teaspoon baking soda
¾ cup milk
2 cups chopped pecans
2 teaspoons pecan-flavored extract or vanilla

Preheat oven to 325°F. Butter & flour a 10-inch tube or bundt pan.

Cream butter & shortening. Gradually add sugar, beating until light & fluffy. Add eggs one at a time, beating after each addition. Sift 2½ cups flour, baking powder & soda. Add to creamed mixture alternately with milk. Dredge pecans in remaining ½ cup flour. Stir into batter. Add extract. Pour into prepared pan. Bake 1 hour & 15 minutes, until toothpick inserted in center comes out clean. It will be very dark brown. Cool in pan 15 minutes. Remove from pan. Cool. Delicious with ice cream. Cake freezes well.

16-24 servings

MENU

Linguini with Lemon Clam Sauce

Mozzarella Garlic Bread

Cauliflower Salad with Black Olives

Waffle Cookies

Espresso with Orange Peel

Italian White Frascati

•

Family or friends can enjoy the pleasures of the Italian table where food "satisfies the stomach and respects the mind." Savory but simple, rich but not too heavy, the spirit is light & casual. Use fresh fruit as the centerpiece to accompany the Waffle Cookies.

PASTA

Linguini with Lemon Clam Sauce

•

- ½ cup butter, divided
- 3 tablespoons olive oil
- 2 cloves garlic, minced
- 1 shallot, minced
- 2 cans (8 ounces each) minced clams, drained, reserve liquid
- 3 tablespoons fresh lemon juice
- 1 tablespoon chopped parsley
- 2 teaspoons grated lemon peel
- ¼ teaspoon ground pepper
- 1 bay leaf
- 1 pound linguini, cooked & drained
- grated Parmesan cheese

Heat 3 tablespoons of the butter & the oil in a heavy pan. Sauté garlic & shallot until tender. Add the liquid from clams, lemon juice, parsley, lemon peel, pepper & bay leaf. Simmer until liquid is reduced to 1 cup. Remove bay leaf. Stir in clams. Heat thoroughly. Add remaining butter. Stir. Serve sauce over linguini. Sprinkle with Parmesan.

4-6 servings

SALAD

Cauliflower Salad with Black Olives

•

- 1 head cauliflower, broken into large flowerets
- 6 tablespoons olive oil
- 3 tablespoons white wine vinegar
- 1 teaspoon dry mustard
- ½ teaspoon fresh ground pepper
- 1 tablespoon capers
- 1 tablespoon minced parsley
- 1 jar (2 ounces) chopped pimientos
- 3 scallions, sliced
- ½ teaspoon salt
- ½ cup sliced, pitted black olives

Drop cauliflowerets into boiling salted water. Cook 5 minutes. Drain & rinse under cold water. In the bottom of a round bowl, reassemble flowerets into a head, stems up. Combine oil, vinegar, mustard, pepper, capers, parsley, pimientos, scallions & salt. Pour over cauliflower. Cover & chill at least 2 hours or overnight. To serve, drain off marinade into a small bowl. Place serving dish on top of cauliflower & invert. Add olives to marinade. Spoon over cauliflower.

6 servings

DESSERT

Waffle Cookies

•

- 1½ cups butter, softened
- 1¾ cups sugar
- 5 eggs, separated
- 1 teaspoon vanilla, anise, lemon, orange, or other extract
- 2 teaspoons baking powder
- 5½ cups flour

waffle iron

Cream butter & sugar in large bowl until fluffy. Add egg yolks one at a time. Beat well. Add vanilla or extract. Combine flour & baking powder. Add flour to egg mixture. Beat egg whites until stiff. Fold into batter until smooth. Form into walnut-size balls. Bake in a waffle iron until brown.

2½ dozen

MENU

Rouladen of Beef

Spätzel

Rött Kraut

Rümtopf

Püher Schnitten

German Rheinhessen Spätlese

•

Nothing says "Milwaukee" better than German food. Embroidered tablecloth, hock wine glasses, pretty china, a loaf of rye bread & plenty of butter set the perfect tone. A stein of beer & soft, hot pretzels are faultless preludes to gemütlichkeit—an atmosphere of warmth & fellowship.

Rouladen of Beef

•

- 2 pounds thin round steak, pounded into 6-8 square pieces
- salt & pepper
- Dijon-style mustard
- 6-8 slices bacon
- 1 medium onion, chopped
- ½ pound carrots, chopped
- 6-8 dill pickle spears
- 2 tablespoons vegetable oil

Sprinkle meat with salt & pepper. Spread each piece with 1 tablespoon mustard. Lay 1 slice bacon across each piece of meat. Top with chopped onion, carrots & 1 spear pickle. Roll up & secure with toothpick. Sauté rolls in oil until brown. Add 1-inch water to pan. Simmer, covered, 1½ hours until tender. Thicken pan juices with cornstarch if desired.

6 servings

Pictured page 176.

Rött Kraut

•

- 1 3-pound head red cabbage, finely shredded
- 2 large cooking apples, peeled & chopped
- 1 large onion, chopped
- ¼ cup sugar
- ¼ cup vinegar
- 6 slices crisp-cooked bacon, crumbled
- 2 tablespoons bacon drippings
- 1 teaspoon salt
- ground pepper
- ½ cup boiling water

In a large saucepan, combine all ingredients. Add water. Bring mixture to a boil. Reduce heat. Let simmer 1 hour.

8 servings

Püher Schnitten

•

- ¼ pound butter, softened
- ½ cup sugar
- 6 eggs, separated
- ¾ cup flour
- 1 teaspoon baking powder
- grated peel of ½ lemon

Topping:

- 1¼ cups sugar
- 3½ cups ground, toasted hazelnuts (filberts)
- 1 teaspoon vanilla

Preheat oven to 350°F.

Beat butter & sugar until light & fluffy. Add egg yolks one at a time. Add lemon peel, flour & baking powder. Mix until smooth. Spread into 13x9-inch pan.

Beat the egg whites until soft peaks form. Gradually add sugar. Beat until stiff. Fold in hazelnuts & vanilla. Spread onto dough mixture. Bake 30 minutes. Cool. Cut into diamond shapes.

3 dozen

MENU

Herb Roasted Chicken

Ghivetch

Dilled Egg Noodles

Patica

Moravian Sugar Cake

Homemade Plum Sauce

Yugoslavian Red Prokupac

•

From Czechoslovakia to the Adriatic coast, Eastern Europe is well represented in Milwaukee. Church festivals are celebrated with customary gusto & with foods like these. Serve tiny glasses of clear plum brandy to whet the appetite!

Ghivetch

•

1 cup thinly sliced carrots
1 cup sliced green beans
1 cup diced potatoes
½ cup diced celery
2 medium tomatoes, cut into wedges
1 small yellow squash, sliced
1 small zucchini, sliced
1 small Bermuda onion, chopped
½ head cauliflower, broken into flowerets
¼ cup green pepper strips
¼ cup red pepper strips
½ cup green peas

Sauce:
1 cup beef stock
⅓ cup olive oil
3 cloves garlic, minced
½ bay leaf, crumbled
½ teaspoon tarragon
2 teaspoons salt
1 teaspoon ground pepper

Preheat oven to 350°F. Combine vegetables in 13x9-inch pan.

In a saucepan, boil sauce ingredients. Pour over vegetables. Cover with aluminum foil. Bake 1 hour.

8-10 servings

Pictured page 2.

Patica

•

4 cups flour
1 teaspoon salt
½ pound pure lard, room temperature
1 cup warm milk
2 tablespoons sugar
1 package yeast
2 eggs, beaten

Filling:
3 pounds chopped pecans or walnuts
1 heaping cup crushed vanilla wafers
1 tablespoon cinnamon
2 cups butter, melted
8-ounces honey
1 cup packed brown sugar
9 eggs, beaten

In a large bowl, mix flour & salt. Cut in lard until uniformly crumbly. In a small bowl, combine milk, sugar & yeast. Add eggs. Mix flour & milk mixtures together to form dough. Cover tightly & chill overnight.

Preheat oven to 350°F. Butter 2 10-inch tube pans.

Combine pecans, wafer crumbs & cinnamon. Mix melted butter, honey & brown sugar. Add to pecan mixture. Add eggs. Mix well.

Remove dough from refrigerator. On a very large surface, roll dough ¼-inch thick, 4 feet wide. On one long side, spread filling mixture evenly up to the edges of dough. Working left to right, gently pull dough around filling with hands & begin rolling it up into a 3-inch diameter x 4-foot long roll. Divide into two sections. Place in prepared pans, patting edges of dough together where they meet. Cover & let rise in warm place 1 hour. Bake 1 hour. Let cool in pans. When completely cooled, remove from pans. Slice very thin to serve. Double wrap to freeze for up to 6 months.

25-30 servings per pan

Moravian Sugar Cake

•

2 packages quick-rise yeast
1 cup warm water
1 cup sugar
½ teaspoon salt
2 eggs, beaten
1½ cups butter, melted
1 cup hot mashed potatoes
5-6 cups sifted flour
1½ cups packed light brown sugar
1 tablespoon cinnamon

Butter 3 9-inch square or round cake pans.

Combine yeast & water. Let stand a few minutes. Mix together sugar, salt, eggs & 1 cup of the butter. Gradually beat in mashed potatoes. Add 1 cup of flour. Beat until smooth. Stir in yeast. Beat in enough remaining flour to form a light, soft dough. Cover & let rise until doubled, about 1½ hours.

Divide dough into 3 portions. Press evenly into prepared pans. Cover & let rise until doubled.

Preheat oven to 350°F.

Blend together brown sugar & cinnamon. Make indentations 1-inch apart on each cake. Sprinkle sugar mixture into each depression. Drizzle remaining ½ cup butter over top of cakes. Bake 20 minutes. Cakes freeze very well. Serve with plum sauce, or another fruit sauce if desired.

6-8 servings each cake

MENU

Hungarian Steak with Caper-Sour Cream Sauce

Potato Dumplings with Caraway Seed

Herbed Kohlrabi

Pickled Baby Beets

Traudl's Plum Küchen

Viennese Coffee

Hungarian Red
Egri Bikavér
"Bull's Blood"

•

The fare of this menu suggests a hearty family gathering on a Sunday night to celebrate a homecoming or a birthday. Italian plums come into season late summer. Plan ahead & have the Küchen in the freezer. The wine is ancient in Hungarian history & has symbolic masculine overtones. Offer a schnapps (brandy) as an apéritif.

Hungarian Steak with Caper-Sour Cream Sauce

•

2 pounds beef round steak, ¾-inch thick
salt & pepper
2 tablespoons vegetable oil
3 medium carrots, bias-cut 2-inches thick
2 medium parsnips, cut into strips
½ cup sliced celery
1 cup boiling water
1 cup beef stock
½ teaspoon salt
dash pepper
3 tablespoons flour
1 cup sour cream
2 tablespoons capers, drained
paprika

Preheat oven to 350°F.

Cut steak into serving-size pieces. Season with salt & pepper. Heat oil in a skillet. Brown meat. Remove to shallow casserole or Dutch oven. Top with carrots, parsnips, & celery. Combine water, stock, salt & pepper. Pour mixture over steak & vegetables. Bake, covered, 1-1¼ hours. Remove meat & vegetables to platter. Keep warm. To the pan juices, add water if necessary to make 1 cup liquid. Combine flour & sour cream. Stir into pan juices. Add capers. Cook 2 minutes & stir until bubbly. Serve on top of steak & vegetables. Sprinkle with paprika.

6 servings

Herbed Kohlrabi

•

2 tablespoons butter
1½ pounds kohlrabi, cut into julienne strips
⅔ cup chicken stock
1½ tablespoons sugar
½ teaspoon salt
¼ teaspoon pepper
1 tablespoon chopped parsley
1 teaspoon dried chervil

In a skillet, heat butter. Add kohlrabi, stock, sugar, salt & pepper. Bring mixture to boil. Reduce heat & simmer, covered, until tender but still crisp, 7 minutes. Increase heat to high. Cook, uncovered, stirring constantly until liquid evaporates & vegetable is glazed, 5 minutes. Add herbs. Serve at once. Carrots, turnips, or other root vegetables may be used.

4 servings

Traudl's Plum Küchen

•

20 Italian purple plums, pitted & quartered

Pastry:
2 cups flour
1 cup sugar
¾ cup unsalted butter, softened
1 egg
1 teaspoon vanilla
2 tablespoons milk

Custard:
2 egg yolks, beaten
1 tablespoon milk
4 tablespoons sugar

Streusel:
1¼ cups flour
¾ cup sugar
½ cup unsalted butter, softened
1 teaspoon grated lemon peel

powdered sugar
whipped cream, optional

Preheat oven to 400°F. Butter & flour 2 8-inch cake or springform pans.

Combine flour & sugar. Cut butter into flour mixture. Add egg, vanilla & milk. Add extra flour if necessary to make dough very smooth. Divide dough in half. Pat onto bottom & 1½-inches up sides of each pan. Place plums in pans.

Combine custard ingredients. Mix well. Pour onto plums. Combine streusel ingredients until crumbly. Top custard with streusel. Bake 10 minutes. Reduce heat to 375°F. Bake 35-40 minutes until golden brown. Cool on rack. Remove from cake pan. Dust with powdered sugar. Serve on cake plate with whipped cream if desired. Fresh peaches, cherries or blueberries may be substituted for plums.

10-12 servings

MENU

Miniature Spring Rolls

Japanese Beer

Cress-Kiwi Salad with Pineapple Dressing

Batayaki

Steamed Rice

Stir-Fried Oriental Vegetables

Mandarin Orange Cake

French Red Côtes-du-Rhône

•

Sharpen your chopsticks. Set the table with simple elegance for this dinner with an oriental flavor. Three flowers representing earth, man & sky with airy greens for the centerpiece. Plain white dinnerware & pastel linens will lighten the table.

SALAD

Cress-Kiwi Salad with Pineapple Dressing

•

2 large heads Boston lettuce, torn into bite size pieces, reserve large outer leaves
2 bunches watercress, stems trimmed
1 large avocado, cut into 1-inch cubes
2 tablespoons lemon juice
2 cups diagonally sliced celery
4 kiwi fruit, sliced
¼ cup toasted sesame seed

Pineapple Dressing:
¾ cup vegetable oil
¼ cup unsweetened pineapple juice
1 teaspoon grated lemon peel
2 tablespoons lemon juice
1 tablespoon chopped fresh mint
¾ teaspoon salt
½ teaspoon dry mustard
fresh ground pepper

Line a platter with the large outer leaves of lettuce. Add torn lettuce and cress. Toss avocado cubes with lemon juice. Arrange avocado, celery & kiwi on top of greens. Sprinkle with sesame seed. Cover & chill until serving.

Combine dressing ingredients. Chill. Before serving. Gently toss salad with dressing.

12 servings

ENTREE

Batayaki

•

½ cup butter
4 medium onions, thinly sliced
1 pound mushrooms, thinly sliced
2-2½ pounds top sirloin, trimmed & thinly sliced

Dipping Sauce:
juice of 1 lemon
½ cup soy sauce, or amount equal to lemon juice

Melt butter in wok or deep skillet over medium-high heat. Add onions. Cook 10-15 minutes. Add mushrooms. Sauté briefly. Add meat. Cook 1-2 minutes, until meat is lightly browned. Place on serving platter.

Combine lemon juice & soy for dipping sauce. Serve with rice & dipping sauce in small individual bowls.

5-6 servings

DESSERT

Mandarin Orange Cake

•

2 cups flour
2 cups sugar
2 teaspoons baking soda
½ teaspoon salt
2 eggs, beaten
2 cans (11 ounces each) mandarin oranges, drained
1 cup packed brown sugar
4 tablespoons milk
3 tablespoons butter

Preheat oven to 350°F. Butter & flour 2 8-inch cake pans or 1 13x9-inch pan.

Sift flour, sugar, baking soda, & salt. Add to beaten eggs. Add oranges. Beat with mixer four minutes. Pour batter into prepared pans. Bake 40 minutes. Mix brown sugar, milk & butter in small saucepan. Bring to a boil. Pour over hot cake right from the oven. Delicious served with whipped cream.

12-15 servings

MENU

Door County Fish Boil

Coleslaw

Rye Bread & Sweet Butter

Door County Cherry Crisp

Lemon Tea Bread

French White Entre-Deux-Mers

•

The fish boil & Door County are Wisconsin's answer to Cape Cod & the clam bake. Working outdoors, usually behind a restaurant, the chef, a multi-talented person, plays accordion or fiddle when the fish basket goes into a pot over a roaring fire. Dramatically, the music stops, signaling the grand finale. Fuel is thrown onto the fire, allowing the water to boil over, removing the fish oils. The basket is lifted out of the water & whisked into the restaurant where the food is served buffet-style.

ENTREE

Door County Fish Boil

•

18 small new potatoes, scrubbed, unpeeled
18 small onions, peeled
12 whitefish steaks, 1-inch thick
cheesecloth
6-8 quarts water
1 cup salt
melted butter
lemon wedges
parsley

Large kettle with a lift-out basket

Tie potatoes & onions into a cheesecloth bag. Tie fish in another cheesecloth bag. Fill kettle with water. Bring to rolling boil. Add ½ cup salt. Place potatoes-onions in basket. Place basket in kettle. Cook 10 minutes. Add remaining salt. Add fish to basket.

Cook 10 minutes. Skim surface. Lift basket from water. Drain well. Remove cheesecloth. Serve with butter & lemon. Sprinkle with parsley.

6 servings

DESSERT

Door County Cherry Crisp

•

3 tablespoons cornstarch
½ cup sugar
2½ cups pitted Door County tart cherries, including juice
1 cup brown sugar
1 cup flour
½ cup butter, melted
ice cream or sweetened whipped cream

Preheat oven to 350°F. Lightly butter an 8-inch square pan.

In a medium saucepan combine cornstarch, sugar & cherries. Simmer 7-10 minutes until thickened. Pour into prepared pan. Mix brown sugar, flour & butter until uniformly crumbly. Sprinkle evenly over cherries. Bake 25 minutes. Serve warm topped with ice cream or whipped cream.

6 servings

DESSERT

Lemon Tea Bread

•

1 cup butter, softened
1 cup sugar
5 large eggs
2 teaspoons grated lemon peel
2 cups flour
½ teaspoon baking powder
½ cup dried currants
2 tablespoons sugar

Preheat oven to 350°F. Butter & flour a 9x5-inch loaf pan.

In a bowl, cream butter & sugar until light & fluffy. Beat in eggs one at a time. Add lemon peel. Beat until smooth. Sift together flour & baking powder. Gradually add to butter mixture. Stir in currants. Pour batter into prepared pan. Bake 30 minutes. Sprinkle sugar evenly over top of loaf. Continue baking 30 minutes. Remove from oven. Cool on rack 5 minutes.

Remove from pan. Cool. Serve thinly sliced.

1 loaf

MENU

Sauerbraten

Noodle Kugel

Braised Belgian Carrots

Sautéed Cabbage Wedges

Cranberry Ice

German Mosel Auslese

•

The influence of immigrant German families on Milwaukee & Wisconsin is apparent on our tables. Distinctly winter fare, the menu is lightened with vegetables to satisfy today's lighter palate. The elegant Auslese lends sophistication for everyone's enjoyment.

Sauerbraten

•

Marinade:
- 2 cups vinegar
- 2 cups water
- ½ cup chopped onion
- 4 bay leaves
- 2 tablespoons paprika
- 4 cloves

3-5 pounds beef top or bottom round

- 1 cup flour, divided
- 4 tablespoons butter
- ½ cup sliced carrots
- ½ cup sliced onions
- ½ cup sliced celery
- 1 teaspoon thyme
- reserved marinade
- 1 cup water
- ½ cup Mosel wine
- ⅓ cup finely crushed ginger snaps
- ¼ cup brown sugar
- 1 teaspoon salt
- ground pepper

In a saucepan, heat marinade ingredients just to the boil. Place meat in non-metal dish. Pour on hot marinade. Marinate several days, turning meat once a day.

Remove meat. Pat dry with paper toweling. Strain marinade into bowl. Set aside.

Dredge beef in ½ cup flour. In a large pot, melt butter & brown meat on all sides. Add carrots, onions & celery. Cook 5 minutes, stirring vegetables. Add thyme & reserved marinade. Cover. Bake at 325°F. 3 hours.

Remove meat to platter. Keep warm. Strain cooking liquid into saucepan. Combine remaining flour with water. Stir into pan with wine & gingersnaps. Bring to boil. Add brown sugar, salt & pepper. Stir, until thickened & smooth. Slice meat accompanied with the sauce.

6-8 servings

Noodle Kugel

•

- ½ cup butter, melted
- 3 eggs, beaten
- 1 cup sour cream
- 1 cup cottage cheese
- 1 can (8 ounces) crushed pineapple
- 8-ounces medium-wide egg noodles, parboiled 3 minutes, drained

Topping:
- 2 tablespoons butter, melted
- 2 tablespoons brown sugar
- dash cinnamon
- 4 tablespoons cornflake crumbs

Preheat oven to 350°F. Butter a 9-inch square pan.

Combine butter, eggs, sour cream, cottage cheese & pineapple. Add noodles. Pour into prepared pan.

Combine topping ingredients. Spread on top of noodle mixture. Bake 1 hour. Let rest 5 minutes. Cut into squares. May be assembled one day in advance. Bake just before serving. Or, use an 8-cup ring mold with topping added before the noodles. After baking, invert onto platter. Fill center with vegetables if desired.

6-8 servings

Cranberry Ice

•

- 1 quart cranberries
- 2 cups water
- 3 cups sugar
- 2 tablespoons lemon juice
- 2 cups milk

Place cranberries in saucepan with water. Simmer 20 minutes. Cool a few minutes. In small batches, add to processor or blender. Purée. Pour into a sieve over a bowl. Strain & discard skins.

Add sugar to cranberry juice. Stir until dissolved. Add lemon juice & milk. Stir. Pour into a shallow glass or metal pan. Cover. Freeze until firm. Remove from freezer 30 minutes before serving. Scoop into parfait glasses.

10-12 servings

MENU

South of the Border Strata

Lilian's Picadillo Cubano

Rice

Frijoles Molidos Costa Rican Black Beans

Warm Flour Tortillas

Simple Green Salad

Fresh Papaya & Mango with Strawberry Sauce

Mexican Beer with Lime Wedges

•

Mix & match your most colorful dinnerware & napkins to create a casual ambiance for a festive South of the Border menu. Strata is great hot or room temperature.

South of the Border Strata

•

- 4 cups crushed nacho-flavored tortilla chips
- 2 cups grated Monterey Jack cheese
- 6 eggs beaten
- 2½ cups milk
- 1 can (4 ounces) chopped green chilies
- ¼ cup finely chopped onion
- 3 tablespoons chili salsa
- ½ teaspoon salt
- ¼ teaspoon hot pepper sauce
- cherry tomato halves, garnish

Butter a 1½-quart shallow baking dish.

Sprinkle tortilla chips & cheese evenly over bottom of baking dish. In a medium-size bowl, combine eggs, milk, green chilies, onion, salsa, salt & hot pepper sauce. Beat well. Pour over cheese mixture. Cover & refrigerate several hours or overnight. Bake, uncovered, in a preheated 325°F. oven 50-55 minutes, until set & lightly browned. Let rest 10 minutes. Cut into squares. Top each square with cherry tomato half if desired.

6 servings

Lilian's Picadillo Cubano

•

- 3 tablespoons olive oil
- 1 large onion, chopped
- 2 cloves garlic, chopped
- 1½ pounds ground chuck or round
- 1 large green pepper, chopped
- ½ teaspoon basil
- ½ teaspoon oregano
- ½ teaspoon paprika
- ¾ teaspoon cayenne
- 1 can (8 ounces) tomato sauce
- 1 pound tomatoes, peeled, seeded, & chopped
- ½ cup raisins
- ½ cup sliced pimiento-stuffed olives
- salt & pepper

Heat olive oil in large skillet. Sauté onion & garlic 5 minutes. Add meat & brown 7 minutes. Add green pepper & spices. Simmer 15 minutes. Add tomato sauce, tomatoes, raisins & olives. Cook over low heat 1-1½ hours, until mixture is nearly dry. Serve in flour tortillas.

6 servings

Frijoles Molidos Costa Rican Black Beans

•

- 1 pound black beans, washed & soaked overnight in 2 quarts water
- 2 tablespoons butter
- 1 large onion, finely chopped
- 1 large green pepper, finely chopped
- 2 cloves garlic, minced
- 2 quarts water
- 1½ tablespoons salt
- 6 slices bacon
- 1 can (4 ounces) chopped green chilies
- ½ teaspoon paprika
- fresh ground pepper
- grated farmers cheese or any fresh cheese

Drain beans. In a 4-quart pan, sauté onion, green pepper, & garlic in butter. Add beans, water, & salt. Simmer 2½-3 hours until beans are soft. Mash or purée beans. In a large pan, cook bacon until crisp. Remove from pan. Crumble & set aside. Add mashed bean mixture to pan. Add chilies, paprika & pepper. Stir in reserved bacon. Just before serving, sprinkle with grated cheese. May be used as a side dish or as an appetizer with nacho chips. Reheats easily.

6-8 servings

MENU

Feta Mint Salata

Braided Bread

Plaki Baked Fish

Artichokes with Lemon

Sliced Potatoes with Olive Oil & Herbs

Honey Yogurt with Fresh Fruit

California Petite Syrah

•

Bowls of olives & almonds are perfect appetizers. Place the colorful salad in large terra cotta saucers. Use the bread & fresh fruit as the centerpiece. The baked dinner makes entertaining easy.

SALAD

Feta Mint Salata

•

1 large head romaine lettuce, torn into bite-size pieces
2 medium tomatoes, cut into ½-inch wedges
1 large cucumber, sliced
6 large radishes, sliced
1 small bunch scallions, sliced
6-ounces feta cheese, crumbled
4-ounces Kalamata olives
1 tablespoon chopped fresh mint

Dressing:
½ cup olive oil
3 tablespoons fresh lemon juice
2 tablespoons red wine vinegar
1 clove garlic, finely minced
1 teaspoon finely chopped fresh oregano

Place lettuce in large salad bowl. Add tomatoes, cucumbers, radishes, scallions, cheese & olives. Sprinkle with mint. Combine dressing ingredients. Mix well. Toss with salad. Salt & pepper to taste.

8 servings

ENTREE

Plaki Baked Fish

•

1 onion, thinly sliced
1 clove garlic, minced
2 tablespoons olive oil
3 cups peeled, chopped plum tomatoes, with juice
1 tablespoon snipped fresh dill
1 tablespoon chopped fresh oregano
1 teaspoon chopped fresh basil
1 teaspoon ground pepper
2 pounds red snapper fillets

Preheat oven to 350°F. Butter a shallow 2-quart baking dish.

In a medium saucepan, sauté onion & garlic in olive oil until soft but not brown, 5 minutes. Add tomatoes, dill, oregano, basil & pepper. Stir. Cook 5 minutes. Place fillets, skin side down, in prepared baking dish. Pour tomato mixture over fish. Bake, uncovered, 20-25 minutes.

6 servings

POTATOES

Sliced Potatoes with Olive Oil & Herbs

•

8 medium potatoes, thinly sliced
⅓ cup olive oil
1 tablespoon fresh thyme leaves
1 tablespoon chopped fresh savory
1½-2 teaspoons salt
freshly ground black pepper

Preheat oven to 425°F.

Dry potato slices on toweling. Place in large bowl. Mix olive oil, thyme, savory, salt & pepper. Toss with potato slices until each slice is well coated. Spread slices evenly on a baking sheet. Bake 35-40 minutes. Increase heat to 475°F. Cook 5 minutes longer until crisp & golden.

6 servings

MENU

Italian Veal Chops

Garden Pasta with Pesto Sauce

Foccacia Bread

Ricotta Coffee Velvet

Italian Red Pinot Grigio

•

Basil can be purchased at a farmer's market during the summer to make Pesto Sauce for year-long enjoyment. The menu is a snap to put together for family or friends.

Italian Veal Chops

•

6 veal loin or rib chops
1 tablespoon olive oil
salt & pepper
6 fresh sage leaves
1 cup beef stock

In a heavy skillet, brown veal chops on both sides in oil. Season with salt & pepper. Pour off any fat. Add sage & stock. Simmer 20-25 minutes. Add several sliced potatoes, onions & peppers for a one-pot meal.

6 servings

Garden Pasta with Pesto Sauce

•

Pesto Sauce:
2 cups fresh basil leaves
½ cup olive oil
2 tablespoons pine nuts or walnuts
2 cloves garlic
1 teaspoon salt
½ cup freshly grated Parmesan cheese
2 tablespoons freshly grated romano
2 tablespoons butter, softened

1 pound pasta, cooked & drained
1 cup tiny peas
1 cup broccoli flowerets
1 cup chopped tomatoes

In a blender or processor, combine basil, olive oil, pine nuts, garlic & salt. Whirl until smooth. Pour into bowl. Beat in cheeses. When incorporated, add butter. Beat until well blended. To freeze, do not add cheeses or butter. Defrost & add before serving.

To assemble, combine pasta with vegetables. Add Pesto. Toss well. Serve with additional cheese.

6 servings

Ricotta Coffee Velvet

•

1 pound ricotta cheese
4-ounces plain or vanilla yogurt
1½ tablespoons instant coffee
1 cup sugar
⅓ cup bourbon
whipped cream garnish
chocolate sauce garnish

Beat or blend ingredients until very smooth & sugar has dissolved. Chill several hours or overnight. Pour into sherbet glasses or tiny pots de crème. Garnish with whipped cream & a drizzle of chocolate sauce if desired. A light dessert that knows no season.

6 servings

Favorite Gatherings

selections from past JLM cookbooks

MENU

Pear Halves
with
Blue Cheese

Chicken Crab Divan

Wild Rice

Carrots & Onions "Sauter"

Mocha Torte

California Fumé Blanc

•

With this versatile menu you can have an elegant dinner or add wild rice to the Divan, & serve the Pears & Mocha torte for an impressive three course luncheon.

Be Milwaukee's Guest (BMG) 1959

Be Wisconsin's Guest (BWG) 1964

Be Our Guest (BOG) 1976

ENTREE

Chicken Crab Divan

- 2 packages (10 ounces each) frozen artichoke hearts, thawed & drained
- 4 whole skinless chicken breasts, split & boned
- ¼ cup butter
- 1 can (6½ ounces) crabmeat, drained
- ¼ cup dry sherry
- salt & pepper
- 3 tablespoons butter
- ½ cup small whole mushrooms
- ¼ cup finely chopped onions
- 3 tablespoons flour
- 1⅓ cups heavy cream
- 1 cup milk
- ½ cup chopped parsley
- dash cayenne
- ¼ cup grated Parmesan cheese
- paprika

Arrange artichokes on bottom of buttered 12x8-inch baking dish. In large skillet, sauté chicken in butter 15 minutes. Add crab. Cook 5 minutes. Add sherry. Allow to evaporate. Season with salt & pepper. Remove chicken & crab. Keep warm.

Add remaining butter to pan drippings. Sauté mushrooms & onions. Sprinkle with flour. Stir until smooth. Add cream & milk. Stir until thickened. Add parsley & cayenne. Remove from heat. Blend in Parmesan. Cover artichokes with half the sauce. Arrange chicken & crab over sauce. Pour remaining sauce over top. Sprinkle with paprika. Prepare up to 3 days in advance. Bring to room temperature before baking. Bake 375°F. 20 minutes. (BOG)

8 servings

VEGETABLE

Carrots & Onions "Sauter"

- 1 pound carrots, peeled & cut into 1-inch pieces
- ½ pound small onions, peeled
- water to cover
- salt
- 2 bay leaves
- ½ teaspoon thyme
- ½ tablespoon sugar
- 2 tablespoons butter

Put carrots & onions in saucepan. Cover with water. Add salt, bay leaves, thyme & sugar. Simmer until crisp-tender. Drain. Melt butter in pan. Add carrots & onions. Sauté until golden. (BWG)

4-6 servings

DESSERT

Mocha Torte

- 1 cup flour
- 1 teaspoon baking powder
- 6 eggs, separated
- 1 cup sugar
- 1 teaspoon vanilla
- 3 tablespoons cold water

Filling:

- 1 cup unsalted butter, softened
- 1½ cups powdered sugar
- 2 eggs
- 2 tablespoons strong coffee
- 1 cup heavy cream, whipped
- 2-ounces semi-sweet chocolate
- ½ cup ground nuts, optional

Preheat oven to 350°F. Butter & flour 3 9-inch cake pans.

Sift flour & baking powder. Set aside. Beat egg whites to soft peaks. Add sugar gradually. Beat until glossy & stiff. In another bowl beat egg yolks until thick. Add vanilla & cold water. Fold carefully into egg white mixture. Carefully fold in flour. Pour batter into prepared pans. Bake 20 minutes. Remove from pans immediately. Cool.

For the filling, cream butter & sugar. Add eggs one at a time, beating well. Add coffee. Remove ⅓ mixture to a small bowl. Fold ⅓ whipped cream into small bowl. Spread butter-coffee-cream between the 3 cake layers.

Add chocolate to remaining butter mixture. Add remaining whipped cream to butter-chocolate mixture.

Spread chocolate-butter mixture on top & sides of cake. Top with a generous sprinkling of ground nuts if desired. Refrigerate for at least 1 hour. (BMG)

10-12 servings

MENU

Monte's Beef Tenderloin

Julienned Zucchini & Yellow Squash

Mushroom Pie

Lorraine's Philly Velvet

French Red Bordeaux Pauillac

•

Ease in entertaining is the advantage of this menu. Enjoy your guests up to the last minute. Bake squashes in the oven the last 15 minutes while the Mushroom Pie & Tenderloin finish baking. Add a salad course if you like.

ENTREE

Monte's Beef Tenderloin

•

5-pound beef tenderloin, room temperature
larding or bacon to cover meat
1 clove garlic
6 tablespoons butter
3 tablespoons prepared or Dijon-style mustard
½ teaspoon salt
½ teaspoon pepper

Mince or process larding with garlic, butter, mustard, salt & pepper. Mix well to make a paste. Pat over beef. Broil 12 minutes. Bake at 350°F. 15 minutes. Let rest 5 minutes before slicing. Adjust broiling & baking times to size of tenderloin. For 3 pounds, broil 10 minutes, bake 10 minutes. For 6 pounds, broil 15 minutes, bake 15 minutes. (BOG)

10-12 servings

Pictured page 120.

VEGETABLE

Mushroom Pie

•

6 tablespoons butter, divided
2 pounds mushrooms, cleaned & dried
juice of ½ lemon
6 tablespoons flour
1 cup chicken stock
½ cup Madeira sherry
½ cup heavy cream
salt & pepper
1 pie crust to cover baking dish
1 egg, beaten

Preheat oven to 450°F. Butter a shallow 1½-quart baking dish.

In a large skillet, heat 4 tablespoons butter. Add mushrooms & lemon juice. Cover. Cook 10 minutes, shaking pan often. Remove mushrooms to prepared baking dish. Return skillet to heat. Add remaining butter & flour. Stir in stock. Cook, stirring constantly until sauce is thick & smooth. Add Madeira, cream, salt & pepper. Pour sauce over mushrooms. Top with pie crust. Brush crust with beaten egg. Make 4 slits in top of crust. Bake 15 minutes. Reduce heat to 350°F. Bake 10-15 minutes longer. (BMG)

6-8 servings

DESSERT

Lorraine's Philly Velvet

•

1½ cups crushed chocolate wafers
⅓ cup butter, melted
1 package (8 ounces) cream cheese, softened
½ cup sugar, divided
1 teaspoon vanilla
2 eggs, separated
1 package (6 ounces) semi-sweet chocolate chips, melted
1 cup heavy cream, whipped
¾ cup chopped pecans, optional
whipped cream for garnish

Preheat oven to 325°F.

Combine wafer crumbs & butter. Mix well. Press on bottom of 9-inch springform pan. Bake 10 minutes. Cool.

In a large bowl, combine cream cheese, ¼ cup sugar & vanilla. Add egg yolks. Beat until well blended. Add chocolate. In another bowl, beat egg whites until soft peaks form. Gradually beat in sugar. Fold whites into cream cheese mixture. Fold in whipped cream. Fold in pecans if desired. Pour into prepared pan. Freeze. May be made days or weeks ahead of time. Remove from freezer 30 minutes before serving. Garnish with additional whipped cream or chocolate leaves. (BOG)

10-12 servings

MENU

Chicken à la Corral

Sliced Potatoes & Lima Beans Vinaigrette

Broccoli Casserole with Almonds

Raspberry Torte

California Red Merlot

•

Completely portable feast for tailgating. Have thermal coolers for hot & cold foods. Place oven-heated brick in bottom of thermal chest to keep casserole hot. Chicken can be grilled on site or prepared at home. Set the table with finery or disposable dinnerware.

❦

ENTREE

Chicken à la Corral

•

4 pound broiler chicken, quartered
salt & pepper

Sauce:
2 teaspoons oregano
1 tablespoon chopped parsley
2 cloves garlic, minced
¼ cup lemon juice
½ cup olive oil

Place chicken in broiler pan or prepare grill. Season with salt & pepper. Combine sauce ingredients. Broil or grill chicken 20 minutes each side. Baste frequently with sauce. Serve chicken with remaining sauce. (BWG)

4 servings

VEGETABLE

Broccoli Casserole with Almonds

•

2 packages (10 ounces each) frozen chopped broccoli
2 tablespoons butter
2 tablespoons flour
2 cups milk
¾ cup grated Parmesan/romano cheese
1 teaspoon salt
¼ teaspoon ground pepper
¼ pound sliced, sautéed mushrooms
½ cup chopped almonds
4 slices crisp-cooked bacon, crumbled
½ cup buttered bread crumbs
dash paprika

Preheat oven to 350°F. Butter a 1½-quart casserole.

Cook broccoli in small amount of boiling water or steam until crisp-tender. Drain. Place in prepared casserole. In a saucepan, melt butter. Blend in flour. Add milk. Cook, stirring until thick. Add cheese. Stir until melted. Season with salt & pepper. Add mushrooms. Remove from heat. Put almonds & bacon on top of broccoli. Pour cheese sauce over casserole. Sprinkle with bread crumbs & paprika. Bake 20 minutes until browned & bubbly. (BMG)

6 servings

DESSERT

Raspberry Torte

•

1 package (10 ounces) butter or shortbread cookies, crushed
6 tablespoons butter, softened
2 cups powdered sugar
1 egg, beaten
1 teaspoon vanilla
1 quart fresh raspberries or 2 packages (10 ounces each) frozen raspberries, thawed, drained, reserve ½ of juice
1 cup heavy cream, whipped

Put ½ crumbs in buttered 9x9-inch pan. Cream butter & sugar. Add egg & vanilla. Beat until smooth. Spread over crumbs. Top with raspberries & reserved juice. Spread whipped cream over raspberries. Sprinkle with remaining crumbs. Refrigerate overnight. (BWG)

6-8 servings

MENU

Wisconsin Cheddar Cheese Soup

Broiled Mushroom Sandwiches

Spicy Oatmeal Cake

Frosted Mugs of Wisconsin Beer

•

Satisfyingly simple meal for after work soothing, or Sunday night supper.

SOUP

Wisconsin Cheddar Cheese Soup

•

¼ cup butter
½ cup diced carrots
½ cup diced green pepper
½ cup minced onions
⅓ cup flour
4 cups rich chicken stock
6-ounces Wisconsin medium cheddar cheese, grated
6-ounces Wisconsin aged cheddar cheese, grated
salt & pepper
milk to thin soup, optional

Melt butter in 3-quart saucepan. Add vegetables. Sauté until tender but not brown. Add flour. Stir. Add stock. Stir until thickened. Add cheeses, stirring constantly. Season to taste. Simmer 15 minutes. Thin with a small amount of milk if desired. (BWG)

4-6 servings

SANDWICH

Broiled Mushroom Sandwiches

•

1 package (3 ounces) cream cheese, softened
1 tablespoon butter
1 egg yolk
1 teaspoon white wine-Worcestershire sauce
½ cup finely ground mushrooms
6 slices bread, toasted on 1 side

Beat cheese & butter. Add egg yolk & Worcestershire. Stir in mushrooms. Spread mushroom mixture on untoasted side of bread. Broil 5 minutes. Can be served as appetizer. (BMG)

6 servings

DESSERT

Spicy Oatmeal Cake

•

1 cup quick rolled oats
1⅓ cups boiling water
1¾ cups flour
1¼ teaspoons baking soda
1 teaspoon salt
1 teaspoon cinnamon
½ teaspoon nutmeg
⅔ cup butter
1 cup sugar
1 cup packed dark brown sugar
2 eggs
½ cup chopped nuts

Broiled Caramel Topping:
¼ cup butter
1 cup packed dark brown sugar
1 cup flaked coconut
2 tablespoons light cream

Preheat oven to 350°F. Butter a 13x9-inch pan.

Combine oats & boiling water. Set aside. Sift together flour, baking soda, salt, cinnamon & nutmeg. Set aside. Cream butter & sugars. Add eggs. Beat well. Stir in oatmeal & flour mixtures. Add nuts. Stir. Pour into prepared pan. Bake 35-40 minutes. For topping combine butter, brown sugar, coconut & cream. Mix well. Spread on warm cake. Broil on lowest rack until bubbly & golden brown. May also make into cupcakes or muffins, baking 20-25 minutes. (BOG)

12 servings

MENU

Grilled Beef Tenderloin

Horseradish-Cream Sauce

Heavenly Spinach

Stornaway Herb Spaghetti

Fresh Berries & Triple Crème Cheese

French Red Bordeaux - Margaux

•

You can be in complete control entertaining your favorite person, enjoy conversation & relax. Grill meat while heating the Spinach & Herb Spaghetti 20 minutes before serving. Voilà!

Grilled Beef Tenderloin

•

Seasoning Mixture:
¾ cup soy sauce
½ cup sugar
½ cup toasted sesame seed, crushed
¼ cup vegetable oil
¼ cup flour
2 scallions, sliced
1-2 cloves garlic, minced
¼ teaspoon ground pepper

3-4 pounds beef tenderloin, cut into filets

Combine seasoning ingredients. 15 minutes before grilling, spread mixture on filets. Grill to desired doneness. (BOG)

6 servings

Heavenly Spinach

•

6 tablespoons butter, divided
½ pound mushrooms, sliced
½ cup mayonnaise
½ cup sour cream
½ cup grated Parmesan cheese
1 package (10-ounces) frozen artichoke hearts, thawed
4 packages (10-ounces each) frozen chopped spinach, cooked & drained
salt & pepper
3 large tomatoes, sliced ½-inch thick
½ cup dry bread crumbs

Preheat oven to 325°F. Butter a 13x9-inch baking dish.

Sauté mushrooms in 2 tablespoons butter. Combine mayonnaise, sour cream & cheese. Stir in artichokes, spinach, & mushrooms. Season with salt & pepper. Pour into prepared dish. Place tomatoes on top of vegetables. Brown bread crumbs in remaining butter. Sprinkle over vegetables. Bake 20 minutes. (BOG)

10 servings

Stornaway Herb Spaghetti

•

¾ cup olive oil
1 tablespoon butter
1 bunch scallions, finely chopped
1 bunch parsley, finely chopped
1 clove garlic, finely chopped
1½ teaspoons fresh chopped rosemary
1½ teaspoons fresh chopped basil
salt
¼ teaspoon pepper
1 small package (12 ounces) spaghetti, broken into small pieces, cooked & drained
½ cup grated Parmesan cheese

Heat oil & butter in skillet. Add scallions, parsley, garlic, herbs, salt & pepper. Heat through. Pour over hot cooked pasta. Toss with Parmesan. May be reheated in oven at low temperature. (BMG)

6 servings

Photographs

Citrus Chicken Salad, recipe 125
Angel Hair Pasta with Cauliflower & Raw Basil-Tomato Sauces, recipe 132
Chocolate Cinnamon Torte, recipe 105
Cabbage & Grapes, recipe 20
Rouladen of Beef, recipe 154

CHIANTI
I.L.RUFFINO
N° 279238
SERIE J
NESSVNA MANCIA
L'ORIGINALE
IMPERATORE
DELLE FETTUCCINE

Via dei Cerchi
Circo Massimo
P.le Romolo e Remo
Circo Massimo

E.D.
Love, A.D.

Nouille
graines

MENU

Mushroom Soup
with
Homemade Croutons

Hot Crabmeat Sandwich

Crispy Potatoes

Spinach Salad

Warm
Fruit Compote

New York State Seyval Blanc

•

Line up a dart tournament in the basement! At half-time, serve this satisfying Soup-Sandwich-Salad dinner to please all participants, particularly the host or hostess.

Hot Crabmeat Sandwich

•

6-ounces crabmeat
2 packages (3 ounces each) cream cheese, softened
3 tablespoons mayonnaise
1 tablespoon chopped onion
½ teaspoon Worcestershire sauce
4 drops hot pepper sauce
juice of ½ lemon
4 rusks or toasted English muffins
4 slices tomato
salt & pepper
4 slices sharp cheddar cheese

Combine crab, cream cheese, mayonnaise, onion, Worcestershire, hot pepper & lemon juice. Cover & chill overnight. When ready to serve divide crab mixture evenly on top of rusks. Top each with a tomato slice. Season with salt & pepper. Top with cheese. Bake at 300°F. 30-40 minutes. (BWG)

4 servings

Crispy Potatoes

•

4 large unpeeled Idaho potatoes, cut ⅛-inch thick
salt & pepper
½ cup butter, melted
1 cup grated Parmesan cheese

Preheat oven to 350°F.

Arrange potato slices in single layer on baking sheets. Season to taste with salt & pepper. Pour butter over potato slices. Sprinkle with Parmesan. Bake 45 minutes until crisp. Drain on paper toweling. (BOG)

6 servings

Spinach Salad

•

Dressing:
2 hard cooked eggs
1 large apple, chopped
1 small onion, chopped
¼ pound blue cheese, crumbled
½ cup mayonnaise
½ cup sour cream
salt & pepper

1 pound fresh spinach, cleaned & chilled

Combine dressing ingredients. Toss with spinach just before serving. (BMG)

6-8 servings

MENU

Open House Punch

Dairyland Casserole

Brunch Egg Casserole

Mixed Fruit Compote

Fruit Salad Dressing

French Breakfast Puffs

Cherry Muffins

Frosted Pumpkin Bars

French Roast Coffee & Spiced Tea

•

Open House Punch

•

6 bananas
1 can (12 ounces) frozen orange juice
1 can (6 ounces) frozen lemonade
1 can (46 ounces) pineapple juice
3 cups water
2 cups sugar
4 quarts chilled ginger ale

Mash bananas in blender with small amount of orange juice. Combine with remaining orange juice, lemonade, pineapple juice, water & sugar. Mix well. Pour into containers that fit into punch bowl. Freeze until firm. Two hours before serving, place frozen mixture in punch bowl. Add ginger ale. Add vodka, white wine, or champagne, if desired. (BOG)

50 servings

Dairyland Casserole

•

3 tablespoons butter, divided
1½ pounds ground chuck or round
⅓ cup sliced scallions
2 cans (8 ounces each) tomato sauce
dash Worcestershire sauce
1 package (8 ounces) cream cheese, softened
½ cup sour cream
1 cup cottage cheese
8-ounces noodles, cooked & drained

Preheat oven to 350°F. Butter a 2-quart casserole.

In a large skillet, melt 1 tablespoon butter. Brown beef. Add scallions. Add tomato sauce & Worcestershire. Combine cream cheese, sour cream & cottage cheese. Place ½ noodles in bottom of casserole. Cover with cheese mixture. Put remaining noodles on top of cheeses. Top with beef mixture. Bake 20 minutes.

May be prepared in advance before baking. Cover & refrigerate. Bake 45 minutes. (BMG)

8 servings

Brunch Egg Casserole

•

¼ cup butter
¼ cup flour
1 cup light cream
1 cup milk
¼ teaspoon thyme
¼ teaspoon marjoram
¼ teaspoon basil
1 pound extra sharp cheddar cheese, grated
18 hard cooked eggs, sliced thin
1 pound crisp-cooked bacon, crumbled
¼ cup finely chopped fresh parsley
buttered bread crumbs

Preheat oven to 350°F. Butter a 2-2½-quart casserole.

In a medium saucepan, melt butter. Blend in flour. Add cream & milk. Cook, stirring until thick. Add herbs & cheese. Stir until melted. Place ⅓ of sliced eggs in bottom of casserole. Sprinkle ⅓ bacon over eggs. Sprinkle ⅓ parsley. Add ⅓ cheese sauce over all. Repeat 2 more layers. Sprinkle top with bread crumbs. Bake 30 minutes. (BMG)

8-10 servings

Fruit Salad Dressing

•

1 egg, slightly beaten
1 cup sugar
grated peel & juice of 1 lemon
grated peel & juice of 1 orange
2 cups heavy cream, whipped

Combine sugar & egg in top of double boiler. Cook until sugar is thoroughly dissolved. Add grated peels & juices. Cool & store in covered jar in refrigerator. Keeps about 1 week. To use, add 2 tablespoons of this concentrated dressing to each cup of whipped cream. Serve as topping for gelatin or fruit salads. Concentrated dressing also good over ice cream. (BMG)

2 cups concentrate

French Breakfast Puffs

•

1½ cups flour
1½ teaspoons baking powder
½ teaspoon salt
½ teaspoon nutmeg
⅓ cup butter, softened
½ cup sugar
1 egg
½ cup milk

Topping:
½ cup butter, melted
½ cup sugar
1 teaspoon cinnamon

Preheat oven to 350°F. Butter 24 2-inch muffin tins.

Sift flour, baking powder, salt, & nutmeg together 3 times. Set aside. Cream butter & sugar until light & fluffy. Beat in egg. Add flour mixture alternately with milk to egg mixture. Blend well. Fill muffin cups ¾-full. Bake 20 minutes. Remove from tins. Roll each puff in melted butter, then in cinnamon-sugar. Variation: For Apple Muffins, reduce milk to ¼ cup. Add ½ cup grated, peeled apple to batter. (BOG)

2 dozen

Frosted Pumpkin Bars

•

2 cups sugar
4 eggs
1 cup vegetable oil
1 can (16 ounces) pumpkin
2 cups flour
2 teaspoons baking powder
1 teaspoon baking soda
1 teaspoon cinnamon
½ teaspoon salt

Creamy Icing:
1 package (8 ounces) cream cheese, softened
6 tablespoons butter, softened
4 cups powdered sugar
1 teaspoon vanilla

Preheat oven to 350°F.

Combine all ingredients except Icing. Blend well. Pour into unbuttered 15x10-inch jelly roll pan. Bake 25-35 minutes until toothpick inserted in center comes out clean. Cool. For icing, cream the cheese & butter. Gradually add sugar. Beat until well blended. Stir in vanilla. Frost cooled pumpkin bars with icing. (BOG)

4 dozen

Super Bowl Sunday & the crowds have gathered to enjoy a one o'clock buffet brunch. Serve the Fruit Compote as an appetizer with toothpicks to dip in the fluffy Dressing. Make miniature Puffs & Muffins to ease calorie consciences. Cut Pumpkin Bars into diamond shapes & arrange on a platter.

❦

MENU

Cheese & Bacon Puffs

Liverwurst Paté

Siberal Sauce

Lobster, Crab Claws, Mussels &/or Shrimp

Magnums of Iced California Brut Champagne

•

For a reception of exciting dimensions, a retirement, graduation or wedding, guests can help themselves or pass appetizers on silvery trays. Arrange moiré ribbons in soft colors on the serving table to match the flowers. Shimmering champagne flutes, white plates & a tiered ivory cake greet guests to the delights awaiting them.

Cheese & Bacon Puffs

•

1 pound crisp-cooked bacon, crumbled
1 cup mayonnaise
1 cup grated sharp cheddar cheese
4 scallions, sliced
1 tablespoon sherry
1 teaspoon white wine Worcestershire sauce
few drops hot pepper sauce
melba rounds

Combine bacon, mayonnaise, cheese, onions, sherry & seasonings. Chill 3 hours or overnight. Keeps up to 3 days. Spread on melba rounds. Broil until bubbly, 3 minutes. (BOG)

50 servings

Liverwurst Paté

•

1 teaspoon unflavored gelatin
5 teaspoons Cognac
1 pound fresh, unsmoked liverwurst
¼ cup sour cream
1 teaspoon dry mustard
¼ cup minced onion
2 truffles, finely chopped, optional

Soften gelatin in Cognac. Heat over low temperature until gelatin completely dissolves. Mash or process liverwurst with gelatin mixture & remaining ingredients. Pour into a plastic-lined 1-pint mold. Chill, covered, several hours or overnight. Unmold. Serve with toast points or crackers. (BWG)

6-8 servings

Siberal Sauce

•

1 cup mayonnaise
2-3 tablespoons spicy tomato relish
1 tablespoon lemon juice
few drops white wine Worcestershire sauce
3 tablespoons thick, rich cream
generous splash of gin

Combine ingredients. Cover & chill. Serve with a selection of iced, cooked shellfish, "to make a treat for royalty." (BMG)

1½ cups

MENU

Liptauer Cheese
on
Tiny Pumpernickle

Hungarian Veal Goulash

Boiled
Parsley Potatoes

Sprouts Emerald Isle

Pecan Roll

French Red
Rhône Gigondas

•

Make a family event even more special by preparing this menu. Spread the kitchen table with cloth, candles & a small bowl of flowers. Memorable.

Hungarian Veal Goulash

•

1 clove garlic
1 tablespoon bacon fat or shortening
3 medium onions, finely chopped
1 tablespoon Hungarian sweet paprika
salt & pepper
2 pounds veal stew meat, cut into 1-inch cubes
1½ tablespoons tomato paste
1½ cups tomato juice
2 tablespoons sour cream

Rub heavy skillet with garlic. Discard garlic. Heat bacon fat. Add onions & paprika. Cook until onions become transparent. Season meat with salt & pepper. Add meat to onions. Stir until meat is coated. Add tomato paste & juice. Bring to boil. Reduce heat. Simmer 1½ hours until meat is tender. Stir in sour cream. Continue cooking at a very low heat 30 minutes. Do not boil. To prepare in advance, stir in sour cream. Pour meat into 3-quart casserole. Refrigerate. Bake 50 minutes at 300°F. (BWG)

6 servings

Sprouts Emerald Isle

•

4-ounces cream cheese
¾ cup milk
1 tablespoon sherry
1 tablespoon chopped fresh parsley
1 tablespoon minced onion
½ teaspoon salt
¾ pound fresh brussels sprouts or 1 package (10 ounces) frozen, cooked crisp-tender
¼ cup bread crumbs

Melt cream cheese in milk over low heat. Add sherry, parsley & onion. Stir until smooth. Pour ½ sauce into bottom of small baking dish. Arrange sprouts over sauce. Add remaining sauce. Top with bread crumbs. Bake 325°F. 30 minutes. (BMG)

4 servings

Pecan Roll

•

6 eggs, separated
¾ cup sugar
1 teaspoon baking powder
1⅔ cups finely ground pecans
2 tablespoons powdered sugar
1 pint French vanilla ice cream, softened

Caramel Sauce:
2 tablespoons butter
1 cup heavy cream
¾ cup sugar
1½ cups light brown sugar
pinch salt

Preheat oven to 375°F. Line bottom of 15x10-inch jelly roll pan with well-buttered wax paper.

In a bowl, beat yolks until light & lemon-colored. Gradually add sugar. Beat until mixture is very thick. Add baking powder. Add pecans. Combine well. In another bowl, beat egg whites until stiff but not dry. Fold egg whites into yolk mixture until smooth & evenly distributed. Pour mixture into prepared pan. Spread smooth. Bake 20 minutes. Sift powdered sugar onto kitchen towel. Turn cake out immediately onto towel. Cool 5 minutes. Remove paper. Roll cake inside towel. Cool. Unroll. Spread with softened ice cream. Re-roll cake. Freeze until serving. For the Sauce, melt butter. Add cream. Stir in sugars & salt. Cook, stirring, until sugar is thoroughly dissolved. Slice cake & serve with Caramel Sauce. (BMG)

10-12 servings

Artichokes Adored

- 1 cup mayonnaise
- 1 cup Parmesan cheese
- bread rounds, toasted on one side
- 1 package (10 ounces) frozen artichokes, cooked, drained & quartered

Combine mayonnaise & cheese. Spread small amount on untoasted side of bread rounds. Top with artichoke quarter. Top with additional cheese mixture. Broil until lightly browned. As a dip for assorted crackers, combine cheese mixture & artichokes. Put in small ovenproof dish. Bake until bubbly. (BOG)

8 servings

Spaghetti à la Crab

- ¾ cup butter, divided
- 2 tablespoons olive oil
- 5 large shallots, minced
- 2 packages (6 ounces each) frozen Alaskan king crab, thawed, not drained
- ½ cup chopped fresh parsley
- 1 jar (2 ounces) chopped pimientos, drained
- 2 tablespoons lemon juice
- ½ teaspoon Italian herbs
- 1 pound vermicelli, cooked & drained
- croutons
- grated Parmesan cheese

Heat ½ cup butter & oil in medium saucepan. Sauté shallots. Add crabmeat. Stir in parsley, pimientos, lemon juice & herbs. Heat 8-10 minutes. Toss hot pasta with remaining butter. Ladle sauce over pasta. Top with croutons & Parmesan. (BOG)

4-6 servings

Sherry Cream Puffs

- ½ cup butter
- 1¼ cups flour, sifted
- 1 cup boiling water
- ¼ teaspoon salt
- 4 eggs, room temperature

Filling:

- ½ cup butter
- ½ cup flour
- 1½ cups milk
- dash salt
- ⅔ cup sugar
- 2 eggs, beaten
- ½ cup sweet sherry
- 1 cup heavy cream, whipped
- chocolate sauce

Preheat oven to 450°F. Lightly butter a baking sheet.

Combine butter & water in saucepan over medium heat. Stir until butter melts. Add flour & salt. Stir vigorously over low heat until mixture forms a ball & leaves sides of pan. Remove from heat. Cool slightly. Add eggs, one at a time, beating well after each addition. Drop by tablespoonfuls 2-inches apart on prepared pan. Bake 15 minutes. Reduce heat to 350°F. Bake 25-30 minutes longer. Cool.

For filling, heat butter in medium saucepan. Stir in flour. Add milk. Remove from heat when thickened. Add salt, sugar & eggs, beating well. Add sherry. Cool. Fold in whipped cream.

Split & fill puffs. Serve with a chocolate sauce. (BWG)

12-18 puffs

MENU

Artichokes Adored

Spaghetti à la Crab

Sautéed Veal Rib Chops

Marinated Hearts of Palm on Boston Lettuce

Sherry Cream Puffs

Italian White Pinot Bianco or Pinot Grigio

•

Sumptuous dining by candlelight. Impressive to guests yet easy on the hosting duties. Tie ribbon around the middle of folded square napkins, folded point to the bottom. Pull open points away from ribbon to form a 4-point fan or flower.

Acknowledgements

Editor
F. Lynn Nelson

Assistant Editor
Carol Manegold

Chapter Chairmen

Quiet Gatherings
Janet Emmerson

Casual Gatherings
Susan Slocum

Simple Gatherings
Suzi Levendusky

Luncheon Gatherings
Diane Armstrong

Celebration Gatherings
Colleen Mortenson & Julie Meier

Elegant Gatherings
Jane Segerdahl & Jaymie Upton

Notable Gatherings
Minnie Chambers & Missie Hawley

Buffet Gatherings
Anne Gallagher & Chris Mitchell

Ethnic Gatherings
Mary Ornst & Mardi Kemp

Favorite Gatherings
Nancy Szatkowski

Production Panel
Diane Armstrong
Valerie Clarke
Rita Larsen
Susan LeFeber
Janet Roethle
Leslie Schumacher

Proofreaders-Indexers
Diane Armstrong
Catherine F. Bauer
Susan Hopwood

Wine Consultant
Daniel H. Nelson

Chairman
Christine S. Krieg

•

Marketing Chairman
Katherine S. Reising

•

Operations Chairman
Allison M. Dittmann

Retail Marketing
Manager
Nancy M. Schmidt

•

Suzi W. Levendusky
Colleen S. Mortonson
Mary M. Ornst

Wholesale Marketing
Manager
Nancee B. Gorenstein

•

Jennifer F. Hillis
Kaye S. Kovacs
Elizabeth R. Loder
Carol A. Mayer
Jaymie I. Upton

Public Relations
Manager
Debra K. Sosey

•

Nancy N. Stall

Operations
Susan H. Covi
Susan D. Jones
Susan L. LeFeber
Marilynn J. Wilke

Fundraising
Jeanne L. Grist
Jane L. Rice

Special Advisors
Vice President Supportive Services
Louise G. Dill

•

Director of Ways & Means
Judy A. Hansen

•

Treasurer
Mary Anne K. Wawrzyn

The GATHERINGS committee would like to commend on behalf of the Junior League of Milwaukee the following people for their recipes & invaluable assistance in testing & typing recipes:

Stephanie Ackerman
Susan Aiken
Patricia S. Algiers
Linda Allen
Helen Baur Allis
Louise Q. Anderson
Susan Anderson
Kathleen Arenz
Diane Armstrong
Patsy Aster
Amy Balge
Beth Bauer
Cathy Bauer
Leslie Barkow
Linda Barlow
Donna Baumgartner
Helen B. Bechthold
Charlotte Becker
Diane Bedran
Nancy Bell
Cathy Bellovary
Jodi Bender
Terry Beneske
Louise Berg
Mary Bero
Lucy Bibby
Kathe Biersach
Fran Birchhill
Holly Blake
Blue Mound Country Club
Janet Bode
Boder's on the River Restaurant
Kathleen Bonady
Patricia Bond
Carolyn Borelli
Barbara Borges
Georgia Bouda
Bee Boyd
Kathleen Callan Brady
Holly Braun
Claudine Eldred Breidster
Allison Briber
Denise Brondino-Carini
Cathy Brown
Joanne Brown
Eleanor Hamilton Browne
Bobbie Buening
Janet Burdick
Barbara Busch
Paula Calhoun
Denise Cassidy
Minnie Chambers
Annemarie Gabor Christiansen
Jeanne Christiansen
Nancy Nichols Christy
Pam Chumbley
Nancy Collopy
Mary Lou Borders Cook
The Corral Restaurant
Anne Courtney
Debbie Crane
Patty Curtes
Judy Dalecky
Kathy Daly
Alberta Statkus Darling
Mary Darling
Linda Davis
Maureen Day
Agatha Dehmel
Nancy DeMarsh
Mary Russel Dengel
Linda DeRosa
Louise Dill
Melody B. Dill
Deloris Donnelly
Louise Doornelk
Kathy Drum
Patti Dwyer
Pam Elliott
Janet Emmerson
Diane R. Emory
Mary Emory
Joy Duquette Engroff
Gala Eppstein
Lynn Epstein
Stephanie Eron
Laura Fabick
Marjorie S. Feerick
Christine Ferber
Jane Fitzgibbons
Teena Flanner
Diane Foley
Tory Folliard
Patricia Ivins Foster
Jocelyn Kilham Fothergill
Marjorie Fowler
Liz Frank
Linda Lease Franklin
Debbie Freeman
Barb Fuldner
Connie Merker Fullwood
Kate Gaertner
Ann Gallagher
Janet Garmer
Marilyn Gary
Micky Gerschke
Rose Glaisner
Beth Gochnauer
Anne Godsey
Ann Gorenstein
Nancee Gorenstein
Gerorgianna Gormley
Mary Montgomery Goulet
Betsy Gritzmacher
Joan Krejci Grzesiak
Ellen Gutierrez
Lindi Haag
Charlene Haas
Keri Hadler
Judy Hansen
Sue Harrington
Judy Haugsland
Missie Hawley
Virginia Wild Hayssen
Jill Sherry Heavenrich
Holly Helf
Peggy Helz
Jill Herbst
Janet Herr
Susan Wilson Hertzberg
Jenny Hillis
Dolores Hodnet
Jane Hodnik
Beth Hoffman
Susanne Holsen
Barbara Holtz
Patricia Holtzmann
Susan Hopwood
Kathy Howell
Penny Isermann
Francie Ishmael
Valerie Jablonka
Dee Jamison
Jane Jansen
Barbara Janssen
Jody John
Cindy Johnson
Julie Johnson
Peggy Johnson
Vicki Johnson
Sue Jones
Margaret Joppe
Sue Jordan
Laura Jorgensen
Holly Jurss
Karen Juzenas
Kitti Kadlec
Phoebe Kaminsky
Ginny Kannenberg
Susan Kaufman
Karen Keating
Mardi Kemp
Sandra Ketter
Maryglen Kieckhefer
Shelly Bundy King
Lucinda Kitzke
Linda Klimowicz
Aimee Klundt
Genevieve G. Koenig
Kaye Ellen Kovacs
Lora Watts Krauthoefer
Marina Krejci

Chris Krieg
Barb Krueger
Gerri Krysiak
Anne LaBudde
Edith Courteen Landis
Vita Langenkamp
Mary Lardner
Rita Larsen
Mary B. Laudon
Marge Laughlin
Raquel Garcia Lauritzen
Susan LeFeber
Suzanne LeFeber
Pixie Leland
Ann Levendusky
Doray Levendusky
Susan Levendusky
Elizabeth R. Loder
Lola Loepfe
Patricia Longabaugh
Sharon K. Lundgen
Chris Lyndon
Patricia Lyons
Vita MacArthur
Janey Minahan MacNeil
Madelieine's Restaurant
Carol Manegold
Sally S. Manegold
Andrea Topetzes Mann
Mary Marshall
Jane Martin
Marcia Matchette
Tracy Mayfield
Diane McCormick
Karen McCormick
Paulie McCown
Patricia G. McCulloch
Marilyn McGriff
Joan Meehan
Julie Meier
Astrid Schlicke Mellencamp
Ann Miller
Mary Keith Miller
Patricia Minks
Anita Mitchell
Gloria Mitchelson
Holly Moebius
Chris Mitchell
Judy Moon
Marjorie Moon
Betty Moore
Lyndon Moore
Deborah Mortensen
Colleen Mortenson
Jill Muehlmeier
Laurie Mueller
Mary Ellen Mueller
Mary Mulcahy
Nadine Mundt
Mary Myers
Liz Neff
Beverly Nelson
F. Lynn Nelson
Kay Nordeen
Phoebe Norton
Katharine Elwell Noyes
Pam Olsen
Linda Olson
Bonnie Ornst
Mary Ornst
Mildred Ornst
Eugenie Bournique Pabst
Joyce Pabst
Kathy Palmer
Marti Palmer
Katie Parent
Jane Wykle Parker
Lynne Pearcy
Nancy Peters
Salli Watts Peterson
Julie Petri
Jane Phillips
Nancy Phillips
Jacquelin Pillsbury
Ildy Poliner
Barbara Quilling
Deborah Quirk
Mary Raitt
Patricia Ranger
Karin Raymond
Laura Rees
Deanna Crary Reeser
Katherine S. Reising
Anne Rice
Mary Rickmeier
Laurie Roberts
Janet Roethle
Cathy Rowe
Susan Ryan
Kathy Sammons
Linda Sapp
Marlene Schilffarth
Mary Marcato Schley
Jan Schmidt
Mary Kay Schmidt
Nancy Schmidt
Maureen Schroeder
Leslie Schumacher
Patty Schuyler
Meredith Scrivner
Jane Seaman
Jane Segerdahl
Andrea Sellinger
Virginia Rahel Shackleton
Judy Sherman
Maureen Sievers
Vicki Sileno
Jane Simpson
Susan Slocum
Beth Smith
Mary Smith
Sue Smith
Linda Solveson
Elizabeth Van Antwerp Sorgi
Joan Spector
Janet Spero
Barbara C. Steinmetz
Susan Steldt
Judith Stephens
Trisha Stephenson
Kim Stobbs
Lynn Stuhr
Dolly Sullivan
Karen Sullivan
Nancy Szatkowski
Kekee Szorcsik
Gale Tanger
Val Teague
Barbara Terschan
Barb Timmerman
Derse Todd
Roseann Tolan
Elaine Toledo
Angela Topetzes
Patricia Treiber
Terry Trott
Shari Truitt
Pam Uihlein
Polly Strauss Uihlein
Jaymie Upton
Nancy Vetter
Kathleen Greene Vogel
Cindy Wachs
Laurel Walker
Carol Walthers
Mary Anne Wawrzyn
Jean Weissmueller
Barbara Moquin Whealon
Grace Smith White
Lesley White
Marilynn Wilke
Connie Willems
Katie Withers
Gail Miller Wray
Christie Wrenn
Mary Wuesthoff
Mary York
Letitia S. Young
Jan Zakrajsheck
Eileen Ziegler
Penny Ziegler
Sharon Zurawski

The Junior League of Milwaukee would like to thank the following people for submitting recipes & providing suggestions to GATHERINGS:

Molly Abrohams
Debbie Antonio
Sharon Armas
Blythe Bathrick
Priscilla Beadell
Lynne Belcher
Linda P. Bell
Mary Borges
Betsy Boswell
Patricia Brash
Mary Brobson
Gordon I. Burgess, M.D.
Patricia M. Burgess
Marguerite L. Burghardt
Julie Carpenter
Ardis Cerny
Linda Christensen
Judy Christl
Martha Conrad Clark
Sandy Dawson
Laurie Digate
Mary Dolaharty
Myra Dorros
Madeline Ells
Sue Erlacher
Barbara Faude
Christine Ferber
Connie Frank
Susan Freedy
Trudy Frentz
Sandy Garmer
Helen Genskow
Judy Gilg
Karen Glanert
Constance Godfrey
Mary Beth Goodspeed
Judy Gorsuch
Suzanne Greene
Eileen Gruesser
Tina Hartwig
Gretchen Henry
Marlene Hirschberg
I'Nell Hogue
Jayne Jordan
Laura LaVanway
Kathy Lee
Betsy Lierk
Eilene Lust-Stevens
Jeanne Machata
Lois Marincic
Cindy Martin
Mary Mayer
Ruth McCoy
Kathy Mesick
Ada Moegenburg
Jean Neal
Kathy Nelson
Katherine Peppler
Judy Perry
Carol Petersen
Karen Petersen
Elly Pick-Jacobs
Pam Pierce
Julie Polakowski
Mary S. Pollock
Jeanne Reed
Judith Ross
Holly Ryan
Patricia Sara
Mary Lee Schweiger
Barbara Shearer
Deborah Singer Silvestri
Lynn Skeen
Lyn Slater
Judith Stark
Marion Stewart
Nancy Sturm
Sue Swindells
Nicole Teweles
Kathleen Timberman
Joan Villavicencio
Sherida Wank
Jean Wenkler
Tracy Wickwire
Ellen Wiese
Laurel Wilkens
Peg Willson
Ann Winchell
Geraldine Woody
Cheryl Worthington

The cover has been donated by the Brooks family in memory of:

Genevieve H. Brooks

We would like to thank the following sponsors for their generous contributions to GATHERINGS:

Anheuser-Busch, Inc.
Somebody Still Cares About Quality
Milwaukee, Wisconsin

First Wisconsin Foundation
Milwaukee, Wisconsin

The Grenadier's Restaurant, Inc.
Milwaukee, Wisconsin

Marshall Field's
Milwaukee, Wisconsin

Usinger's Famous Sausage
America's Finest Since 1880
Milwaukee, Wisconsin

Recipes Sponsored in Honor of:

Mrs. Robert Auspach
Mrs. Douglas A. Baske
Wilma K. Bauer
Nan Blackburn
Barbara Blutstein
Happy Levis Booth
Mrs. Marie Botsch
Josephine Wigdale Brennan
Mrs. Felix Brown
Mary Lou Cardio
Bobbie T. Cosper
Mrs. Owen Crenshaw
Anne Crowley
Margadette M. Demet
Betty Dill
Matsy Ells
Elizabeth Ann Fortmann
Louise Fortmann
Mrs. Robert G. Friedman
Eileen E. Gardner
Sally Levis Gerlinger
Gladys Grist
Mrs. Leonard Gorenstein
Lillian Stroschein Guthnecht
Mrs. Robert L. Hillis
Amelia Hodnik
Jo Hyman
Emma S. Kaszubowski
Mrs. William Keith
Marquirite Killian
Lauren Krieg
Raymond Krieg
Simone Koch
Billie Ann Kubly
Forence Lahman
Kathleen Brennan Lee
Helene Lesynski
John Levendusky
Tess Lewis
Sandra Liebkemann
Mary Lipnicke
Mrs. Fred Lipscomb
Janet Loosen
Emily Luczak
Mary Ann Krembs McDevitt
Bernice L. Meehan
Kathy Mesick
Mrs. Keith Miller
Lyndon Moore
Mary Mortonson
Pat Norris
Mrs. Daniel P.J. O'Connor
Allison Ornst
Bob Ornst, Jr.
Isabelle Polacheck
Karole Read
Ruth Rice
Terrence K. Rice
Leona K. Roussy
Bob Schmidt
Mary Kay Schmidt
Robby Schmidt
Yeddy Schmidt
Peggy Schuster
Mrs. Douglas Seaman
Margery Sengbusch
Carolyn Skuara
Alma Slatten
Walter J. Smith
Edward Larscheid Styles
Julia Larscheid Styles
Dolly Sullivan
Theresa Thiele
Mrs. Joseph E. Tierney, Sr.
Fay Kalafat Topetzes
Maurine Harvey Truitt
University of Illinois-
College of Communications
Mrs. Cora Walker
Connie Welch
Grace S. White
Donna Wieland
Olga Wilke
June Zinkgraf

Production Credits

Typesetting
Zahn-Klicka-Hill

Color Separations
Mandel Company

Keyliners
Barb Adams & Jerry Adams

Printing
Schilffarth & Kress

Binding
W.A. Krueger

Photographic Properties

Dave Boyles
Kathleen Hibscher
Scott Lanza
Sharon K. Lundgren
Carol Manegold
Lorene Johnson
Effie Meyer
F. Lynn Nelson
Steven Plater
Kathryn Sherwood
Rachel J. Stephens
Hans J. Ziegler

Acknowledgements

Patricia R. Connors
Diane Germanotta
Glenn Gilchrist
Don Hill
Dick Kress
Rick Mandel
Kathleen Marquardt
Effie Meyer
Robert L. Meyer
Ellen Rolfes

Index